T0299356

Project Risk Analysis Made Ridiculously Simple

World Scientific–Now Publishers Series in Business

ISSN: 2251-3442

The complete list of titles in the series can be found at
http://www.worldscientific.com/series/ws-npsb

World Scientific – Now Publishers Series in Business: **Vol.13**

Project Risk Analysis Made Ridiculously Simple

Lev Virine

Michael Trumper

Project Decisions, Calgary, Canada

 World Scientific

Published by

World Scientific Publishing Co. Pte. Ltd.
5 Toh Tuck Link, Singapore 596224
USA office: 27 Warren Street, Suite 401-402, Hackensack, NJ 07601
UK office: 57 Shelton Street, Covent Garden, London WC2H 9HE

and

now publishers Inc.
PO Box 1024
Hanover, MA 02339
USA

Library of Congress Cataloging-in-Publication Data
Names: Virine, Lev, 1964–   author. | Trumper, Michael, 1963–   author.
Title: Project risk analysis made ridiculously simple / Lev Virine (Project Decisions,
    Calgary, Canada) & Michael Trumper (Project Decisions, Calgary, Canada).
Description: New Jersey : World Scientific, 2016. | Series: World scientific-now publishers
    series in business ; Volume 13 | Includes bibliographical references and index.
Identifiers: LCCN 2016013143| ISBN 9789814759373 (hc : alk. paper) |
    ISBN 9789814759229 (pbk : alk. paper)
Subjects: LCSH: Project management. | Risk management.
Classification: LCC HD69.P75 V56827 2016 | DDC 658.4/04--dc23
LC record available at https://lccn.loc.gov/2016013143

British Library Cataloguing-in-Publication Data
A catalogue record for this book is available from the British Library.

Desk Editors: Dipasri Sardar/Philly Lim

Typeset by Stallion Press
Email: enquiries@stallionpress.com

Printed in Singapore

About the Authors

Lev Virine has more than 20 years of experience as a structural engineer, software developer, and project manager. In the past 10 years he has been involved in a number of major projects performed by Fortune 500 companies and government agencies to establish effective decision analysis and risk management processes as well as to conduct risk analyses of complex projects.

Lev's current research interests include the application of decision analysis and risk management to project management. He writes and speaks to conferences around the world on project decision analysis, including the psychology of judgment and decision-making, modeling of business processes, and risk management. Lev received his doctoral degree in engineering and computer science from Moscow State University.

Michael Trumper has over 20 years of experience in technical communications, instructional and software design, and training project risk and economics software and theory. Michael has authored papers on quantitative methods in project estimations and risk analysis. He is a co-author of two books on project risk management and decision analysis.

Contents

Introduction

You left for the airport two hours early, but were then stuck in traffic and missed your flight. You borrowed tens of thousands of dollars to open a restaurant that specializes in perogies, but no one was interested. You hired a programmer to develop new CRM software, but he spent more time messaging his new girlfriend than on his work and the project was delayed indefinitely.

All these things are characterized by two words: stuff happens. "Stuff happens" could be due to your own mistakes, but it could be due to events outside of your control. Regardless of why, "stuff happens" is a source of a huge burden on our life. Imagine a world without risk, we would save not only huge amounts of time and money, but also reduce our stress and improve our quality of life. Alas, life is not without risk, so the question is "Can we do something about these risks?" The short answer is yes, we can. We can identify, analyze, and manage them in such a way that when done properly, it will greatly improve our project's chances of success.

If you want to be successful in your personal and professional life including your projects, you need to know the answers to these three questions:

- What could happen?
- What is be probability that it could happen and what will be the impact?
- What can you do about it?

This book is the third in our series about project risk and decision analysis and project risk management. The first book *"Project Decisions: The Art and Science"* (Virine and Trumper, 2007) is focused on project decision analysis. The second book called *"ProjectThink: Why Good*

Managers Make Poor Project Choices" (Virine and Trumper, 2013), where we covered the psychology of project risk management. This book is about project risk analysis or the process of determining project risk probabilities and impacts, risk prioritization, and analysis of mitigation plants.

In this book, we discuss both qualitative and quantitative risk analysis with a greater emphasize on the quantitative risk analysis. In many cases, projects are relatively simple and only require very basic mental processes. For example, if you think that the probability of being stuck in traffic on your way to the airport is significant, you could leave your home earlier. But, in many projects related to your business, you would better advised to use more advanced techniques, particularly different quantitative methods as they will provide your analysis more certainty. Therefore, the primary focus of this book is on quantitative project risk analysis. The subjects will include analysis of risk events with Monte Carlo simulations, sensitivity analysis, and other related concepts. In addition, we will pay a lot of attention to Event chain methodology, a technique that is focused on identifying and managing events and event chains that affect project schedules.

Project risk analysis is closely related to risk management, which we briefly discuss in this book as well. Risk management is focused mostly on what to do with risks, particular risk communication, response planning and governance. Risk analysis can be a part of project risk management.

If this all sounds a bit complicated, you would be correct as in many cases with complex projects the process must be equally complex. However, for both qualitative and quantitative project risk analysis, the concepts are quite straight forward and use very basic mathematical concepts. Luckily, there are a lot of very good and proven software in the market that will do the heavy lifting for you. All examples in this book were performed using RiskyProject project risk analysis and risk management software by Intaver Institute Inc. However, you can use any risk analysis software, a list of which is included in the appendix of this book. Our goal is to provide a straightforward approach to project risk management for project managers, business analysts, and other project team members without requiring mathematical or statistical background of a risk specialist.

We hope you will enjoy our book.

Lev Virine and Michael Trumper
Calgary, Alberta, Canada

Test Your Judgment: Why Do You Need Project Risk Analysis

Here is a quiz to test your judgment. All these problems can be easily solved using quantitative project risk analysis. However, some people believe that project risk analysis is unnecessary because they can make accurate estimates without any analysis. You may be one of them, so let's see how you feel after this quiz.

1. Billionaire Roland Drump wants to build a new Cleopatra casino in Pacific City. He estimates that casino will cost only $200 Million dollars. However, he plans to do some additions:

   - 200 ft. Golden statue of Cleopatra and Drump together has an estimated cost of $40 M, but the probability that he will build this statue is 30%.
   - 1000 sq ft. fresco "Drump in the Swimming Pool" has an estimated cost of $30 M, with a 20% probability that it will be constructed.
   - 300 ft. Gallery with portraits of Drump and other executives of Drump Enterprises has an estimated cost of $50 M with a 10% probability that it will be completed.

   What is the expected cost of casino?

   A. $223 M
   B. $320 M
   C. $252 M

2. A group of gangsters are planning to rob Washington–Washington casino in Las Vegas. Their initial plan:

   - Task 1: John and Don will plant the explosives and blow up a power transmission line going to Las Vegas. It will take 30 min to 1 h.
   - Task 2: Starting the same time Danny and Lenny will steal a getaway car and park it near the casino, which will take 10–20 min.
   - Task 3: After power is knocked off, Terry and Barry will rob the casino. It will take 5–10 min.

   Uncertainties in duration of which task will affect total robbery time the most:

   A. Tasks 1
   B. Only task 2 and 3
   C. All tasks

3. Billionaire Roland Drump decided to arm all casino dealers in his new Cleopatra casino in Pacific City with assault rifles so they can kill unruly clients or preemptively kill clients they suspect might become unruly. Killing clients are:

   A. Mitigation Plan
   B. Response Plan
   C. Both Mitigation Plan and Response Plan

4. Mexican drug lord El Stuppo and his associates are digging an escape tunnel from his prison cell. He found that his project risks will fall into three categories: duration (tunneling could take too much time), cost (tunneling could cost too much money), and security (somebody in prison will discover this project). Duration is two times more important for him than cost and security are three times more important than duration. What are the priorities of these categories?

   A. Duration 29%, Cost 26% and Security 45%
   B. Duration 30%, Cost 20% and Security 50%
   C. Duration 35%, Cost 20% and Security 45%

5. The Beast must learn to love another and earn her love in return before the rose's last petal falls. He has 10 days, remaining, but developing a loving relationship with Beauty most likely will take 6 days but could be completed as early as 4 days or take up to 12 days and it is defined by triangular distribution. What it the chance that the Beast will be able to break the spell?

   A. 87%
   B. 92%
   C. 95%

6. The famous magician David Ironfield is planning to see the body of his assistant in two during the show. Usually, it takes him 1 min to cut the body in half, but this time he has a new magic box and expects two potential delays. There is a 30% chance that assistant may not be able to bend her legs inside the box fast enough. This would delay the trick by 20%. There is also 20% chance that the second assistant, whose legs are supposed to stick out after body is cut, would not be able to hide

her head. It will delay the trick by 50%. How long the trick would take on average:

A. 1 min 30 sec
B. 1 min 10 sec
C. 1 min 5 sec

7. Young wizards Jerry Throter is trying to defeat a troll, which usually takes 10–12 min. So far, fight continues for 8 min and Jerry Throter estimates that only 50% of his battle is complete: the troll is badly wounded, but continues fighting and making inhuman sounds. How much time would it take to defeat the troll with certainty of 70%:

A. From 15.2 min
B. From 18.3 min
C. From 20.5 min

8. Famous crook Terry Fadoff is working on new financial pyramid scheme. He is planning to pump and dump stock of Fadoff Enterprises and get $10–12 M from it. The issues is his must to pay $4–5 M in bribes, $3–4 M to his associates, and $1–2 M to develop an accounting software to hide his activities. All uncertainties are uncorrelated and defined by uniform distributions. What is his maximum payout after all expenses with 80% probability:

A. $1 M
B. $2 M
C. $3 M

9. Two pirates, Jonny Death and Orlando Plume are preparing an expedition to Treasure Island. The Expedition would cost in dollar equivalents $80,000–$120,000 and take 5–6 months, but most likely 5.2 months. What would be the chance that cost will be below $100,000 and duration will be below 5.4 months at the same time?

A. Around 60%
B. Around 50%
C. Around 30%

10. Popular singer, Tracy Terry is planning a new Global Tour, which would take 60 days.

    - Her stopover in Bujumbura (Burundi) could be delayed by 5 days with a probability of 50% if her local fans demand another concert.
    - Her stopover in Tobolsk (Russia) could be delayed by 2 days with a probability of 80%, as she may miss a flight due to signing autographs for her fans.
    - Her stopover in Nuku'alofa (Kingdom of Tonga) could be delayed by 3 days with a probability of 60% because the King may invite her for a lunch.

    Which stopover could cause the longest delay on her tour?

    A. Bujumbura
    B. Tobolsk
    C. Nuku'alofa

Answers to Judgment Quiz

1. Correct answer is (A). You need to multiply probability on cost, sum them and add original $200 M. We will learn about project expected value in Chapter 12.
2. Correct answer is (A). Task 1 has most uncertainties. Task 2 is not on the critical path at all. We will learn about sensitivity analysis in Chapter 9.
3. Correct answer is (C). If dealer kills client before he or she becomes unruly, it is a mitigation plan. If dealer kills client after he or she become unruly, it is a response plan. In this case, it is both mitigation and response plans, because dealer will be shooting on all types of clients. Read Chapter 4 for more information.
4. Correct answer is (A). This can be calculated using Analytic Hierarchy Process, which we will discuss in Chapter 3.
5. Correct answer is (C). You may use analytical solution, but it is simpler to do using Monte Carlo simulation. We will learn about distributions and Monte Carlo simulations in Chapter 5 of this book.
6. Correct answer is (B). This is a cumulative effect of two uncorrelated risks. You need to perform Monte Carlo simulations with risk events. We will discuss it in Chapters 6–8.
7. Correct answer is (B). This is related to automatic calculation of remaining duration for partially completed tasks, which we will discuss in Chapter 10.
8. Correct answer is (B). You need to perform Monte Carlo simulation and calculate 80th percentile (P80) of the statistical distribution of project cost. You may read percentiles in Chapter 5.
9. Correct answer is (C). This question is related to Joint Confidence Level analysis which we will discuss in Chapter 13 of this book.
10. Correct answer is (A). It is related to ranking risks for quantitative risk analysis. You will learn about it in Chapter 9 of the book.

Now score yourself and see where you fall on the table below:

# of correct answers	Some advice
1–3	Don't worry, most of people have difficulties answering these questions without computer analysis. In this book, you will learn how such types of analysis is performed.
3–7	Not so bad. If decision makers as CEO and politicians would have such good judgment and ability to analyze things, our salary would go up and taxes down. However, we still recommend you to read this book, there is always a space to improve your analytical abilities.
7–10	You don't need to use any computer software for project risk analysis, because your brain is a computer. Your analytical abilities are superior. You can tell your management that they don't need to buy a computer for you and can give you the money they saved.

Part I

Project Risk Management and Qualitative Project Risk Analysis

Chapter 1

What is Project Risk Management and Risk Analysis?

Why do certain projects fail where other similar projects succeed? Is it the skills of the project manager and team members, availability of resources (including financing), clearly defined objectives, or stakeholder engagement? It could be many factors, but one of the critical ones is a well conducted project risk management and risk analysis process. In this chapter, with the help of a couple of examples, we will explain the basic concepts of risk management and risk analysis. We will also discuss the concept of risk (what is it?), risk properties, risk categories, and risk mitigation and response planning.

Entebbe Raid 1976

On June 27, 1976, an Air France Flight flying from Tel Aviv to Paris with 248 passengers was hijacked by the Popular Front for the Liberation of Palestine (PFLP) who demanded the release of 40 Palestinian fighters held in Israel and 13 other militants held in several other countries. After a brief stopover in Athens and Tripoli, the aircraft and its hostages landed in Entebbe, Uganda which shows the government supported the militants. While the majority of the passengers were released, the 106 Israeli hostages and the plane's crew remained in Entebbe and the captors threatened to kill the hostages if their demands were not met. After it became apparent that diplomatic efforts were not succeeding, the Israeli army (IDF) decided to attempt a rescue of the hostages. This was an extremely audacious and high risk operation and has become a model for successfully planning and executing similar special operations activities (Dunstan, 2012; Smith, 1976).

3

The hostage release operation took place on July 4, 1976. Four Israeli planes (four C-130 Hercules and two Boeing 707 for support) left Sharm el-Sheikh in the Sinai Peninsula and flew along an international route over the Red sea. To avoid radar detection, the majority of the flight was at a height of no more than 30 m (100 ft.). The rescue plan required that the Israeli planes fly 4,000 km across unfriendly and potentially hostile territories, land the planes at Entebbe and simultaneously assault the terminal and extract the hostages, control the airport, repel attackers and potential pursuers, and finally fly back. The flight would take approximately 8.5 h, the forces would be on the ground at Entebbe for approximately 55 min, and finally the hostages would be flown away. All told, the operation would be completed in a single night under the cover of darkness.

The Israeli C-130 planes landed at Entebbe. Their cargo bay doors were already open. The Israelis knew that Idi Amin, the president of Uganda, had purchased a black Mercedes. A black Mercedes that looked like the president's and Land Rovers that usually accompanied the president's vehicle were to drive from the planes towards the terminal. By pretending to be Idi Amin's entourage, the Israelis hoped to approach the terminal building without being detected. However, near terminal two, Ugandan guards ordered the vehicles to stop. The commandos opened fire on them and quickly killed them. After they had dispatched the guards, the Israelis approached the terminal and swiftly entered the main hall where the hostages were located. Using a megaphone, they shouted, "Stay down!," in both Hebrew and English. During the ensuing gun battle inside the terminal hall, three hostages and all seven hijackers were killed.

Meanwhile, the other three C-130 planes landed in Entebbe. They unloaded armored personnel carriers, which would be required to provide defense against Ugandan forces during the hour required for refueling. The commandos also destroyed around 11 Ugandan MiG-17 fighter planes to prevent any pursuit and swept the airfield to gather intelligence. While the Israelis were loading the hostages onto the planes, Ugandan forces started to direct fire at them from the Airport Control Tower (Figure 1.1). The Israelis returned fire and killed 33–45 Ugandan solders. Only one Israeli, Yonatan Netanyahu, a brother for future Israeli Prime Minister Benjamin Netanyahu, was killed and at least five other commandos were wounded. The rescued hostages were flown to Israel via Nairobi, Kenya.

Figure 1.1. Control tower and terminal of Entebbe airport now.

Shabwa Raid 2014

Here is another story. On December 6, 2014, US Special Forces attempted to free hostages captured by Al-Qaeda from a location on the Arabian Peninsula (AQAP) in Shabwa Governorate of Yemen. The first attempt on November 26, 2014 rescued eight hostages, but five hostages, including the American journalist Luke Somers and South African teacher Pierre Korkie, were moved by AQAP to another location before the first raid (Martinez *et al.*, 2014). Luke Somers was abducted in Yemen in 2013. On December 4, 2014, AQAP threatened to execute Somers within three days unless the US met some demands. AQAP also warned that Somers would be killed if another attempt to rescue the hostages was made.

On December 6, 2014, 40 US Navy SEALs in a V-22 Osprey aircraft landed a distance from the compound where the hostages were kept. An AQAP fighter apparently spotted them while relieving himself outside. According to some reports, it also may have been the barking of a dog that alerted the hostage takers. Whatever the source, the hostage takers were alerted, which had dire consequences for the success of the raid. The assault lasted around 10 min when finally US troops were able to enter the building where they found Somers and Korkie gravely injured. They were evacuated to the Ospreys and a medical team tried to perform surgery in transit. However, both Somers and Korkie succumbed to their injuries. Six AQAP fighters were killed and an unknown number of US troops were killed or injured in the raid. Importantly, the operation's planners were unaware of the identity of Korkie and that a charity group had been negotiating with his captors and his release was imminent (BBC News, 2014). Apparently, the payment had already been made and his release was just a formality.

Why was the Entebbe raid successful, where the Shabwah raid suffered such losses? May be it was just luck? This could have some merit as recent historical analysis partially supports this theory (David, 2015). But perhaps, the difference could be due to superior risk management in the Entebbe case. For example, the Yemeni captors must have been expecting a second attempt to rescue the hostages and this was a major obstacle to successfully executing the plan. However, it appears that this risk was not completely mitigated. Is it possible to mitigate the risk with the chance that one of the captors would be relieving himself outside or catching the attention of a dog? We do not know. But let us examine the successful operation (Entebbe raid) from risk management and risk analysis perspective.

A Qualitative Project Risk Analysis Perspective

We do not know what type of project risk management and risk analysis was done by operation's planners. But we believe that it was done and done quite rigorously. We would like to use this example to demonstrate you how project risk management and analysis works and why it can be so beneficial. But before we begin, a small disclaimer: we will perform a relatively simple analysis and we do not claim to possess to have exact information in respect to the probabilities and impacts of certain risks; and therefore, cannot give a definite answer from the historical point of view. This example is only intended to illustrate the project risk analysis methodology.

With this high level understanding of the plan, we have enough information to apply a simple forensic risk analysis. Normally, project risk analysis would be performed prior to the start of a project, or during execution, to generate probabilities of meeting project objectives. But in this case, we are trying to determine in hindsight whether the decision to launch the rescue attempt was a well taken chance or a reckless gamble given the extraordinary risks that the team had to overcome.

In the risk analysis process, we have to identify the critical risks, or those risks that will have the most potential to affect key objectives and add them to the *risk register*, or the list of risk with their properties. In this case, the main objective is to retrieve the hostages with the minimal loss of life. To achieve this, the team would have to avoid early detection, execute the plan on the ground quickly and efficiently, and secure their departure from pursuers. With these objectives, the first major risk identified is "Flight is detected in the air" and element of surprise is lost. The second risk would be to the execution of the actual assault. "Poor or incorrect intelligence" could greatly increase the time to execute or even failure of the assault. For example, hostages could be moved to a different location and the commandos would arrive to an empty terminal. Hijackers could also become aware of the raid when the planes land and this forewarning could endanger the hostages. Bad weather is an additional risk that could cause problems with the flight, landing, assault, and departure. Finally, Ugandan forces might try to pursue departing commandos and hostages on land and in the air.

At this stage of the analysis, we can assign *probability* and *impacts* to these risks. *Risk scores* can be calculated as risk probabilities multiplied by risk impact. Probability of 100% indicates that the risk has occurred. An impact of 100% indicates a total failure of the operation due to this risk. The risk scores indicate which risks have the highest potential to affect the project, these are the critical risks and must be managed to ensure the highest chance of success. Table 1.1 shows how very high level risk register may look like:

Table 1.1. Risk register with pre-mitigated probability, impacts, and scores.

	Risk	Probability	Impact	Score
1	Planes are discovered during flight	50%	80%	40%
2	Poor or incorrect intelligence	70%	60%	42%
3	Hijackers are alerted early	50%	70%	35%
4	Bad weather	30%	30%	9%
5	Ugandan forces pursue departing commandos and hostages	50%	50%	25%

Before risk plans are in place, they are considered "*pre-mitigated*" risks. Risk planning is a process where the team decides how to handle the risks. Risks can be eliminated, transferred, mitigated, or accepted. Prior to putting the risk plans in place, the critical risks have a high probability of causing projects to fail to meet one or more key objectives. However, by formulating risk plans, the team is either able to eliminate them or minimize the probability of them occurring. We can rank risks based on their post-mitigation scores. In most cases, mitigation plans are costly and mitigation plans are reserved for critical risks that cannot be eliminated or transferred.

Risk mitigation is an activity which is performed before a risk occurs; risk response is performed after a risk occurs. For example, to avoid detection and maximize surprise, the planes took a circuitous route under the cover of darkness at an extremely low altitude. This is a mitigation plan whose objective was to lower the possibility of detection from a near certainty to a reasonably low possibility. Firing on the Ugandan forces in the control tower was a response plan: it was executed after the risk occurred. Mitigation plans reduce the probabilities and impacts of risks and become what we refer to as "*post-mitigated*" probability and impact. For example, destroying MiG-17s on the ground can reduce the "Ugandan forces pursue departing commandos and hostages" risk probability from 50% to 10%. We can also rank risks based on their post-mitigation scores as it provides an opportunity to assess effectiveness of the mitigation plans.

The process just described is referred to as *qualitative project risk analysis*. It does not involve any complex mathematical calculations. In reality, it is just a "mental exercise" where we are encouraged to think about potential risks and what to do about them. Though it is a mental or thinking process, in practice, most projects will maintain a risk register using some type of software.

A Quantitative Project Risk Analysis Perspective

In reality, planning for a complex project, such as the raid on Entebbe is much more elaborate process. It includes one very important step: scheduling the operation. Figure 1.2 shows how a schedule of the raid might have appeared.

The issue we want to look at is how risks can have different impacts on tasks and resources. The same risk may have different impacts on different

	Task Name	Low Duration	Base Duration	High Duration	Gantt Chart 11 PM	12 PM
1	First Plane Landing in Entebbe	4.5 min	5 min	5.5 min		
2	**Assault Element**		30 min			
3	Unload Vehicles	1.8 min	2 min	3 min		
4	Drive to Terminal	4.5 min	5 min	7.5 min		
5	Approach Terminal	1.8 min	2 min	3 min		
6	Enter Terminal	0.9 min	1 min	1.5 min		
7	Secure Hostages	18 min	20 min	30 min		
8	**Securing Element**		45 min			
9	Securing Forces Planes Land	5 min	5 min	5 min		
10	Secure Civilian Airport Field	18 min	20 min	30 min		
11	First Plane Landing in Entebbe	9 min	10 min	15 min		
12	Clear and Secure Runways	9 min	10 min	15 min		
13	Securing Hercules Aircraft for Hostages	9 min	10 min	15 min		
14	Manoeuver Hercules Close to Terminal	9 min	10 min	15 min		
15	Clear Military Airstrip	9 min	10 min	15 min		
16	Destroy MIG Fighters	9 min	10 min	15 min		
17	Defend Against Ugandan Forces	17 min	30 min	45 min		
18	**Departure**		15 min			
19	Load Hostages	4.5 min	5 min	7.5 min		
20	Defend Planes	9 min	15 min	17 min		

Figure 1.2. Schedule of the raid.

tasks. Some tasks may not be on or near the critical path, or in other words, if the task duration increases if a risk occurs, the final project duration may not be impacted. In addition, multiple risks may impact the same tasks. As a result, an assessment of the cumulative impact of all risks on project can be quite complex.

Here is how it can be done. After we identified risks and risk responses, we need to assign these "post-mitigated" risks' probability and impact to tasks and resources. For example, the risk "poor or incorrect intelligence" can cause an increase of duration of the task "driving to terminal" as the assault team takes longer to locate and secure hostages. This risk actually did occur when the Mercedes was stopped at the check point.

In addition, risks can be related to each other, for example, one risk can be correlated with another one. The risk "Poor or incorrect intelligence" could occur when the risk "Ugandan forces pursue departing commandos and hostages" occurs. Risks can occur at a certain moment during the course of a task. The same risk may have different alternative outcomes, for example, 10% cancel task, 20% delay task, and 5% accelerate task (an opportunity). The process of modeling schedules with risks and identifying the relationship between the risks is called *Event chain methodology*, which we will review in later chapters of the book.

The risk register should only include important and readily identifiable risks. There might have been a risk that a commando could fall down and sprain his ankle (causing a delay), but our ability to manage these events is extremely limited and many cannot be foreseen. To model these "noise" events, we can use ranges of task duration by defining low and high duration of each task. In our example, we can define low and high duration. For example, for activities that we believe have little uncertainty, we can multiply the base duration by 0.9 and 1.2 to produce a low and high duration respectively. Alternatively, in activities that have a higher level of uncertainty, we use 0.7 and 2.0 to calculate low and high durations.

The next step is to perform a mathematical calculation with the project schedule and these risks as an inputs. This mathematical calculation can give us answer on few very important questions:

1. What are the most critical risks that can have the largest impact on our project? The entered and calculated risk probabilities and impacts may differ for risks as when we assign risks they may be assigned to multiple tasks or resources. From our analysis, the most critical (the one with the highest score) risk is "Planes are discovered during flight." Indeed, this appears to be not only the most critical risk in our analysis, but was also recognized as such by the original planners who went to great lengths to reduce the probability of this risk for if it occurred it would probably have caused the rescuers to abandon the raid.

2. What is the duration of project with all risks and uncertainties? This realistic or risk adjusted project schedule should be managed.

3. What is chance that project will be completed within a certain period of time? For example, before more Ugandan ground forces could arrive to support troops stationed in the airport. In reality, the assault portion of the mission took 53 min. But from our analysis there was only a 20% chance of the successful completion of the operation with this period of time. Perhaps, the planners knew something we do not or had a very high risk tolerance.

4. What is the success rate of the project? Success rate is the chance that project objectives are met.

Two things are apparent (at least from our analysis): first, the Israelis' were extremely efficient and executed a successful rescue in about as short period as possible; second, that the mission was very risky and is an example of how careful planning and almost perfect execution can overcome formidable odds.

What we just discussed is called quantitative project risk analysis or a process of assigning numerical probabilities to the risks and uncertainties and applying quantitative methods to determine impact of those risks on the project schedule. Even though we used a simplified analysis of this historic event, it does shows how quantitative risk analysis will gauge how much risk your project has, how you can minimize risk, and what the chances are that you can meet a particular deadline.

Project Risk Management Perspective

The success of Entebbe raid was the result not only of a successful analysis of the risk as part of planning the operations, but also in execution of the plan. We are sure that Israeli commandos were prepared for many eventualities. Risks, including their probabilities and impact, change over time. If a risk occurs it is converted to an issue and a response plan is executed. If the issue is resolved, it becomes a lesson learned (Figure 1.3). US Admiral Bill McRaven, who was the commander of the raid that killed Osama bin Laden in Pakistan in 2011, published a book almost two decades ago, Spec Ops: Case Studies in Special Operations Warfare (McRaven, 1996). This book is regarded as the bible for how to plan special operations.

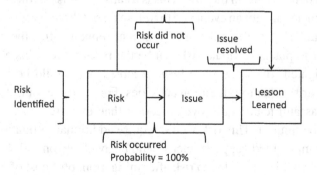

Figure 1.3. Project risk management life cycle.

McRaven interviewed the key participants in a number of special operations including the Entebbe raid. Some risks and particularly the risk "Hijackers became aware" has become a lesson learned: successful operations must be done with great speed and generate complete to adversaries (Bergen and Sterman, 2014).

All other information associated with risks, for example, dates when risk active, risk description, objectives, dates when risk is active, can change as well. Risks should be reviewed over time of the course of a project. Risks may have owners that are responsible for activities associated with the risk. This process of identification, analysis, assessment, and control of the risks in projects is called *project risk management*.

Before we move further, we need to mention few important concepts, related to risk management:

1. **Trigger** is an event, which can cause a risk. In some cases, triggers can also be a risk. Identification of triggers is very important because it allows project members to identify events which will increase the likelihood that a risk will occur. For example, in the Shabwa raid, when the dog started barking it was a trigger for the risk of lost element of surprise. Indeed, you do not need to be an expert in risk management to understand that there could be a chain of events or triggers that occurred. The rescuers made too much noise, caused the dog to bark, which alerted the captors. Would it be possible to get rid of the initial trigger? Possibly.

2. **Cause:** The risk can be caused by something that is not a trigger. For example, a special operations force member's rifles jams because of design deficiencies in the rifle. This is a cause of a risk. However, design deficiencies are not an event and therefore do not directly trigger the jam.

3. **Residual risk** is the amount of risk that remains after the risk plans are put in place. Residual risk can be the risk that remains after a risk is mitigated, risks that have been accepted or it could be a new risk which arises due to mitigation activities. For example, in Entebbe raid, if the assault team is discovered earlier than expected, many hostages could be injured. This risk would require additional mitigation efforts, for example, medical personnel should be available on C-130 planes.

4. **Cost of risk** is a loss due to risk after mitigation, plus cost of mitigation and response plans, plus cost of residual risks. The "expected" cost of

risk is the potential cost of the risk multiplied by the probability of the risk. For example, in Shabwa raid, the cost would be calculated based on whether V-22 Osprey aircraft is damaged or destroyed. Actual cost of V-22 Osprey aircraft is around $70 million (AeroWeb, 2015). Chance that that aircraft will crash after mitigation efforts could be reduced to 1%. So, the expected loss is $700,000. In addition, the cost of mitigation efforts and residual risks might be $100,000. So, the cost of the risk is $800,000.

5. **Risk Category:** Risks can impact different project parameters: duration, cost, safety, security, technology, etc., which are referred to as categories. Categories can be related to schedules such as duration and cost. If risk belongs to schedule related category, the risk impact may change, if schedule changes. Alternatively, non-schedule risk categories are not directly related to a project schedule. These include safety, technology, public relations, quality, legal, security, and others.

Risks and Their Attributes

On November 4, 1979 students seized the US Embassy in Tehran, Iran along with 52 hostages. In response, US President Jimmy Carter ordered Operation Eagle Claw (or Operation Evening Light or Operation Rice Bowl) in an attempt to release the diplomats held captive at the embassy of the United States in Iran (Bowden, 2006). The operation took place on April 24, 1980.

Originally, the planning for the operation was very complex. It was to take place over two nights. On the first night, the aircraft, including eight helicopters RH-53D Sea Stallions (Figure 1.4) would enter Iran and fly to a designated refueling point Desert One. Jet fuel and troops would be brought to the area by C-130 and EC-130E aircraft. The second stage of the operation would be focused on the hostage rescue itself. It was planned to start from a point closer to Tehran named Desert Two Tehran. With the troops loaded on, the helicopters were to fly from Desert One to Desert Two, to be met by trucks driven by CIA agents stationed in Iran. At this time, the CIA agents and ground forces would travel from Desert Two into Tehran. AC-130 gunships would be deployed around the site in Tehran where the hostages were being held. At the same time, other US troops would disable electrical power in the area. Finally, another group of troops would capture

Figure 1.4. Helicopters RH-53D before the mission on the USS Nimitz.

Manzariyeh Air Base near Tehran to allow the arrival of several C-141 Starlifters. Once this was all in place, the US troops in Tehran would assault the embassy and release the hostages. The hostages and troops would be evacuated immediately by helicopters stationed across the street from the embassy and flown directly to the Manzariyeh Air Base. Finally, C-141 Starlifters would fly hostages to troops to a designated safe location. How risky does this plan appear? One principle tells us that the more complex a project, the higher number of risks and chance of project failure.

So what happened? After the planes landed at Desert One, the helicopters were sent to the area. One helicopter was forced to land in the desert due to a cracked rotor blade. The crew was picked up by another helicopter. Another helicopter encountered a sand storm and had to return to the Nimitz aircraft carrier. A third helicopter arrived at Desert One with broken hydraulic system. Although five other helicopters successfully arrived at Desert One, commanders decided that five helicopters would not be enough to continue the operation and received a presidential confirmation to abandon the mission. As the aircraft were preparing to leave, a plane and helicopter collided killing eight soldiers and destroying both aircraft. An official investigation blamed deficiencies in mission planning and command and control for the failure of the operation.

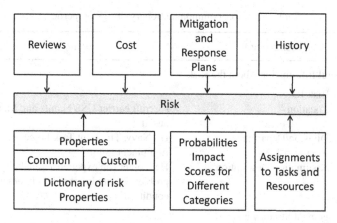

Figure 1.5. Risk attributes.

Risk is not just a name of event with probability and impact. It has many attributes. Let us take a look on one risk associated with the operation — mechanical problem with the helicopters. Figure 1.5 shows the set of risk attributes as shown below:

1. **Risk Properties** includes general qualitative information about risk. This information comes from a dictionary that can be customized for every organization. For example, if you do not need to record the cost of risk, this property can be optional or not be included at all. The risk properties can be used to filter the risk register. For example, you may want to see all risks assigned to a particular owner or those who share a certain trigger. Table 1.2 shows most common risk properties.

2. **Risk Probability, Impacts, and Scores for Different Categories:** Each risk has a certain probability, impact, and score (probability multiplied on impact). If probability equals 100% the risk become an issue. Each risk could a threat, opportunity, but in most cases both threat and opportunity. The opportunity always exists for all risks, although is many cases it is very minor. The same risk can affect different categories. Table 1.3 shows common set of risk categories, which can be customized for different organizations.

3. **Assignment to Task or Resources:** Risks can be assigned, or linked to tasks and resources. For example, the risk "Mechanical problem with the helicopters" can be assigned to a number of tasks, including Flight to

Table 1.2. Most common dictionary of risk properties.

	Risk property	Example
1	General Information About the Risk	
	1.1 Risk ID	
	1.2 Location	Aircraft carrier USS Nimitz and Iranian desert
	1.3 Division/Department	US Navy, The Joint Task Force
	1.4 Area of risk	Equipment failure
	1.5 Assumption/Description	Helicopter can experience reliability problem due to longer flight in desert condition
2	Management Strategy and Objectives	
	2.1 Threat management strategy: avoid transfer, mitigate, accept	Avoid risk or mitigate mechanical failure depending on severity of the problem
	2.2 Opportunity management strategy: exploit, share, enhance, transfer	
	2.3 Objectives	Ensure that mechanical failure does not involve more than 2 helicopters
	2.4 Duration of mitigation efforts	During entire operation
3	Risk Cause and Effect	
	3.1 Cause	Manufacturing defect
	3.2 Trigger	Insufficient testing
	3.3 Effect	In case of mechanical failure, helicopter must return to USS Nimitz, land in a desert and be destroyed
4	Resources Associated with the Risk	
	4.1 Recorder	Helicopter pilot
	4.2 Owner	The helicopter commander Marine Lieutenant Colonel Edward R. Seiffert
	4.3 Contact	Operation controller
	4.4 Manager	Marine Lieutenant Colonel Edward R. Seiffert
5	Risk Timeline	
	5.1 Date identified	During operation planning
	5.2 Date recorded	During operation planning
	5.3 Date closed	Never closed, used a lesson learned

(Continued)

Table 1.2. (*Continued*)

	Risk property	Example
5.4	Date converted to issue	At the benign of operation when one helicopter (Bluebeard 6) was grounded to abandoned in a desert when experienced cracked rotor blade
5.5	Date converted to lesson learned	At the end of operation
5.6	Last review	During operation
5.7	Review frequency	Frequency increase when active phase of the operation start
5.8	Next review	During operation
6	Pre-Mitigation Analysis	
6.1	Start time — pre-mitigation (sunrise)	Before eight US Navy helicopters from HELMINERON 16 would arrive to the USS Nimitz
6.2	Finish time — pre-mitigation (sunset)	End of operation
6.3	Exposure period — post mitigation	During preparation and operation itself
7	Post-Mitigation Analysis	
7.1	Start time — post-mitigation (sunrise)	Before eight US Navy helicopters would arrive to the USS Nimitz
7.2	Finish time — post-mitigation (sunset)	End of operation
7.3	Exposure period — post mitigation	During preparation and operation itself
7.4	Residual risk	Probability of mechanical failure will remain until the end of operation

Desert One, Flight to Desert Two, Flight to Tehran, etc. The risk can also be assigned to the resource "Troops", so the risk can occur in any tasks where the troops are transported by the helicopter. The risk assignment is very important for quantitative risk analysis, where we need to know how risks would affect particular tasks.

4. **Risk Reviews:** The character of risks are always changing during the course of a project. After the risk "Mechanical problem with the helicopters," is identified and included to the risk register, during operation

Table 1.3. Risk categories.

	Risk category	Example, how risk "Mechanical problem with the helicopters" affect most important categories
1	Project duration or scope	Mechanical failure would delay landing at Desert One and all subsequent activities. It can cause cancelation of activities
2	Cost and income	Helicopters can be lost or require costly repair
3	Safety and security	Mechanical failure could not only jeopardize safety of troops, but also safety of hostages
4	Legal	
5	Quality	
6	Technology	
7	Public relations	Significant public relations issues for US military and Carter administration
8	Environment	

planning, everything could change multiple times. For example:

- Risk probability and impact, and other attributes could be updated because the scope of the mission can change, for example in case the helicopters need to fly to Desert Two at a different time.
- Mechanical conditions of helicopters must be checked after helicopters arrive to Nimitz.
- New experts can give another opinion on risk properties.
- Quantitative schedule risk analysis can be performed and yield different probability and impact.
- New mitigation and response plans can be generated, for example in the case where new or updated intelligence is received from the CIA agents in Iran.

> If impact is negative, the risk would become a *threat*. If impact is positive it is an *opportunity*.

5. **Risk History:** Is essentially a set of change records for each risk? Each time a risk is modified either as a results of review or without any formal review, it needs to be recorded as one of the attributes of the risk. For example, during a review after the completion of any special operation

such as Operation Eagle Claw, it is important to understand if certain risks were identified and assessed, and if yes, when and by whom. Risk history is also important for risk audit or complete review of all risks.

6. **Risk Cost:** Information about risk cost, including expected loses, cost of residual risks and mitigation plans is also a risk attribute.

7. **Mitigation and Response Plans:** The same mitigation and response plans can be used in different risks. Therefore, it is easier to record them in a separate list. The references to these mitigation and response plans are an attribute of a risk. One risk may have multiple mitigation and response plans that can be executed sequentially. When mitigation or response plan is assigned to the risk, it could include such attributes as probabilities and impact reduction due to mitigation efforts, dates when plans were executed, and action plan if it is specific for the risk.

Chapter 2

Risk Identification, Monitoring, and Control

In this chapter, we will discuss the basic processes of project risk management. Although this book is focused on project risk analysis, which is one component of project risk management, it is important to understand the associated processes of risk identification and communication as they are used as the inputs and outputs of the project risk analysis. These processes require an understanding of how to identify risks including probabilities and impacts, the roles or risk reviews, risk audit, and risk commission.

Tzar Bomba

Can you guess what is the monstrous contraption? It is the casing of Tsar Bomba, a Soviet Union-made hydrogen bomb, the most powerful nuclear weapon ever detonated. The bomb had a yield of 50 megaton s of TNT and was tested in the Novaya Zemlya archipelago in Arctic Ocean on October 30,1961. Just for comparison, the nuclear bomb in Hiroshima of 16 kilotons of TNT was a mere spark in comparison, the Bomba was 3,000 times more powerful, which represents 10 times the combined energy of all the conventional explosives used in World War II (Andryushin *et al.*, 2003). The bomb was dropped from an altitude of 10.5 km using s parachute and was detonated at an altitude of slightly above 4 km. The fireball reached nearly as high as the altitude of the release plane and was visible at almost 1,000 km away. The height of mushroom cloud reached 67 km at its maximum or more than seven times the height of Mount Everest.

I think that we can all agree that designing and testing hydrogen bombs involve a lot of risk. Therefore, if you are working on project that is this complex, has never been previously performed, and involves extreme hazards, this requires very careful and stringent risk analysis and management. (*Note*: if you are planning to build a hydrogen bomb in your garage, this book will come in handy). We can assume that the risk management on all phases of the project was done properly as there was a successful result. Here are a few examples of the risks the project has that were identified and partially mitigated.

1. The design of the bomb was capable of yielding approximately 100 megatons TNT, but engineers discovered that plane delivering the bomb would not have enough time to escape the explosion (no kidding!). Moreover, there was a legitimate concern that huge blast would cause too much nuclear fallout, so the decision was made to reduce the power of the bomb.
2. The heat from the blast would be so significant that to protect both the delivery and observer plane were painted in reflective white paint to provide an additional protection.
3. The bomb weighed 27 metric tons, was 8 m (26 ft.) long and had a diameter of 2 m (6.6 ft.). It was so large that the plane's bomb bay doors and internal fuel tanks had to be removed, which in turn created additional risks related to flying the aircraft.
4. There was a chance the parachute would not deploy properly, so special measures were taken and if there was a malfunction, the bomb would be disabled.

Nevertheless, in spite of their risk planning, some risks did occur. For example, contrary to original calculations, the fireball caused by a bomb did not hit the ground because its own shock wave reflected back and prevented it. The shock wave caused the plane to drop one kilometer in altitude. Moreover, the actual yield was 57–58.6 megatons of TNT, around 15% greater than the calculated theoretical yield.

Risk Identification Techniques

Even though it was not perfect, the history of this particular H-Bomb testing project underscores the importance of risk identification processes. Without going through this process, it is probable that many risks would not have been mitigated or avoided and the result would have been disaster and almost was for the plane. Project Management Body of Knowledge (Project Management Institute, 2013) describes a number of risk identification techniques:

- **Documentation review** is a review of relevant project documents associated with current and previous projects. For example, if a plan is inconsistent with its requirements, that can be a source for potential risks. One such document is a project schedule. It is much easier to identify risks if they are related to project activities.
- **Information-gathering techniques** include brainstorming, the Delphi technique, interviewing, decision conferencing, and strengths, weaknesses, opportunities, and threats (SWOT) analysis.
- **Checklist analysis:** Organizations can create checklists using risks and lessons learned from previous projects. Despite its simplicity, checklists can be a very powerful tool. It was even the subject of a very persuasive book "The Checklist Manifesto" (Gawande, 2011) about importance of checklists in the business world.
- **Assumption analysis** identifies risks by reviewing inconsistencies or inaccuracies in original project assumptions.
- **Diagramming techniques** include flow charts, cause-and-effect diagrams, influence diagrams, event chain diagrams, mind maps, and others.

Group Integration Techniques for Risk Identification

Research in group judgment and decision-making confirms that group discussions can lead to better decisions (Virine and Trumper, 2007). Here are few techniques which can be used for risk identification:

1. Consensus: These are face-to-face discussions between group members where one judgment is eventually accepted by all members. Team members meet regularly to identify and review risks in anticipation that they will come to a consensus. However, this method has a problem which is called "We discussed and I decided." Some team members, who often happen to be managers, can monopolize the discussion and significantly influence the final judgment.

2. Delphi: The Delphi method named after Oracle of Delphi was developed at the RAND Corporation, a non-profit global policy think tank, at the beginning of the Cold War to forecast the impact of technology on warfare. The Delphi process helps to protect against the "We discussed and I decided" effect, because group members do not meet face-to-face. Instead, they provide their opinions anonymously, perhaps on paper or some other method that ensures anonymity, in a series of rounds until a consensus is reached. The facilitator sends out a list of questions about potential risks or just asks "what risks can occur" to a panel of experts. Responses are then analyzed and common and conflicting viewpoints are identified.

3. Dialectic: In this technique, members are asked to discuss those factors that may be causing biases in their judgments. Group members who hold differing opinions on what risks can affect the project and how will try to understand each other and resolve their differences by examining contradictions in each person's position. For example, during the H-Bomb testing, some team members may have disagreed with each other about the safety implications of a certain design. It would be important to discuss these issues.

4. Interviewing: The moderator can individually interview project experts to elicit information about risks. Many risks are related to personal issues related to different team members and management in particular. Often these interpersonal issues are better to discuss in confidence. In 1989 movie "Weekend at Bernie's", two low-level financial employees Larry Wilson and Richard Parker discovered insurance fraud in a company run by CEO, Bernie Lomax. Bernie, realizing he had been discovered, considered Larry and Richard as a threat and asked his mob partner Vito to kill them. However, Vito has a different view of where the real risk lies: he believes that Bernie has been attracting too much attention with his opulent lifestyle and spending habits (plus his relationship with Vito girlfriend Tina), and orders a hit on Bernie instead. Obviously, Vito probably considered this risk as confidential and would not include this on the more general organization risk list.

5. Dictatorship: This process uses face-to-face discussions that lead to the selection of one group member whose judgment will represent that of the group. Psychologists found that judgments produced by the dictatorship technique are generally more accurate than those produced by any of the other techniques (Sniezek, 1989). The dictatorship technique may be useful when a project team is trying to identify risks that require specific knowledge or expertise. In this case, it is important to identify the person with the best knowledge of the subject and discuss potential risks under his or her guidance.

6. Decision conferencing: Decision conferencing involves having experts get together for 1–3 days in face-to-face meetings that are moderated by a decision analyst (Phillips, 2006). The analyst creates computer-based models that incorporate the risks identified by experts. We will discuss these models in later chapters of this book. The main advantage of this approach is that the creation of the model goes in parallel with the discussions, so that the experts can examine the results as the discussions progress and provide a quick reality check. It is an iterative process that allows experts to identify risks and then review results of analysis and update their original assumptions if required.

7. Brainstorming techniques: There are a number of different brainstorming techniques (Clemen, 1997). The main goal of these techniques is to promote creative thinking among group members. The three main rules about brainstorming are:

- Do not present detailed analysis of the ideas.
- All ideas are welcome, even the absolutely "far out" ideas; groups should come up with as many ideas as possible.
- Group members are encouraged to come up with ideas that extend the ideas of other members.

Psychologists have discovered that brainstorming can be more effective if several people work on a problem independently and then share and discuss their ideas (Hill, 1982). One of brainstorming techniques is called the *nominal group method* (Delbecq *et al.*, 1975). In the beginning, each group member writes down as many potential risks as possible. During the meeting, the members present these risks, the group evaluates them, and the moderator records the result of the discussion. After the discussion, every group member ranks the risks. These rankings are then combined mathematically to select what risks could be used in further analysis.

Diagramming Tools for Risk Identification

A number of diagramming techniques are used for risk identification. All these tools can be used as part of risk identification workshop where moderators enter information about risks during discussion and present it to the experts. This can be performed with specialized software or simply a paper and a pen.

One of the diagramming techniques is called *Event chain diagrams*, where risks are presented on a Gantt chart. We will discuss this technique in detail in Chapter 7 of this book. The issue with this technique is that relies on a project schedule that may be not yet be ready for a specific phase of the project. In the absence of detailed project schedule, it is possible to use flow charts, which show major phases or milestones of the project and relationship between them. It is possible to also use the WBS elements as the basis of this analysis. With these charts, it is easier to identify risks associated with particular project phases, deliverables, or objectives. Flow charts are especially good at showing how branches could impact a project. For example, if a H-Bomb is too large for the plane, another project needs to be conducted to upgrade the plane.

Recently, one of the most popular graphic tools for project risk identification has become mind maps (Figure 2.1). In a mind map, the central theme is often illustrated with a graphic image. The ideas related to the main theme radiate from that central image as "branches." Topics and ideas of lesser importance are represented as "sub-branches" of their relevant branch.

Cause-and-effect diagrams are the brainchild of Kaoru Ishikawa and are sometimes called "fishbone" diagrams (Figure 2.2).

If you are trying to identify the relationship between risks, for example, what risk could trigger another risk, you may find cause-and-effect diagrams useful.

Judgment Elicitation Techniques

After you identify a list of risks, the next step it to determine the risk properties, in particular, risk probabilities and impacts. We recommend that the identification of risk and the subsequent determination of probability and impacts take place in two separate steps, and if possible in separate meetings. This can help to create a psychological breathing room for your

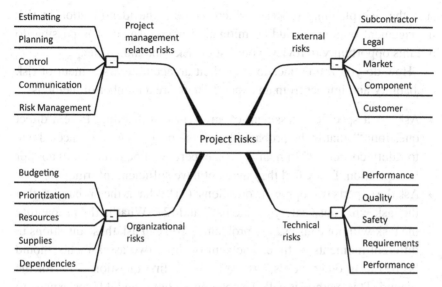

Figure 2.1. Generic mind map for risk identification.

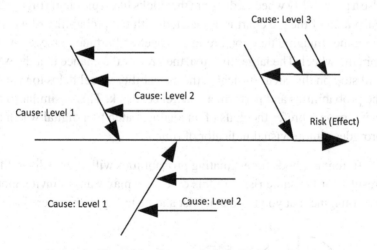

Figure 2.2. Cause-and-effect diagram.

team allowing them to put them in context as well as set the stage to review the existing list. In the next meeting, before you start the process of assigning probabilities and impact, you can review the original list, perhaps you missed a few or are redundant or irrelevant. Finally, you can then start the risk planning process, which includes the identification of risk management options, including mitigation plans. Again, it is possible to use this opportunity to review your list of risks one more time.

How do you frame questions to elicit an accurate assessment of risk probability and impact from an expert? There are a number of methods:

- Ask for a specific assessment of an event's probability. Pose a direct question: "What is the probability that the project will be canceled due to safety concerns?" In many cases, experts will be reluctant to answer this question if they feel they may not have sufficient information.
- Ask the experts two opposing questions: (1) "What is the probability that the task will cause safety problems?" and (2) "What is the probability the task will not cause safety problem?" You can ask these questions in different moments of time. The sum of these two assessments should be 100%. In other words, say 30% for the first question, 70% for the second. This method is called a coherence check, and it helps experts to starting thinking about this risk.
- Use a probability wheel, a diagram that looks like a pie chart (Figure 2.3). Each area of the pie chart is associated with the probability of a certain outcome. Imagine that you are in a Wheel of Fortune game show. You spin the wheel. The larger the area, the greater the chance that the wheel will stop on this area. Basically, the probability wheel helps to visualize the probabilities and perform a coherence check. This is similar to how many people prefer the dials of an analog watch to a digital watch as it provides a more visual indicator of time.

Different methods for estimating probabilities will often deliver different results for the same risks. In this case, you may want to invite another expert. Imagine that you to go a dentist and he tells you that there is a 90%

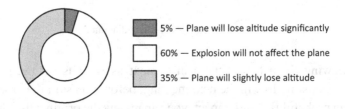

Figure 2.3. Probability wheel.

probability that you will lose a tooth and he needs to extract it. Dismayed as you do not like the image of a big gap in your smile, you head next door to another dentist and his assessment is 50%, but also offers a root canal as an alternative. Finally, you visit a third dentist and the prognosis is now 5% and you probably do not require any remedy other than a new toothbrush. What should you do given this conflicting advice? Often, the last one who has less motivation bias (profit) is most likely correct, but who knows. You may want to arrange a conference between the experts to discuss their assumptions and how they came to their conclusions, but this may not be practical.

Our preferred method to deal with this problem is to break down the risk into simpler risks and review them separately. For example, instead of asking a single question about the probability that the project will be canceled due to safety problems, you may ask two questions:

- What it is the chance that a safety problem will occur?
- What is the chance that the safety problem will lead to a project cancelation?

Psychologists found that identifying probabilities can be accurate as long as information is properly elicited (Cooke, 1991; O'Hagan *et al.*, 2006). Essentially, the accuracy of the judgment depends on how questions are framed. If you have a strategic or a complex project, we recommend the use of risk workshops with a moderator who is an expert in judgment elicitation.

Risk Reviews, History, and Audit

Risks in complex projects require constant monitoring, because all information about the risks, including probability, and impact may change during the course of a project. It is important that information about the actual status of risks is not ignored and slips through the cracks. Most changes occur as a result of performance management: different management decisions or actual performance can cause the probability of some risks to change, risk owners can change, some risks may be closed, mitigation or response plans may be updated.

A common phenomenon in many movies is that the level of suspense constantly grows. For example, a standard movie scene is where one character has a hold of another's hand to keep them from plummeting from a skyscraper, cliff, helicopter or other prop. To build up the suspense, at the beginning of the scene the grip is usually strong, then as time goes by, the grip loosens and a long fall, scream, and death seem imminent. Miraculously though, when all seems lost and the one character's life starts to flash before their eyes, they are pulled up from danger. How, a sudden jolt of adrenalin, strong coffee, or a shot of steroids? Who knows, but everyone is safe and high fives all around. If this was a project "Pull character hanging from helicopter into safety" we would see that the probability of the risk changes over the life of the project. At the beginning, the risk probability is low as the hero's grip seems to be quite strong, but then as he or she starts to get tired and the grip weakens the probability increases gradually until it rises almost to 100%. Here is how your risk history log would look like

21:43:15 — Risk "fall from the plane", probability 50%. Impact: instant death.

21:43:16 — Risk "fall from the plane", probability 70%. Impact: instant death.

21:43:17 — Risk "fall from the plane", probability 99.9%. Impact: instant death.

21:43:18 — Risk "fall from the plane," Probability 0%. Impact: None. The risk is converted to lesson learned "When flying, make sure you are on the inside of the plane".

If you find yourself in this situation, desperately clutching onto the hand of an unfortunate team member who has found themselves on the outside of an airborne plane, you can probably defer on updating your risk status. However, when situations are not so dire and you have more time (and hands) to spare, if your risks are experiencing changes to probability or other attributes, you better update them, otherwise the results of any future risk analysis, including risk ranking may be incorrect.

Risk reviews can be conducted as part of regular project tea meetings or individually by risk owners or risk managers. Usually, risk management software sends a notification when risk needs to be reviewed. It can be done periodically, weekly, monthly, etc. All parameters of the risk should to be reviewed and updated if required. Risk reviews are usually augmented with information that describes the current project situation as it impacts the particular risk. For example, during a particular period risk mitigation activities are completed successfully. In this case, you need to update the risk to reflect any changes to probability or impact due to these activities. Each time a parameter of the risk is updated, a change record needs to be created, which becomes the risk history. This risk history is important for auditing purposes as it will describe who, what, when, and, most importantly, why the changes were made?

Risk Committee is a group of experts, which ensures that risk identification, analysis and communication are done consistently across organization. For example, a risk committee can facilitate risk reviews and approve risks for inclusion to the risk lists.

A *risk audit* is a review of some or all of the risks by an independent body. Risks are usually entered to the list by different people who have different perceptions of risks and different risk tolerance. Remember, the 1964 movie "Dr. Strangelove or: How I Learned to Stop Worrying and Love the Bomb"? Apparently Dr. Strangelove, the President's scientific advisor and former Nazi, liked nuclear explosions, but others had different feelings about it. Because of individual differences in perception and risk tolerance, it is important to ensure consistency in all risk properties. Organizations usually have *risk committee* or a group of experts that are responsible for risk audits and overseeing other aspects of the risk management process. In many cases, risk committees also review and approve risks that have been identified and entered into the system. In this case, until they are approved they are not considered open and visible to anyone but members of the committee. The reason for this committee is that risks can be misnamed, misidentified, duplicate, or even irrelevant. For example, we often come across situations where the same risk has been given a different name, so in the risk register they appear as different risks, but are in actuality the same risk. One expert may identify a general risk as "Bad weather," but another may identify it more specifically as "Frost can affect release of

H-Bomb parachute." It may be the first general risk needs to be broken down into smaller risks, frost being one of them. It is the job of the risk committee to ensure that risks are identified with correct level of granularity. In addition, it needs to review risk information to ensure all required properties have been added.

Chapter 3

Risk Registers and Risk Prioritization

The goal of risk analysis is to prioritize risks. Risk prioritization is an output of qualitative or quantitative risk analysis. Risk prioritization facilitates project decisions, particularly with regards to risk mitigation and response planning. There are a number of tools which can help with risk prioritization, particularly the risk register and the risk matrix.

Why We Should Prioritize Risks

Let us assume that this summer you are planning a road trip from Boston to New York that will primarily travel along the I95. The weather forecast is promising, nothing spectacular, but good for travelling. Before embarking on your trip, you perform *ad hoc* risk assessment. Like a good project manager, you want to minimize the chance of delays and determine what you might require in case of an emergency. Here is an example of risks that you might encounter:

1. You run out of gas and your trip could take a lot longer. This could be especially concerning if you find yourself out of gas while on the I95 as this means that you will have increased the probability of other risks occurring as you are stranded precariously on the side of the freeway.
   Mitigation plan: Start with a full tank of gas and, if you are extremely risk averse, you might choose to carry an extra gas caner or two.
2. Your car breaks down. As with the above, this has the potential to seriously impact your schedule (as well as your budget).
   Mitigation plan: Perform all scheduled maintenance and perhaps ask your mechanic to inspect all major systems. However, even a well

maintained vehicle can suffer a breakdown, so you may want to carry a few spare parts. For example, some light bulbs, spark plugs, a crankshaft, and an alternator, just in case.

3. You get a flat tire. You already have a spare one, but you could get a second flat.

    Mitigation plan: Carry a second spare tire.

4. In spite of the forecast, the weather is unpredictable and may turn for the worst.

    Mitigation plan: Pack some extra supplies, candles, warm blankets, rain gear, extra food, and other items that will help you survive a couple days in case of a major hurricane and floods. Take a raft and life jacket.

5. You could be robbed. Could it happen on your way to New York? Absolutely.

    Mitigation plan: Wear body armor and carry your stun gun, pepper spray, and horn with you. Just in case things get really ugly, you probably should have your machine gun and enough rounds of ammunition to survive a long siege — think the "Walking Dead."

6. The roads could be blocked. Think of what happened to the King of France, Henry the IV. Well travelling down a road, he found it blocked by several logs. When they stopped, an assassin jumped into the carriage and stabbed the king. Henry IV was not good in risk management, but you are.

    Mitigation plan: Take a chainsaw and, just in case, your mother-in-law can ride in the back as a body guard.

7. You could get a speeding ticket. You could go the speed limit and eliminate the risk altogether, but your plan calls for a speed of 15% over the posted limit. It will get you to New York quicker, but close to a speed that will put you at risk for a ticket.

    Mitigation plan: You could buy some anti-radar devices, but better yet, you can install stealth technology and your car will be invisible to police radar.

You might be starting to see a problem here. If you try to avoid and/or mitigate all of the risks you have identified, this will result in two things. Your car will be so laden down with supplies it will be unable to move and the expense of all your mitigation efforts will mean that you will not have any funds to enjoy the sites if you manage to get to New York. For example, though we have not checked, we believe stealth technology would take a considerable chunk out of your budget. The reality is that you must deal with constrained resources (budget, time, etc.) and it would be impossible to completely mitigate all of your risks. The solution is to prioritize your risks to determine which are the most important, so that given your limited resources you can minimize your risks in the most cost effective manner possible. Now the question is, how do you determine what risks are the most important? This is where the risk register comes in as it is the key to prioritizing your risks.

Risk Scores

We discussed risk registers when we talked about risk identification. Now, we can use the risk register as part of the risk analysis, including risk response planning, and risk monitoring and control. To prioritize risks, you need to assign each one a risk score. The risk score is calculated using a risk's probability and impact.

$$\text{Risk score} = \text{Risk Probability} \times \text{Risk Impact}.$$

If a risk occurs, it will have varying impacts on different project objectives (such as duration, cost, and safety). For example, the risk "run out of gas" may have a significant impact on your trip duration, but very little on cost or safety. Therefore, the risk score should be calculated separately for each objective. If you calculate the all probabilities and impacts of a risk, you can calculate its overall risk score. Table 3.1 shows an example of the risk register with risk scores calculated based on overall probabilities and impacts. The bar on the right column is an easy way to present risk scores. To make the score easier to understand, you can multiply them by a certain value (e.g. 100). Please note that risks in the risk register are sorted based on risk score. As a result, Table 3.1 is a *tornado diagram* for risk scores.

Risk score is relatively simple and yet powerful indicator of the order in which we should prioritize our risk response planning activities. Done properly, it provides a realistic measure of the potential impact and its relative importance as compared to other project risks. There are many cases in projects where a risk's impact is very significant but the probability of

Table 3.1. Example of risk register and risk scores.

	Risk	Probability	Impact	Score	
1	Run out of gas	5%	10%	50	
2	Flat tire	3%	15%	45	
3	Mechanical problem	2%	18%	36	
4	Bad weather	2%	15%	30	
5	Speeding ticket	0.5%	50%	25	
6	Armed robbery	0.1%	80%	8	
7	Log on the road	0.1%	50%	5	

occurring is very small. Psychologically, people overestimate the "score" of risks very high because the impacts arouse emotions like fear and anxiety. The classic situation is the risk of a terrorist attack on an aircraft. Although the impact of the risk can be very significant, the probability is very small. The score of a risk "terrorist attack" is lower than many other risks related to the operation of aircraft, such as mechanical problems or a sleep deprived pilot. As a result, people often support greater expenditure towards the elimination of terrorist attacks as opposed to improving maintenance programs or monitoring sleep diaries of pilots. In our road trip example, though an armed robbery would have a significant impact on our project, the probability of it occurring is extremely low. Therefore, its overall risk score is lower compared to the other risks. If you have to make a choice between bringing extra rain gear or wearing body armor, rain gear should be your priority.

Risk scores can be calculated separately for threats (negative risks) and opportunities (positive risks). For example, on a trip from Boston to New York there are a couple of opportunities an early departure to avoid heavy traffic and constant monitoring of traffic reports to avoid accidents or congested areas. The score for opportunities is calculated similar to scores for threats and helps to determine which opportunity should be exploited first.

Risk Impact Types

To come up with a meaningful risk impact and risk score, we need to learn how risk impact is calculated for different categories. In Chapter 1, we

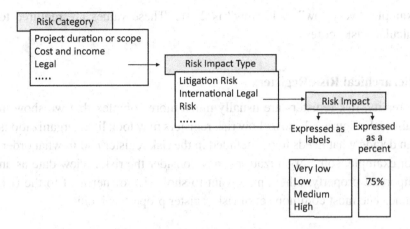

Figure 3.1. Relationship between risk category and risk impact.

learned about risk categories, such as "project duration or scope," "cost and income," "safety and security," and others. These are very general groups of project parameters or objectives that risks can affect. For example, a risk "bad weather" can affect project duration and cost. The question is how. "Bad weather" can cause an increase in duration by a certain number of days, task cancelation, or restart a task. These impacts belong to the same category "project duration or scope" and are measured and calculated differently. The same is true for the cost risk category. "Bad weather" can lead to fixed or relative (%) increase in costs. These impacts are called *Risk Impact Type*. One category may have multiple risk impact types (see Figure 3.1).

Risk impact type or outcome type is the result if a risk occurs.

Each risk has a particular value associated with the risk impact type. This is an actual risk impact. Risk impact can be expressed as a label or as a value. For example, risk "use overseas supplier" belongs to legal category and has "international legal risk" impact type. Actual impact of this risk can be "medium" or 75%. The actual value of the risk impact depends on the risk category and what risk impact type to which it belongs. Usually, each impact label represents a numerical value "behind the scenes". For example, "very low" is 1, "low" is 2, etc. These values are required to calculate risk scores.

Hierarchical Risk Registers

In reality, risk registers are usually much more complex that we show in Table 3.1. Figure 3.2 shows how risk registers may look like. Organizations can decide what needs to be included in the risk register and in what order. For example, some organizations may consider the risk review date as an important property, others may want to show risk owner next to the risk name. The most common set of risk register properties include:

- Risk name.
- Risk description.
- Risk probability, impact, score, and cost before mitigation.
- Risk cost before mitigation.
- Risk probability, impact, score, and cost after mitigation.
- Cost of mitigation.
- Open or closed risk, Is this risk a threat, opportunity, or both? Is it a risk, issue or lesson learned?

Risk registers can be based on risk status or categories and presented in a hierarchical format. In Figure 3.2, this hierarchy is based on Open and Closed risks. In this case we have two groups: Open risks and Closed Risks. Hierarchies can be created using:

- Risk categories — the most common risk hierarchy; please note that since one risk can belong to different categories, the risk can be repeated in different groups; for example "bad weather" may appear in groups "project duration or scope" and "cost and income".
- Open/Closed risks.
- Risk/Issues/Lessons learned.
- Risks assigned to managers.
- Risks assigned to owners.
- Hidden and Visible risks — risks might not visible to specific users and risk register administrators may want to see which risks are hidden or visible.

	Risk Name	Open/Cl	Risk/Issue	Threat/Opp	Probab	Impact	Score	Score	Cost
1	⊟ Open								
2	Delay in Financing	Opened	Risk	Threat	65.0%	63.6%	41.3%		$10,000
3	Other risks, related to the project	Opened	Risk	Threat	20.0%	87.4%	17.5%		$5,000
4	Not enough information about competitors	Opened	Issue	Threat	88.9%	18.2%	16.2%		$8,000
5	Selected name is taken	Opened	Risk	Threat	30.0%	13.4%	4.0%		$7,000
6	Lack of knowledge of the specific area	Opened	Risk	Threat	9.0%	40.5%	3.6%		$6,000
7	Risks affecting whole company/division	Opened	Risk	Threat	4.0%	55.6%	2.2%		$6,000
8	Cost information is not available	Opened	Risk	Both	8.9%	0.0%	0.0%		$10,000
9	Delay in getting level advice	Opened	Risk	Threat	85.0%	0.0%	0.0%		$3,000
10	Delay in patent and trademark search	Opened	Risk	Threat	30.0%	0.0%	0.0%		$4,000
11	Not enough data to analyze demand level	Opened	Risk	Threat	75.0%	0.0%	0.0%		$3,000
12	Not enough data to plan management of de	Opened	Risk	Threat	20.0%	0.0%	0.0%		$3,000
13	Staff turnover	Opened	Issue	Threat	10.0%	0.0%	0.0%		$6,000
14	⊟ Closed								
15	Problem with hiring	Closed	Risk	Threat	0.0%	0.0%	0.0%		$0.00

Figure 3.2. Example of risk register.

If a risk register hierarchy is based on a risk category, it is usually called *Risk breakdown structure*.

In addition to the hierarchical presentation, risk registers can be sorted or filtered. For example, it is possible to view risks, issues, lessons learned separately. It is also possible to filter risks using properties: for example, review date, mitigation cost, etc. Risk register sorting is usually done based on pre-mitigation or post-mitigation risk score, but it can be also done alphabetically to make it easy to locate risks using names or other properties.

Risk Matrixes

Risk matrixes are another tool used to visualize and prioritize risks, as well as to decide on their mitigation strategies (Figure 3.3). Risks are plotted on a chart where the horizontal axis represents impact and the vertical axis represents probability. Therefore, this chart is called a *probability and impact matrix*.

Risk matrixes are usually subdivided into a number of cells: risks with low scores are associated light grey or green cells, risks with medium scores

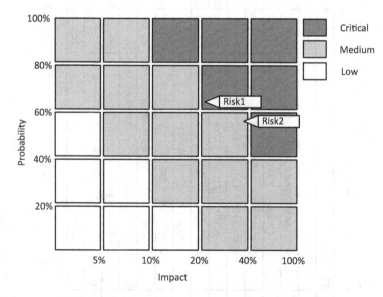

Figure 3.3. Probability vs. impact matrix for threats.

are associated with darker or yellow cells, and risks with high scores are associated with dark or red cells.

This color coding can provide the basis for your overall risk management strategy. In this case, the color of the cell dictates the risk priority and level of planning and/or strategy that must be applied to a risk. For example, all risks that land on the red cells in your risk matrix are considered high priority and must have a defined risk plan (avoid, transfer, or mitigate). Risks that land in the yellow or green are of lesser importance and require less management scrutiny. Management can be accepted and put on your watch list.

You may show additional information on a risk matrix (Figure 3.4):

1. Risk matrices may also show the risk history how risk probability and impacts changed over time; usually, the history is shown as a line intersecting with points indicating times and risk scores.
2. Risk matrices may include the number of risks in each cell; this can be a useful indicator as risk registers can have many risks and in which case it can be difficult to show all the risks on the same matrix.

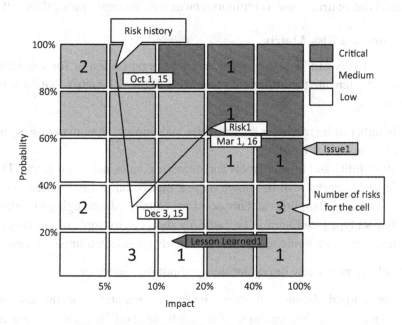

Figure 3.4. Additional information on a risk matrix.

3. Risks, issues, lessons learned, as well as opened and closed risks can be shown on risk matrixes using different symbols or colors
4. Other risk properties, such as owner, manager, risk, cost, etc. can be shown on risk matrixes as well.

Risk Matrix Phenomenon

Let us take a look at Figure 3.3 again. It shows two risks:

- Risk 1. Impact = 22%, Probability = 64%, Score = 14%.
- Risk 2. Impact = 38%, Probability = 46%, Score = 17%.

So, the risk score for Risk 2 is greater than for Risk 1. Nevertheless, Risk 2 lands on the medium risk area of the risk matrix and Risk 1 is on the critical area. The reason why we have this effect is because we are showing the risks on discrete cells rather than on continuous green–yellow–red (white–grey–dark grey) chart. In most cases, this is acceptable, as impact and probabilities are not defined very precisely anyway. If you really concern about this effect, we recommend increasing the number of cells in risk matrix or use a continuous chart with gradients rather than cells.

Setting-up a Risk Matrix

Risk matrixes can be setup up for an entire organization or for a specific program. Here are the important parameters of the risk matrix that must be defined:

1. Number of intervals for probabilities and impact. How many rows and columns will it have?
2. Probability and Impact labels and numerical value of each interval. The label of interval will be shown on risk matrix, but it can be used when you enter probabilities and impacts for a certain risk belonging to certain impact type (see Figure 3.1). Table 3.2 shows an example of probability and impact on numerical scales and labels for selected impact types:

Please note a few important things about risk matrixes:

- You should define and name intervals separately for threats and opportunities. For example, the safety interval definition requiring hospitalization may not be suitable for opportunities (unless this is

Table 3.2. Definition of probability and impact interval labels.

Risk probability label	Probability labels				
	Very low	Low	Medium	High	Very high
Numerical value of probability	0–5% or less than 1 in 20 chance of occurring	5–10% or 1 in 10 chance of occurring	10–25% or 1 in 4 chance of occurring	25–50% or 1 in 2 chance of occurring	50–100% Better than ever chance of occurring
	Impact labels for selected impact types				
Numerical value of impact	0–3%	3–10%	10–30%	25–50%	50–100%
Delay duration impact	<1 month delay	1–2 month delay	2–4 month delay	4–12 month delay	>1 year delay
Safety impact	Non-injury accident	Required medical attention	Required hospitaliza-tion	Loss of work date	Fatality
Quality impact	One or few minor requirements not met	Minor requirements not met	One major requirement not met	More than one major requirements not met	Project cannot be completed

Department of Defense project related to the outcomes of battle tactics). As a result, an organization may need to define many interval names for multiple objectives, for impacts and probabilities, and for threats and opportunities. However, you only have to do this once and it can be used for all of our projects. In addition, you can use the overall rank indicators for objectives that do not require specific intervals.

• In many cases, the intervals for numerical scales are nonlinear. In particular, higher impacts are associated with larger intervals. For example, if you travel from Boston to New York and you delayed on 30 min it may be acceptable, however, it you delayed on 1, 2, or more hours, it is a serious impact to your schedule, and you should avoid such risks.

How to Define Risks in the Risk Register

Let us assume that Indiana Jones is on another mission to recover an ancient artifact and has the risk "Unwanted encounter with the scary guy." Here is how would he might define the risk in a risk register.

1. Enter the risk in the risk register.
2. Identify risk properties. For example, risk "Encounter with the scary guy" will occur only when Indiana Jones is in enemy's airport; Indiana Jones will be an owner and manager of this risk; he is the one man in the airport, and nobody can help him.
3. Select which risk categories this risk will impact. In this case, it is duration and safety; we doubt that Indiana Jones had any concerns about cost, environment, or public relations.
4. Define the type of impact for the impact type related to category project duration:

   a. Relative delay.
   b. Fixed delay.
   c. Restart task.
   d. Cancel task.

5. Define the impact type for safety. Indiana Jones is quite risk tolerant and decides that a fight with huge scary guy is not a problem for him and should not have a high impact on his mission. He can choose how to define safety for:

   a. Safety of himself.
   b. Safety of others.
   c. Safety of equipment and tools.

   Since there is nobody else there that he cares about and he does not have any equipment or tools rather than his hat, he chooses "Safety of himself".

6. Define impact value. For each impact type, Indiana Jones must define an actual impact value. For delay, he enters 10%. For safety, he has five different choices (see Table 3.2). He chooses "Non-injury accident" meaning he probably gets knocked down a few times, but prevails without any grievous wounds as this is the usual outcome of his fights with villains regardless of their size, skill, and weapons. According to

Table 3.2, it is associated with 1.5% (middle value of the range between 0% and 3%).

7. Enter probabilities for risk impacts. Indiana Jones enters probabilities for both risk impacts. Usually, risk has one probability number for all risk categories. So Indiana Jones enters that there is a 50% probability that he will meet a large and dangerous villain.

Ranking Risks Which Belong to Difference Categories

What is more important for Indiana Jones, spend an extra couple of minute to fight a dangerous villain or have a non-injury accident? In other words, what category is more important: Duration or Safety? This is a more difficult question. What if Indiana Jones has several risks, as shown in Table 3.3?

Let's assume that probability of both risks is the same. If we compare risks only within a specific category, it would be very easy prioritize them. For the safety category, the most important risk would be "Encounter with the snake" (as you probably remember Indiana Jones has a phobia of snakes). For the duration category, the most important risk would be "Encounter with the villain." It will just take longer to defeat the villain than avoid the snake. The issue is what is the most important risk if we take all risk impacts for all categories into consideration? Here is how we can solve this problem.

Each category has a priority. These priorities are used to adjust risk scores. Let us assume that we have five categories as it is shown in Table 3.4. Theoretically, we can just assign priority values to each category:

- Duration and scope: 20%.
- Safety: 40%.
- Cost: 20%.
- Legal: 10%.
- Quality: 10%.

Table 3.3. Two risks have different impacts in different categories.

Risk	Impact for safety category	Impact for duration category
Encounter with the villain	1.5%	10%
Encounter with the snake	7%	5%

Table 3.4. Calculation or priorities for risk categories using pair wise comparison.

Risk category	Priority	Safety	Duration and scope	Cost and income	Quality	Legal
Safety	25.2%	1	3	1	1	1
Duration and scope	16.4%	0.33	1	1	1	1
Performance	19.5%	1	1	1	1	1
Quality	19.5%	1	1	1	1	1
Legal	19.5%	1	1	1	1	1

It could be quite accurate if we have just two or three categories, but if we have more categories we can do a more precise calculation. We can ask people, how much more critical to your project or organization is Safety compared to Duration. We might say Safety is three times more important. We would then enter this number into the cell of Table 3.4 associated with Duration and Scope and Safety categories. The corresponding cell associated with both categories will equal 1/3. We can repeat this process on all pairs of categories. In case of five categories it will result in 10 pairs of values. These numbers will be used to calculate priority for each category. This process is called pair-wise comparison. Why is it better than just entering priority as a single value? The reason is it is much easier to elicit relative importance of one category compared to another one. In other words, people will provide much more accurate values if they are asked to compare one category vs. another rather than if they are asked just to provide a priority for each category. A similar process was proposed by Thomas L. Saaty in the 1970s for decision making. It is called *analytic hierarchy process* (AHP) (Saaty and Peniwati, 2008).

Here is how actual priorities are calculated:

1. Calculate the sum of all values for each column. For example, for first column it will be 4.33.
2. Normalize the values in each column. For example, the first value in column "Duration and Scope" will be 1/4.33 = 0.23.
3. Calculate the sum of normalized values for each row. Now that we have priorities, we can use it to calculate impacts for both risks in Table 3.3. Impacts of each risk for each category will be multiplied on the priority

Table 3.5. Calculation of combined risk impact.

Risk	Impact for safety category	Impact for duration category	Total impact
Encounter with the scary guy	1.5% × 0.252	10% × 0.164	2.02%
Encounter with the snake	7% × 0.252	5% × 0.164	2.60%

of this category. For example, we have impact, in our Indiana Jones example we have risk "Encounter with the scary guy." This risk has two impacts:

(a) Impact on duration = 10%.
(b) Impact on safety = 1.5%.
    Now we can multiply these numbers on the prioritization weights for each category (16.4% and 25.2% consequently). The results will be:
(c) Impact on duration = 10% × 0.164 = 1.64%.
(d) Impact on safety = 1.5% × 0.252 = 0.378%.
    Then we can repeat these calculations for the second risk "Encounter with the snake."

4. Sum up the results as shown in Table 3.5.
5. Normalize the results if we want to reset them to a 0–100% scale. This step is optional and not required if we just need to rank the risks.

Based on our analysis, the most important risk for Indiana Jones would be "Encounter with the snake."

Chapter 4

Risk Mitigation and Response Planning

I do not believe in taking foolish chances, but nothing can be accomplished without
taking any chances at all.

Charles Augustus Lindbergh,
American aviator, author, inventor

The main purpose of risk analysis is to decide what to do about your
risks. Unfortunately, often people properly identify risks, but do not pay
very much attention to risk planning because of optimism bias or wishful
thinking. Risks can be avoided, accepted, transferred to another party or
mitigated. If you decide to avoid or transfer a risk, then you can close them
on your risk register. If a risk is accepted, that is, you will not perform any
prior actions to minimize it occurring, then a response plan may be put in
place in case the risk does occur. If you choose to mitigate a risk, then this
indicates you will put in place activities that will reduce the probability
or impact of the risk occurring. In this chapter, we will learn a few basic
concepts of risk mitigation and response planning, such as mitigating risks
in stages, using a risk matrix to depict mitigation plans and storing all plans
in a risk mitigation and response registry.

Why Perform Response and Mitigation Planning?

On May 20–21, 1927, Charles Augustus Lindbergh (Figure 4.1), a
25-year-old US Air Mail pilot, made a solo non-stop flight from New York's
Long Island to Le Bourget Field in Paris, France, a distance of nearly 3,600
statute miles (5,800 km). He used a single-engine, purpose-built monoplane
called the Spirit of St. Louis. This record setting flight took 33 h and 30 min.

Figure 4.1. Charles Augustus Lindbergh.

Lindbergh became the first person in history to be in New York one day and Paris the next.

Preparation for the flight and the flight itself was quite an accomplishment in terms of project management and, in particular, risk management (Charleslindbergh.com, 2015). It was not the first attempt to fly between New York and Paris. Previous attempts failed for various reasons. Lindbergh and his team knew about the potential risks and focused on mitigating them. For example, Lindbergh's crew had strained and restrained the fuel to eliminate as much sediment as possible to prevent any fuel line blockages during the flight. They also ensured that the weight of the plane and fuel was light enough to allow it to take off. Lindbergh's flight was a very risky proposition, but its success in many aspects can be attributed to the risk mitigation.

Both in their everyday lives and in project management, people often do not pay enough attention to risk mitigation and response planning. Our lives might be completely different if we focused on limiting the impact of risk (risk mitigation) rather dealing with them after the fact. We would spend more time cleaning our teeth rather than repairing cavities. We would focus on conserving energy rather than dealing with effects of smog. We would foresee potential delays in our projects and minimize root causes of these delays rather than applying huge resources at the end of our projects trying to complete them on time.

The Psychology of Risk Mitigation

Remember, Q (standing for Quartermaster) the gadget man who gives Bond different weapons, cars and other spy gear for his missions? Here is a snippet from one of their conversations in "The World Is Not Enough":

Q: "I have always tried to teach you two things: First, never let them see you bleed;"

Bond: "And second?"

Q: "Always have an escape plan"

In fact, Q briefs Bond on risk mitigation and response strategies and offers some risk mitigation tools in the form of his gadgets. However, as is often the case in real life, Bond does not really pay any attention to Q and has less respect for Q's equipment (it is never returned in pristine shape). This is an interesting phenomenon: in most cases people are able to identify risks, but they pay much less attention to risk mitigation. This is a common situation in project management: project managers create elaborate risk registers, but their efforts mostly end there. They do not use if for its most important function which is to prioritize and manage the risks, Why is this the norm?

The reason lies in human psychology, particularly in what is called the *Optimism Bias*. According to optimism bias, people tend to believe that they are less exposed to risk than others. For example, smokers believe that they are less likely to suffer or die from smoke related diseases than other smokers. So people know about their risks, but do not want to do anything about them because they think that it will not happen with them. James Bond suffers from the same shortcoming, probably because he had never paid much attention to Q's advice and instructions and was still well and alive after two dozen movies. A real James Bond would probably have died from any combination of gunshots, bombs, alcoholism, and sexually transmitted diseases before he completed his first.

This effect is very common in project management. For example, a company decides to launch a new line of products. The main risk is that market does not like it. Everybody, from the CEO to assembly line workers are aware this is a risk. However, the company management often does not have any mitigation plans to minimize this outcome. For example, they could ensure that the product can be easily updated in case the market does not accept it. In 2005, the toy manufacturer Lego produced an action figure called Galidore based on a TV series (Robertson and Breen, 2013). It was not well accepted by the market, which was one of the primary reasons of the very significant decline in Lego revenue in 2002–2007. The TV series was cancelled after 26 half-hour episodes. The issue is that the design, manufacture, and introduction of products to the market is a long and very expensive process. If mitigation plans for the risks related to product sales are not in place, this could lead to major revenue problems.

Risk Management Strategies

Before landing in US federal jail for 150 years, Bernard Lawrence "Bernie" Madoff was a successful investor. On December 2008, it was discovered that the asset management unit of Bernard L. Madoff Investment Securities LLC was a massive Ponzi scheme, which cost investors billions of dollars. In 2009, the FBI arrested two computer programmers Jerome O'Hara and George Perez on criminal charges of conspiracy for falsifying books in Madoff's company in New York. Computer programing is one of the most secure professions from the liability point of view. Programmers are rarely arrested because of their work. But in this case, O'Hara and Perez developed custom software to deceive investors and regulators and conceal Madoff's crimes. Their computer code made false customer statements, trade confirmations, and other documents that tricked customers and authorities.

> Risk management strategy is a set of activities or projects designed to deal with threats and opportunities.

So when Madoff was planning his scheme, he probably was considering how he would conceal his ill-gotten gains. This concealment was essentially risk management strategy related to the risk "Ponzi scheme is discovered".

Interestingly, this risk, as with most risks related to criminal activities, included both threats and opportunities:

- Threat: Conviction and imprisonment.
- Opportunities: Large amounts of money.

The computer program developed by O'Hara and Perez was designed to address both threats and opportunities at the same time. Here are different mitigation potential strategies for threats:

1. *Accept Risk*: Madoff could choose to do nothing with regard to the documents they issued to regulators or customers. But in this case he might be quickly discovered. So avoiding the threat would not be a viable strategy in this case.
2. *Transfer Risk*: Madoff could ask somebody else to deal with risk, at least partially. For example, he could have purchased an insurance policy, except there is no insurance for the fraud. Perhaps, this could be a new market for insurers: if a fraud scheme is discovered, the policy would pay the crook's legal bills.
3. *Avoid Risk*: Avoiding risk would mean that Madoff abandon the Ponzi scheme and try to run an honest business. But this probably did not appeal to him.
4. *Mitigate Risk*: This is exactly what he did with the custom made computer program. With this program, it was much easier to deceive the authorities and clients and make it very difficult to trace the money. But it was impossible to completely eliminate the risk because the fraud actually took place and there was still a possibility (residual risk) he would be discovered.

Now let us see different management strategies for opportunities.

1. *Accept Opportunity*: The same as for threats, this would entail Madoff doing essentially what he did, just running his Ponzi scheme.
2. *Share Opportunity*: Sharing opportunities in this case would mean sharing the profit as well. In this case, very few people knew about Madoff Ponzi scheme, and he probably was not willing to give up to much of his profits if he was taking most of the risk.

3. *Exploit Opportunity*: This strategy does not work very well in a case of fraud. A good example for exploiting opportunities would be discovering some new investment potential.

4. *Enhance Opportunity*: This is exactly what Madoff did. By providing carefully crafted, but false statements Madoff was able get more clients, avoid detection and operate his scheme longer.

Risk Mitigation vs. Risk Response Planning

When *Q* suggested to James Bond that he should always have an escape plan, he in fact was referring to risk response plan. Here is the difference between mitigation and response:

- *Mitigation plans* are executed *before* a risk occurs; they usually include a list of activities, which are part of project schedule.
- *Response plans* are planned in advance but executed *after* a risk occurs.

Sometimes we call response plans "Plan B", implying that "Plan B" will be executed if "Plan A" fails. Interestingly, Plan B is a trademark of the morning-after birth control pill by Paladin Labs Inc., which is a risk response-type remedy in case other birth control "evening-before" options either were not used or failed.

Because response plans do not need to be executed in advance and don't require actual actions, due to optimism bias people tend to put greater emphasis on planning risk responses rather than mitigation.

Determining which option to take, mitigation or response depends on cost. In many cases, it is cheaper to execute mitigation plans in advance, rather than response plans after the fact. But in project management, it is very important to perform detailed analysis of multiple scenarios with mitigation and response plans to choose the most cost effective course of action.

Registry of Risk Mitigation Plans

In the same manner as risks, mitigation plans can be stored in the registry. Why do we need it? In many projects, one mitigation plan can be used to mitigate many risks. So the process of mitigating planning includes the following steps for each risk:

- Identify a risk strategy.
- Find mitigation and response plans in the registry that include this strategy. Add new plans to the registry if compatible ones do not currently exist.
- Calculate cost of each of these plans.
- Select the best plans.
- Assign mitigation or response plans from the registry to the risk.
- Add new mitigation or response plans to the registry.

Risk mitigation and response plan registries can have hierarchical structures to make it easier to organize and find plans.

Q from James Bond movies offers a complete risk mitigation and response registry. The only thing required of James Bond is to select an appropriate item from the registry and use it in case of particular risk. Table 4.1 shows what *Q*'s risk mitigation and response registry might look like.

Other items in the risk mitigation and response registry could include:

- The Risks to which each plan is assigned; for example, mitigation plan "Use of shooting pen" will be assigned to the risk "James Bond is attacked in the Villain's Kitchen."
- Default probability and impact reduction. For example, the pen gun should reduce the threat from the kitchen staff and therefore the probability that Bond would be killed in the villain's kitchen by 20%. Probability and impact reductions may be different if the mitigation plan is assigned to a different risk.
- Mitigation or response plan description: where and how mitigation plan will be executed.

Risk Mitigation in Stages: Waterfall Charts

On August 24, 2011, Russia launched an unmanned spacecraft Progress M-12M at the International Space Station (ISS). Progress's mission included resupplying ISS with 2.67 tons of supplies: oxygen, food, and fuel. The planned mission also included three reboosts to the ISS. Approximately

Table 4.1. Risk mitigation and response plan registry for James Bond.

Mitigation or response plan name	Type (mitigation response or both)	Cost	Action plan
Use of shooting items			
• Pen gun	Mitigation	$30	Shoot kitchen staff at villain's headquarter
• Machine gun disguised as a tree brunch	Mitigation	$500	Shoot all enemies at the same time in villain's headquarter
Use of Transportation Items			
• Explosion-proof self-driving Rolls-Royce	Both	$100,000	Drive to and from villain's headquarter
• Helicopter the size of beach chair	Response	$200,000	Escape from aforementioned headquarters when romance with villain's girlfriend does not go well

325 s into the flight, a malfunction was detected in the engines of the third stage of the Soyuz-U rocket (Figure 4.2), which caused the onboard computer to terminate the flight. As a result, the vehicle failed to achieve orbit, reentering over the Altai region of Russia. On September 9, the Russian space authorities announced that the crash was caused by a blocked fuel duct. Remember, this is the same risk that Lindbergh's crew was trying to prevent: a fuel line blockage. Perhaps, Russian engineers 84 years later did not consider this risk worth mitigating. Fortunately, the failure did not to have any immediate impact on the crew of the ISS and the spacecraft was insured for US $103 million. Therefore, the question was what to do next.

The problem was that the same or similar rockets were planned for multiple launches including manned missions to ISS. As a precaution, the launch of a GLONASS satellite on a Soyuz-2-1b/Fregat, which had been scheduled for August 26, was delayed until the engines could be inspected. This launched occurred only on October 2, 2011. Similar rockets were then

Figure 4.2. Soyuz Rocket.

used in launches for unmanned missions on October 21, 2011 and October 30, 2011. Finally, on November 14, 2011, when it was clear that the problem that caused the crash of Progress M-12M was resolved, Russia launched a manned flight with three cosmonauts to ISS.

Each space mission has different technological risks and some of them may have a catastrophic impact, such as termination of the mission or failure of the launch. These risks can be mitigated in stages. At each stage, the probability and impact of the risk can be reduced. Each stage of this mitigation may take some time. For example, in the first stage probability and impact may be reduced by 2%, in the next stage probability and impact can be reduced by additional 2% more, and so on. Essentially, each stage of risk mitigation is an execution of a separate risk mitigation plan.

Risk mitigation in stages is a very common strategy in different industries, even though we may not refer to it this way. For example, to develop new drugs pharmaceutical companies use multiple phases, each of them must follow certain protocol and be approved by authorities, such

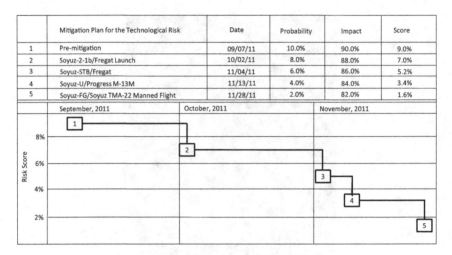

	Mitigation Plan for the Technological Risk	Date	Probability	Impact	Score
1	Pre-mitigation	09/07/11	10.0%	90.0%	9.0%
2	Soyuz-2-1b/Fregat Launch	10/02/11	8.0%	88.0%	7.0%
3	Soyuz-STB/Fregat	11/04/11	6.0%	86.0%	5.2%
4	Soyuz-U/Progress M-13M	11/13/11	4.0%	84.0%	3.4%
5	Soyuz-FG/Soyuz TMA-22 Manned Flight	11/28/11	2.0%	82.0%	1.6%

Figure 4.3. Risk mitigation chart: Waterfall diagram.

as Federal Drug Administration in US (FDA). The first phase is focused on drug safety; the second phase is on to test the drug's efficacy, and the third phase focuses on developing safe dosage levels. Essentially, this is multi-stage risk mitigation process.

Multi-stage risk mitigation processes can be graphically presented using Risk Mitigation Waterfall charts (Figure 4.3). The horizontal axis on this chart is time, the vertical axis is risk probability, impact, or score. This chart provides an intuitive visual representation on how and when risk probability and impact will be reduced.

Each stage of risk mitigation is usually associated with different project activities or even projects, as occurred with the sequential launches of the Soyuz-U rockets. Each mitigation plan has a certain cost attached to it. If for some reason execution of mitigation plan fails, the total mitigation cost of the risk will increase. Risk mitigation in different stages helps to lower overall cost of project risks.

Cost of Risk and Its Mitigation

Because of risk mitigation and risk response cost of risk is not a simple loss due to risk. It needs to be calculated by the following ways (Figure 4.4).

1. *Potential Loss*: The loss in monetary terms if the risk occurs.

  For example, for the risk "low quality component," the potential loss is

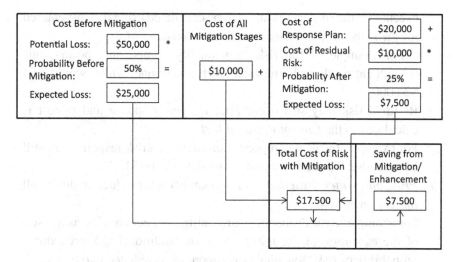

Figure 4.4. Cost of risk calculation.

$50,000. It is the cost that you would incur if a low quality component were supplied.

2. *Risk Probability (pre-mitigation)*: Used to calculate Expected Loss.

3. *Expected Loss* takes into account that the risk may not occur. It is an indicator that helps you to compare the costs of different risks.

   Expected loss = Potential Loss × Probability (pre-mitigation)

   For example, probability of risk "low quality component" equals 50%.

   Potential loss equals $50,000. Expected loss will be $25,000 = $50,000 × 50%.

4. *Cost of Mitigation* is the cost of all stages of efforts to reduce the probability and impact of the risk.

   For example, mitigation plans will include "Additional QA procedure" and "QA audit of supplier's operation," which would cost $10,000 in total.

5. Even if a mitigation plan is executed as planned, there will still be a cost associated with the risk as while it is possible to reduce risk, it is normally not possible or even preferable to eliminate it (unless you are able to avoid the risk, typically by eliminating those activities or deliverables that are exposed to the risk). The *response plan* may be

executed if the risk occurs and will be calculated using the cost entered for the response plan associated with this risk.

For example, if the risk "low quality component" occurs, this component needs to be replaced with a new one, which would cost $20,000.

6. Residual risk may still occur after the risk response and is cost is calculated as the *Cost of Residual Risk.*

    For example, the new component installed as a risk response can still be defective. The residual cost of the risk will be $10,000.

7. *Probability after Mitigation* is a probability after reduction due to all mitigation efforts.

    For example: Risk Probability after mitigation equals 25% as a result of the execution of the mitigation plan "additional QA procedure" probability of risk "low quality component" is reduced two times.

8. Expected loss after mitigation takes into account that the risk may not occur.

    Expected loss after mitigation = (Cost of Response Plan + Cost of Residual Risk) × Probability after mitigation.

    For example, probability of risk "low quality component" after mitigation equals 25%. Expected loss after mitigation will be $7,500 = ($20,000 + $10,000) × 25%.

9. *Total Risk Cost after Mitigation* = Expected loss after mitigation + Cost of Mitigation.

    For example: Total cost after mitigation of risk "low quality component" will be $17,500 = $7,500 + $10,000.

10. *Saving from Mitigation* is the difference between costs with and without mitigation. If this number is negative, mitigation efforts will not lead to cost saving.

    Saving from Mitigation = Expected Loss − Total Risk Cost after Mitigation.

    For example, total cost after mitigation of risk "low quality component" will be $17,500. Expected loss is $25,000. Saving from Mitigation is $7,500. Because this number is positive, it makes sense to perform the mitigation efforts. It is one of the most important indicators to estimate efficiency of mitigation plans.

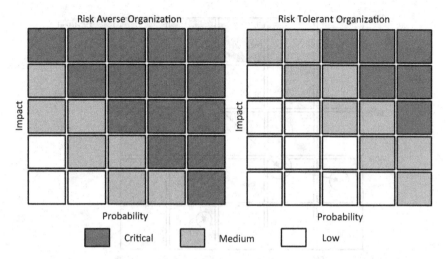

Figure 4.5. Risk matrix for risk averse and risk tolerant organizations.

Table 4.2. Example of mitigation strategies for different objectives for threats.

Factor	Color		
	Green — low risk	Yellow — medium risk	Red — high risk
Overall	Accept	Accept	Avoid > transfer > mitigate
Schedule	Accept	Accept > mitigate	Avoid > transfer
Cost	Accept	Accept > mitigate	Avoid > transfer
Safety	Accept	Accept	Avoid > transfer > mitigate
Quality	Accept	Accept	Avoid > transfer > mitigate

Using the Risk Matrix for Risk Mitigation Planning

Risk matrixes are very useful tools to support decisions regarding what risk management strategy should be taken. Each mitigation strategy can be associated with different colors on the risk matrix. First of all, the organization needs to define which cells will be assigned with color. This will reflect their risk tolerance. If many cells are red or dark it means that organization is risk averse and tends to avoid most risks (see Figure 4.5). If many cells are green or light it means that organization is risk tolerant and ready to accept many risks. Each color will be associated with mitigation strategy for each factor as shown in Table 4.2. These set of colors could be different for threats and opportunities.

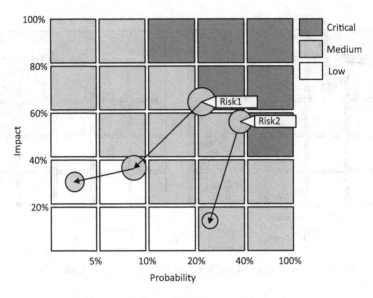

Figure 4.6. Risk mitigation on a risk matrix.

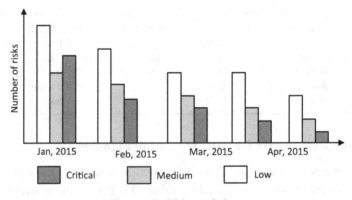

Figure 4.7. Risk trend chart.

You may show additional information on risk matrix (Figure 4.5):

1. Mitigation plans can be shown as arrows and lines on a risk matrix. They show how risks' probabilities and impacts can be reduced as a result of mitigation efforts over time. Different phases or actions of mitigation efforts can be shown on this chart as well.

2. Risk costs can be shown as a circle on the risk matrix (Figure 4.6). Larger costs can be associated with bigger circles. The cost can be reduced as a result of mitigation efforts, so it is possible to display cost for different stages of the mitigation.

3. Another useful way to present post mitigated risks is called a risk trend chart (Figure 4.7). Over the course of a project, risks can be open and closed, mitigation, and response plans can be executed. Risk trend charts show how risks changed over time. In general, the trend is to reduce the number of open risks over the course of a project or program. Also, some risks can be re-categorized based on risk reviews e.g. critical to low.

Part II

Quantitative Project Risk Analysis

Chapter 5

Monte Carlo Schedule Risk Analysis

Monte Carlo simulations of project schedules have become one of the foundations of quantitative project risk analysis. In this chapter, we will learn everything you need to know about Monte Carlo simulations and how to perform them, even if you have never heard about it before. This will include a number of important concepts related to the Monte Carlo methodology, such as statistical distributions, sampling, conversions, and more.

Why Quantitative Risk Analysis?

Let us take a look at the project schedule (Figure 5.1).

This project is affected by two risks:

1. Risk 1 increases the duration of Task 2 on 2 days with 80% probability.
2. Risk 2 increases the duration of Task 3 on 1 day with 10% probability.

Based on qualitative analysis, which we discussed in Part I of this book, Risk 1 has a greater score and needs to be mitigated first. But Risk 1 does not affect the finish time of the project: even if this risk were to occur, Task 2 duration will be 5 days while Task 3 duration will be 6 days minimum. In other words, Task 3 is on the critical path of the schedule. So, the project finish will always be determined by the Task 3 finish time. So, based on analysis of the project schedule, only Risk 2 will impact project schedule and therefore needs to be mitigated first.

Here is another situation. What if uncertainties in tasks are defined as a range of values? For example, duration of Task 1 could be between 2 and 6

67

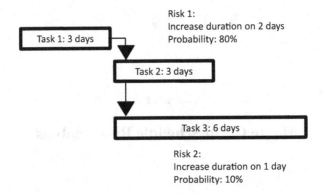

Figure 5.1. Risk 1 does not affect project schedule.

days and duration of Task 2 could be between 2 and 12 days. What would be the chance that our project would be completed, for example, in 9 days?

These are only two examples of problems related to risks in project schedule. There are quite a few situations which cannot be easily analyzed using qualitative methods. In such cases, you can use some quantitative methods. One of the most popular quantitative methods is Monte Carlo simulations.

A Little Bit of History

As with many other things, Monte Carlo methodology does not have a single inventor. One of the early variants of Monte Carlo was developed by the Italian physicist and mathematician Enrico Fermi in the 1930's. In 1946, the Polish-American mathematician Stanislaw Ulam (Figure 5.2) tried to calculate the chance of winning based on original hand of cards dealt. He discovered that the number of combinations was too large to use traditional combinatorial calculations and started to work on a more practical method: Is it possible to play the hand hundreds of times and count the number of successful plays? (Ulam, 1983). Later, he shared his idea with another famous mathematician John von Neumann. They were both working on physics research related to nuclear bomb designs at the Los Alamos Scientific Laboratory. Ulam and von Neumann applied this method to the neutron diffusion problem to calculate the distance that neutrons would likely travel through various materials. They published their work

Figure 5.2. Stanislaw Ulam — one of the inventors of Monte Carlo methodology.

in 1947. The catchy name "Monte Carlo" came up because any research in Los Alamos required a code name. The name was suggested by another physicist Nicholas Metropolis and referred to the Monte Carlo casino in Monaco. Apparently, Ulam's uncle liked to borrow money from the relatives because he "just had to go to Monte Carlo" (Metropolis, 1987).

Monte Carlo method was used extensively as part of nuclear and thermo-nuclear bomb designs. In the 1950's, numerous papers were published in physics literature on the Monte Carlo method. Later, interest in Monte Carlo spread to different areas including engineering, computational biology, computer graphics, business, and finance. A number of software tools implemented Monte Carlo simulation. Spreadsheet-based software, such as Crystal Ball by Decisioneering (later acquired by Oracle) and @Risk by Palisade became standard tools for many engineers and economists. Palisade developed one of first project risk analysis software, called @Risk for Projects. It was an add-in to Microsoft Project and allowed users to perform Monte Carlo simulations of project schedules. @Risk for Projects implemented a number of important concepts related to Monte Carlo method, particularly probabilistic and conditional branching, probabilistic calendars, correlations, critical indices, and others. Another successful commercial tool for project schedule risk analysis was Pertmaster, which later was integrated with Oracle Primavera. RiskyProject by Intaver Institute became one of the first software tools to use risk events or risk drivers to define project uncertainties. It implemented Event Chain Methodology, which significantly simplifies the modeling of project risks and uncertainties. We will learn about Event Chain Methodology in the next chapters of the book. Currently, there are a number of software applications in the market, which perform Monte Carlo schedule risk analysis. You will find a list of them in the appendices of this book.

Statistical Distributions

Look at this police lineup picture (Figure 5.3). All these people have different heights:

1. 5'10"
2. 6'3"
3. 5'7"
4. 5'11"
5. 5'5"

Let us group these numbers:

Group 1: From 5'0 to 5'6" — 1 person.
Group 2: From 5'6" to 6'0" — 3 persons.
Group 3: From 6" to 6'6" — 1 person.

Now we can present these groups in a chart (Figure 5.4):

> Statistical or probability distribution is the relationship between data samples or outcome of a statistical experiment and its probability of occurrence.

Figure 5.3. All people have different heights.

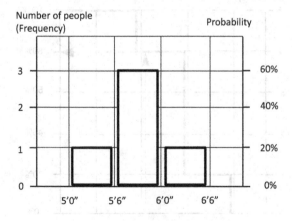

Figure 5.4. Frequency histogram.

Horizontal axis of this chart shows the actual value, which is the in this case height of the person. The left vertical axis shows the number of people for the range. It is called the frequency. The right vertical axis shows the probability. Probability is the chance that something will happen or has occurred. In our case, the total number of people is five. Number of people between 5'6″ and 6'0″ is three. Therefore, the probability will be 3/5 = 60%. It means that based on this sample of people, the probability that height will be between 5'6″ and 6'0″ is 60%.

The chart in Figure 5.4 is called Frequency Histogram. It was first introduced by the British mathematician and statistician, Karl Pearson. This histogram and data table represents a statistical or probability distribution or relationship between data samples and their probability of occurrence. It is important to remember that distribution can be applied to any ranges of values, which can be an input or an output (results) of analysis.

The chart shown in Figure 5.4 can be drawn differently. We can sum up a number of samples or probabilities from the left to the right and present the result as a line (see Figure 5.5). This is called a *Cumulative Probability* chart. Why should we do it? Using cumulative probability plots, it is easy to determine how values are associated with probability. Just select

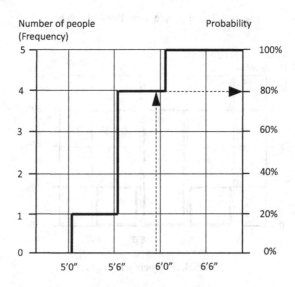

Figure 5.5. Cumulative probability plot.

a value on the horizontal axis then draw a vertical line until it crosses the cumulative probability line and you will find the probability and frequency associated with a selected value. In our example (Figure 5.3), there is an 80% probability that a person's height will be less or equal to 5'11". Cumulative probability plots are useful when you compare different uncertain variables, for example, when you compare multiple scenarios.

Discrete and Continuous Statistical Distributions

The distribution we discussed before is discrete. It means there is a certain probability or frequency associated with a range of values. Usually, such distributions can be generated based on a set of empirical data. But distributions can also be defined by a formula. Formulas will give us a relationship between value and probability. If you have a set of empirical data, it is possible to fit some known continuous statistical distribution to the data. It is not an exact science, but it can improve accuracy of analysis especially if you are trying to use historical empirical data for new projects. Figure 5.6 shows how we can fit a Beta distribution to our data.

Continuous distributions can be bounded or unbounded. Unbounded distributions can reach infinity at its tails. For example, normal distribution is unbounded, which means that there is a very small probability that a value, such as duration, can be extremely large. Beta, uniform, and triangular distributions are bounded. When you perform schedule risk analysis, you

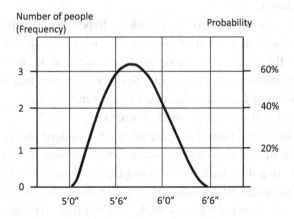

Figure 5.6. Fitting beta distribution.

may need to impose cutoffs or truncate unbounded distributions. Usually, schedule risk analysis software does this by default: cutoff values are associated with input low and high duration, cost, etc.

Statistical Parameters

Each statistical distribution has a number of statistical parameters, which are useful to describe the properties of the distribution. The parameter that first comes to mind when we talk about distributions is the *mean*, or average value. In our example, the mean equals 5'10". However, mean does not tell us how wide the statistical distribution is. It is like the average body temperature in the hospital, which is always very close to normal because while someone may have a fever, somebody is dead and cold.

It is possible to measure the width of the distribution using different values around the extremes. However, in most real life situations, these measures can be misleading. For example, the tallest man in medical history was Robert Wadlow from Alton, Illinois. He was 8'11.1" (2.72 m). Chandra Bahadur Dangi from Nepal was shortest adult person. He was 21.5" (54.6 cm). The difference in height between tallest and shortest people is 217.4 cm or just over 7'. But this range may not be very representative for the analysis that you are doing as there are only few people in the world whose heights are at these extremes. Because of this, we prefer to use other statistical parameters that can be used to address this problem, variance and standard deviation.

Variance — a measure of how widely dispersed the values are in a distribution, and thus is an indication of the risk of the distribution. It is calculated as the average of the squared deviations about the mean. The variance gives disproportionate weight to outlying values that are far from the mean. You will find formulas that describe how to calculate variance and other statistical parameters in the Glossary.

One of the most important parameters for understanding statistical distribution is *standard deviation* — a measure of how widely dispersed the values are in a distribution. For example, if a project's task duration is greater than the standard deviation, then wider statistical distributions, and more uncertainties are associated with the task duration. It is one of the most important parameters of statistical distribution. Standard deviation equals the square root of the variance. *Semi-standard deviation* is a measure of dispersion for the values falling below the mean or another target value. Semi-standard deviation is calculated the same way as standard deviation, except only samples below mean or target values are used in the calculation.

Another statistical parameter is *kurtosis*. Kurtosis is a measure of the flatness or peaked nature of a distribution relative to a normal distribution. A parameter called skewness is a measure of the degree of asymmetry of a distribution around its mean. If the distribution is skewed to the left, it will have a positive skewness. If it is skewed to the right, it will have a negative skewness.

Schedule risk analysis software packages usually present these statistical parameters as the results of Monte Carlo simulations.

Percentiles

Percentiles are another type of statistical parameter. It is a value on a scale of 0–100 that indicates the percentage of a distribution that is equal to or below this value. A value in the 90th percentile (sometimes defined as P90) is a value equal to or lower than 90% of all other values in the distribution. Here is an example. You have the following 10 values:

$$20, 22, 10, 5, 34, 40, 48, 7, 32, 49.$$

To calculate percentiles, all samples need to be sorted:

$$5, 7, 10, 20, 22, 32, 34, 40, 48, 49.$$

Number 22 is P50 because there are five values below or equal or below 22. Interestingly, P50 is not necessarily the mean, which in this case is 26.7.

Probabilistic Parameters of Project Schedules

Project schedules have many uncertain parameters which can be expressed by statistical distribution. Here are some of most important parameters.

1. Task duration. The task can take longer or shorter period of time. It is the most common type of uncertainty in schedule risk analysis. Sometimes, people perform analysis based only on uncertainties in time. If you

have a resource attached to the task there is a rate associated to the resources, uncertainties in variable or time-dependent costs of the task are calculated automatically.

2. Task fixed cost. Fixed cost does not depend on task duration, so uncertainties in fixed cost should be defined by separate distributions.

3. Statistical distribution of moment of risk within a task. Any project task can be affected by events. These events can occur at different times between the beginning and the end of a task. For example, you are painting a room and knock the paint bucket over and spill paint all around. Most likely, this will occur at the end of the task because the bucket will be almost empty and easier to tip it over.

4. Statistical distribution for risk outcome. Risk events may affect tasks or resources in different ways. For example, they can cause task delays or cost increases. This delay can be probabilistic. For example, if you get a flat tire (event), putting on your spare tire may take from 15 to 30 min.

5. Statistical distribution of work. Sometimes, we define how much effort needs to be spent on a particular task, instead of defining task duration.

6. Statistical distribution of lag between tasks. Lag is a delay between the finish of the predecessor and the start of the successor task. This delay can be uncertain and defined by a statistical distribution.

7. Statistical distribution for rate. Material resources may have different cost per unit. For example, you may need to have between 5 and 7 tons of cements for your construction project. Work resources may also have uncertainties in rate. For example, the hourly wage of construction labor can be between \$15/h and \$25/h. Probabilistic rate is very important during project planning and estimating when you do not know exactly how much your resources will cost.

8. Probabilistic calendar. In project management, different calendars can be applied to whole project, tasks, or resources. These calendars will show working vs. non-working hours or shifts. In many cases, particular non-working hours can be uncertain. For example, construction crews cannot work during heavy rain. So to model such situations, you would need to define that during certain seasons some number of days per month will be non-working.

We will discuss probabilistic calendar and uncertainties in rate in more details in Chapter 11 of this book.

How Monte Carlo Works

Now that we have reviewed a few statistics basics, let us take a look at how a Monte Carlo simulation of a project schedule works. Before we start, we need to remind you about the critical path method. *Critical path method* is a scheduling algorithm, which calculates start and finish time of each activity, as well as determining critical path, floats, and other schedule parameters. Input parameters for the critical path method are task durations, start and finish times (if they are known), constraints including resource constraints, etc. In most cases, we know when a project is supposed to start, the duration of activities, any constraints, and the relationships between activities. In project schedules, the relationships between activities are links and these relationships can have different parameters, for example, one activity can start only when the previous one is completed. The relationship between all the activities in a project schedule is called a *precedence network*. Based on these input parameters, the critical path method will calculate detailed project schedule including the start and the finish time of the project and all its activities.

Here is an example of a very simple project schedule. Let us assume that you are going to do the laundry. In this case, you have a project schedule that has only two tasks: wash the laundry in the washing machine and dry it in the dryer. Your washing machine and dryer have sensors: they will automatically shut off when the laundry is finished. Let us assume that both of them will shut off the following way (Figure 5.7):

- low estimate: 30 min,
- most likely: 45 min,
- high estimate: 60 min,

and the uncertainties are defined by a triangular statistical distribution.

We might ask how long it would take to complete both operations. However, in the probabilistic world, this question is not correct. More

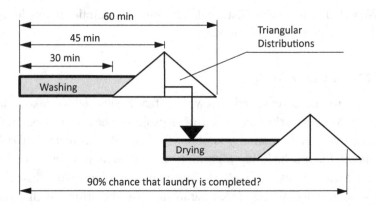

Figure 5.7. Statistical distributions for task duration.

informative questions would be:

- What is the average time in which the laundry will be completed?
- What is the chance that you will complete the laundry within 1 h and 40 min?
- How long should you account for to ensure that laundry is 90% complete?

All these questions can be answered by one type of analysis. Let us focus on the last question. The simplest way to answer this question is to add the statistical distributions together. Total project (laundry) will take between 60 and 120 min. We can then calculate the duration associated with a 90% probability that the project will be completed. But, adding up statistical distributions in project schedules is not always possible. What if you have two or more parallel paths (activities that share the same successor) in your project schedule? One may be completed earlier than the other, in which case it is not possible to add up statistical distributions. Also, different tasks may have different combinations of statistical distributions. For example, one task may have a normal distribution; another will have a discrete distribution. So, in practice, while adding statistical distributions is possible it has very limited application e.g. small groups of tasks.

Monte Carlo offers a universal method to analyze your schedule. It does not matter what combination of tasks you have and what distributions they have, Monte Carlo will be able to calculate an accurate, if probabilistic, answer. Here is how it works:

1. For each task, generate a random number.
2. Based on each task's random number, get a value from the statistical distribution. In our case, we would get duration of washing or drying in minutes from a triangular statistical distribution. This is where the magic happens. Durations will be taken from statistical distributions in such a way that values associated with the "hump" of the distribution will come up more often than numbers associated with the tail of the distribution. The procedure that can produce a sequence of values that can be taken from the probability distribution is called *sampling*. Each distribution has a formula or a number of formulas. The inputs for this formula are random numbers and distribution parameters that define the shape of the distribution. The output is the value. In our example, it is duration in minutes. Figure 5.8 shows results of sampling for one task. Using these values, you can create a frequency histogram. Interestingly, although this histogram is discrete or manually generated, it resembles the shape of the original distributions, which were triangular. In fact, the more iterations we have, the more the resulting distribution will resemble the original input distributions.
3. Repeat this process for all tasks. In this way, all the tasks will have a duration value taken or sampled from the statistical distribution.

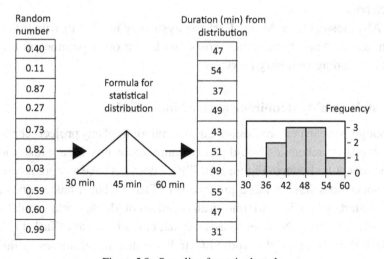

Figure 5.8. Sampling for a single task.

4. Now the duration values obtained from the statistical distribution have a critical path calculation run on them. In our example, you would just need to add up the durations for task washing and drying. The sum will be the total project duration.
5. Repeat steps 1–4 many times, each time getting a new value for the project duration. Using these values, you can create a statistical distribution of the project duration. By analyzing this statistical distribution, you can answer our questions. For example, from the analysis we can show that there is a 90% chance that the project (laundry) duration will be 103 min or less.

The results of a Monte Carlo schedule risk analysis can be thought of as a *risk adjusted project schedule*. Risk adjusted project schedules can be created using mean duration, start and finish times, or a particular percentile of statistical distributions for start, finish time, and duration. It is very convenient to show a risk adjusted project schedule alongside the original deterministic (no uncertainties) project schedule. Both schedules can be shown on a single Gantt chart. This helps to highlight how uncertainties can impact project schedules. In most cases, project activities can be delayed ("shifted to the right") because of threats, but they can also be shorter because of opportunities. You can see this in Figure 5.9, where the original schedule is shown as a white bar and the risk adjusted project schedule are black bars.

Also, results from Monte Carlo analysis may include distributions for duration, start and finish times, costs, work, and other parameters for all tasks, including summary tasks.

Schedule Quality Requirements for Monte Carlo

Although you can perform Monte Carlo simulations of any project schedule, not all project schedules would yield meaningful results. Please take a look at the schedule shown in Figure 5.10. Task 2 does not have any predecessors and successors. Task 4 has a predecessor (Task 1), but it has a constraint "Must Start On", so its start time on all iterations of Monte Carlo simulations is always the same. Now let us assume that at least one task (Task 1) has a statistical distribution. We would like to know how uncertainties in Task 1 will affect project finish time, which is equal to the finish time of Task 3.

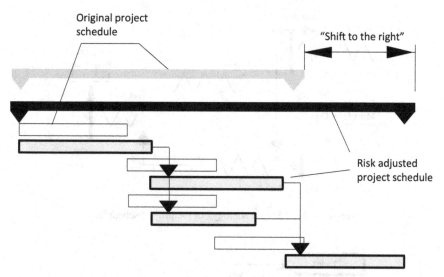

Figure 5.9. Risk adjusted project schedule (black bars) and original schedule (white bars).

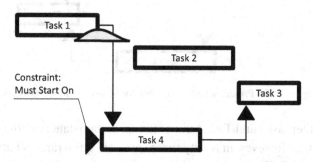

Figure 5.10. Monte Carlo simulations of this project schedule will not yield meaningful results.

Let us imagine that each task is a spring. We will move Task 1 back and forth and measure how Task 3 would respond (Figure 5.11).

It is pretty obvious that Task 3 will not move at all. Since Task 4 is constrained and Task 2 is not linked to any activities, movement of Task 1 will not be reflected in Task 3. It is possible that this project schedule correctly reflects the nature of the project: it is supposed to be this way. Start and finish times of Task 2 are completely unrelated to start and finish

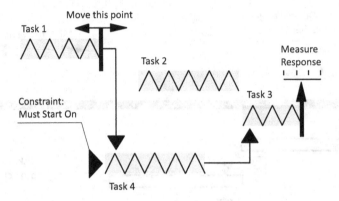

Figure 5.11. "Spring analogy" of the project schedule.

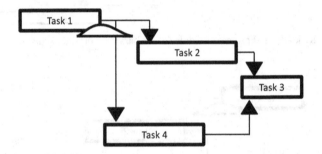

Figure 5.12. Project schedule suitable for Monte Carlo simulations.

times of other tasks and Task 4 must start on certain date regardless of Task 1 finish time. However, in reality these cases are quite rare. What normally happens, especially as schedule becomes more detailed, planners forget to link some activities, and define unnecessary constraints. Figure 5.12 shows a project schedule that is more suitable for Monte Carlo simulation.

If you apply "spring analogy" to this schedule, the finish time of Task 3 will change if we move end point of Task 3 back and forth.

So, at a minimum, to prepare a schedule for Monte Carlo simulations:

1. Avoid unnecessary constraints.
2. Make sure that all activities have predecessors and successors (with some limited exceptions e.g. Project start and finish).

Distributions for Project Risk Analysis

Table 5.1 shows a number of statistical distributions in alphabetical order, which can be used for project risk analysis.

It is important to find an appropriate distribution for whatever you are trying to model. However, actual differences between distributions of the similar shape, such as triangular and lognormal will be very small. If you use triangular distribution for duration of all the tasks in your project instead of lognormal distributions, project duration distribution (result of analysis) will vary only slightly. Specific percentiles (P70 or P90) may differ by a few percent, but it does not significantly affect the overall results of your analysis. However, if you use uniform distribution instead of normal or exponential distribution instead of BetaPert, the difference can be significant.

Three Point Estimates and Uncertainty Bands

The simplest way to define distribution is by providing three point estimates: low, base, and high duration, and cost. Triangular distribution can be set as the default. For other distributions, it is important to identify the meaning of boundary estimates. For example, for normal distribution, low and high estimates can be associated with P5 and P95.

Low and high values can be entered by multiplying base value of certain coefficient, such as 0.9 and 1.2, or may entering absolute increment, for example, -2 days and $+3$ days. It is important to enter meaningful values, which can be different for different tasks. Some people may select a large group of tasks and assign the same coefficient for low and high estimates for all of them. We do not recommend this as it may not accurately reflect differences in uncertainties that are inherent to some activities. Some software tools allow the user to define bands, or different levels of certainties. For example:

Band 1: Low uncertainty: Low $= 0.9 \times$ base; High $= 1.2 \times$ base.
Band 2: Medium uncertainty: Low $= 0.7 \times$ base; High $= 1.3 \times$ base.
Band 3: High uncertainty: Low $= 0.6 \times$ base; High $= 1.4 \times$ base.

This simplifies the process of defining uncertainties: specific band can be assigned to the selected group of tasks. It is also possible to visualize bands using different colors on the Gantt chart.

Table 5.1. Distributions most commonly used for project risk analysis.

	Distribution	Type	Parameters	How to use
1	Beta	Continuous	Alpha and beta parameters	Used for wide range of conditions. If Alpha and Beta are 1, Beta distribution will uniform. If Alpha and Beta are the same, the distribution will be symmetrical.
2	BetaPert	Continuous	Mean parameter	Derived from Beta distribution. Used as "smoother" substitute to Triangular distribution.
3	Cauchy	Continuous	Shape parameter	Used if low duration, cost, or start time represents "best case scenario" value. High value represents a cut off: how long duration, cost, and start time can expand.
4	Custom (Points)	Discrete	Set of points with probabilities	Used to define generic shape of distribution by entering point as a percentage of task duration, start time or cost, and associated relative probability. The distribution is useful when some historical data about task duration and cost is available.
5	Custom (Intervals)	Discrete	Set of intervals with probabilities	Used to define distributions consisting of multiple segments with associated relative probabilities. Each segment is defined by uniform distribution. Interval is entered as a percent of task duration or cost. The distribution is useful when some historical data about task duration and cost is available.

(*Continued*)

Table 5.1. (*Continued*)

	Distribution	Type	Parameters	How to use
6	Exponential	Continuous	Mean parameter	Similar to Cauchy distribution
7	Gamma	Continuous	Alpha and beta parameters	Similar to Cauchy distribution.
8	Gumbel	Continuous	Two share parameters	Skewed distribution. Useful if there is lower chance that task will take longer time than a shorter time.
9	Laplace	Continuous	One parameters	Similar to Cauchy distribution.
10	Lognormal	Continuous	Mean and standard deviation parameter or P1/P99, P5/P95, P10/P90, etc.	Similar to Gumbel distribution.
11	Normal	Continuous	Mean parameter or P1/P99, P5/P95, P10/P90, etc.	Normal distribution that describes situations where values are distributed symmetrically around the mean. 68% of all values under the curve lie within on standard deviation of mean and 95% lie within two standard deviations. Low and high values of duration, cost, and start time serve as cut offs.
12	Rayleigh	Continuous	Standard deviation parameter	Similar to Gumbel distribution.
13	Triangular	Continuous	Most Likely parameter	Most likely parameter overwrites base value of duration, cost, or start time.
14	Uniform	Continuous		Equal probability that duration, cost, or start time will be between low and high values.

Seed and Linear Congruence

When you perform sampling, you need to generate random values for each statistical distribution. This happens every time during each iteration for all variables, for example, for duration and cost of all tasks. This can cause a couple of issues:

1. It may significantly affect calculation performance: however, newer computers are very powerful, so this should no longer be an issue.
2. Every time you run a Monte Carlo simulation, the results will differ because the analysis uses random inputs. This can be a major inconvenience because of the expectation that you will get the same results every time you perform the same analysis on the same schedule. If you run a large number of iterations, there will not be a significant difference between simulation results, but it still can confound your expectations.

The solution to the latter issue is called *pseudorandom number generator*. In this case, the software will generate a random number only once when you first assign a statistical distribution to the task or resource parameter. This number is recorded and is used as a starting point of the calculation. This random number is called the *seed*. After the seed is generated, the next value for the second iteration of Monte Carlo process is generated as a function of the seed. The third value is generated as a function of the second value and so on. In other words, this sequence is predefined.

How do computers generate random numbers? There is a whole field of science dedicated to this process (see Gentle, 2004; McNalley, 2010). Generally, there are two types of random number generators. One type is based on some physical phenomena, such as radioactive decay or atmospheric noise. These physical effects can be programmed in the Monte Carlo software. The second type of random number generators is based on computational algorithms. Some random number generators are not "random enough" for the tasks for which they are intended. Monte Carlo simulation of project schedules does not require a super high quality random number generation algorithm; however, it should be of reasonable quality to ensure that seeds are actually randomly generated.

One of the simplest and at the same time quite common pseudorandom number generators is called *linear congruential generator*. The sequence of numbers is generated using a very simple recursive equation:

$$X_{n+1} = A \times X_n + C,$$

where A is a multiplier, C is an increment, and X is the sequence of pseudorandom values. X_0 is a seed. The value has a limit, for example, 2,147,483,648, which 2^{31}. When a pseudorandom number reaches this limit 2^{31}, it will be subtracted from the result of the formula. For this formula to generate high quality pseudorandom numbers, A and C must be selected very carefully. Example of A is 1,103,515,245 or C is 12,345.

How Many Iterations are Required

Some people believe that if they increase the number of iterations in Monte Carlo simulation, they will have more accurate results. But remember that the accuracy of results depends on the accuracy of input data or in our case, how we define statistical distributions for task cost, duration and other parameters. Let us assume that you estimate low and high durations of task in software development project. Even if you perform this task few times, you cannot tell if the duration is between 4 and 6 days, or between 3.5 and 6.5 days. In this case, the imprecision of the estimate is greater than 10%. This lack of precision is due to the inherent uncertainty in all activities and is different for different projects and different tasks. Sometimes, it may be 1–5% if you maintain records and do repeatable project. However, sometimes, it is a very significant number. If everybody could accurately estimate project durations, we would not need any analysis and you would not need to read this book.

Now let us take a look how much precision additional Monte Carlo simulations would add. When we calculate to perform Monte Carlo simulation, we calculate mean and standard deviation of project duration. There are the results for standard deviation and mean of project duration of very small real software development projects (Figures 5.13 and 5.14).

As you can see here, if the number of iterations is small, there is a significant difference between results on current and previous iterations. However, after few hundred iterations, the difference is reduced significantly. In fact, the difference between standard deviation for 500 iterations and 550 iterations calculation is only 0.4%. The difference between the mean for 500 iteration case and 550 iteration case is even less: 0.04%. Remember the imprecision inherent in input uncertainties is around 10%? When we have run these analysis on actual projects, we have found that in most cases, it

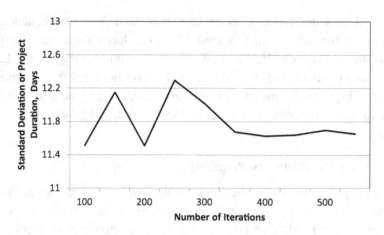

Figure 5.13. Standard deviation of project duration vs. number of iteration.

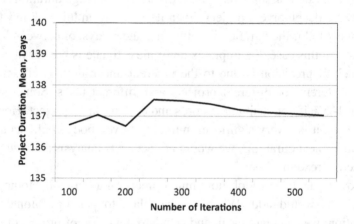

Figure 5.14. Mean of project duration vs. number of iteration.

does not require you to run 1,000s of iterations. In most schedules, 300–500 iterations will be the correct optimal number of iterations. There are two cases where more iterations may be required:

1. You have very rare events which you would like to capture in your schedule risk analysis. For example, earthquake with probability of 0.01% per duration of the project. So your number of iterations should be at least 10,000 iterations in this case.

2. It is important for you to monitor the results at the boundaries or "extreme percentiles," for example, for P1 or P99. If you use distributions with low probabilities on the boundaries, such as triangular, you may need to increase the number of iterations to improve the accuracy of the results.

Modern schedule risk analysis software are extremely fast. The time required can differ depending upon the schedules, hardware, and software packages, but we can give you some idea. It may take 30 s^{-1} min to run 2,000 iterations on a 5,000 task schedule on an average computer. You may run into some problems if you have very large master schedules with many project interdependencies.

Convergence Monitoring

Since we do not know exactly how many iterations are required, there is a way to stop them when additional iterations do not improve accuracy of calculation. This process is called *convergence monitoring*. Since the software usually calculates statistical parameters, such as mean and standard deviation of project duration, it is possible to check if these parameters do not exceed certain limits during x number of iterations.

For example, with convergence monitoring, Monte Carlo simulations can be set to stop if the statistical deviation and mean do not change more than 0.15% on each iteration and this condition is met over 20 iterations. Why do we need a 20 iteration condition? Sometimes, there could be events that can cause significant changes in mean or standard deviation from one iteration to the next. If this happens, we need to wait an additional 20 iterations to monitor if the results are stable or are still fluctuating. If after 20 iterations the standard deviation and mean do not fluctuate by more than 0.15%, the simulation will be considered to have converged and the iterations will stop. Based on our experience, these criteria (0.15% changes over 20 iterations) are a reasonable convergence criteria for most schedules with the exception of schedules that have risks with small probabilities but large impacts, often referred to as Black Swan events. In these cases, you may want to increase the iteration condition to ensure these events are properly accounted for.

It is possible to use other parameters for convergence monitoring: for example, P10/P90. Sometimes, it is necessary to monitor not only project duration, but also cost, work and other project parameters together.

If you use convergence monitoring, you do not have to worry about how many iterations are required for analyzing your schedule.

Chapter 6

Project Risk Analysis with Events: An Introduction to Event Chain Methodology

In Chapter 1 of this book, we briefly discussed quantitative risk analysis with events. Now we are going to explain this process in detail. Risk events from risk register can be used as an input for project risk analysis. You will learn how to perform risk analysis using event assignment to task and duration, and why it can provide better analysis than 'traditional' Monte Carlo simulations. We will also introduce you to "Event chain methodology," which is an extension to traditional quantitative project risk analysis. To begin, we will discuss the first principle of Event chain methodology: managing single risk events.

Project Risk Analysis with Events

On November 22, 1963, President John Kennedy was fatally shot by a sniper in Dallas, Texas. An investigation by the Warren Commission concluded that Kennedy was assassinated by Lee Harvey Oswald acting alone; however, many believe that Kennedy was killed as a result of a conspiracy. Using project risk analysis, we decided to assess whether Oswald would have had a realistic chance of assassinating the president on his own. But before we begin, a small disclaimer: we do not claim to possess exact information especially with regards to the probabilities and impacts of certain risks; and therefore, cannot give a definite answer from the historical point of view. This example is only intended to illustrate project risk analysis methodology.

What we are trying to achieve is called forensic risk analysis. In most cases, project risk analysis is performed prior to the start of a project or

Figure 6.1. Texas school book depository. Photo by Andrew J. Oldaker.

during execution to generate probabilities of meeting project objectives. But in this case, we are trying to determine the chance that Oswald could complete his project — the assassination of President Kennedy — as it actually occurred. The steps which Oswald performed were documented by the Warren Commission with accuracy of plus or minus a few minutes. Oswald was probably on the 6th floor of the Texas School Book Depository at 12:10, 20 min before the first shot was fired. Oswald fired three rifle shots from the sixth-floor window of the Book Depository at 12:30 (Figure 6.1). Immediately after the shooting Oswald went downstairs and at 12:40 boarded a city bus but got off two blocks later. He then hailed a taxi and arrived at his rooming house at 1 p.m. At 1:15 Dallas Patrolman J. D. Tippit was shot by Oswald approximately 1.4 km from Oswald's rooming house. Oswald was arrested at the Texas Theatre after 1:40.

The project schedule is one of the inputs of project risk analysis. The second one is a risk register. In general, the risks may affect project scope, duration, cost, safety, security, quality, etc. But in this case we will analyze how risks would affect the duration of the assassination plan. For example, an important duration risk would be that Oswald would be discovered before the attempt. When Oswald was taking a bus, taxi, or walk, it could take longer. Such risks as "rifle misfires", the "President's motorcade changes planned course" or "missed shot" are not included as they do not directly affect duration.

After we identified risks, we need to assign them to tasks and resources. At this moment, we would enter probabilities and impact of risks. For example, the risk "Oswald discovered earlier" can cause cancelation of the task and all its successors. The risk "Bus does not come on time..." can cause an increase of task duration.

In general, risks can be related to each other, for example, one risk can trigger another risk. Risks can occur at a certain moment during the course of the task. The same event may have different alternative outcomes, for example, 10% cancel task, 20% delay tasks, and 5% accelerate the tasks, which is an opportunity. The risk register includes only the most important risks and may not include many low probability and low impact events. For example, Oswald could trip over while running downstairs, or have difficulty opening the window on 6th floor, which causes a slight delay. To model these "noise" events, we can use a statistical distribution of task duration by defining low and high duration of each task. In our example, low and high duration will be calculated by multiplying base duration on 0.9 and 1.2. However, it is important that this statistical distribution would not include impact of events from risk register, otherwise we would count this impact twice. The next step is to perform Monte Carlo simulation. Figure 6.2 shows the original project schedule. Arrows on the chart represent risks.

Figure 6.3 shows a risk register with calculated risk probability, impact, and score. Calculated risk probability and impact may be different than the risk impact we enter when we assign risk to individual tasks, as one risk may be assigned to multiple tasks or resources.

From our analysis, the most important risk (the one with the highest score) is "Oswald discovered during escape." If this was a normal project, this risk would have the highest priority when performing mitigation and risk response planning; however, it does not look like Oswald put a lot of efforts into mitigating this risk. Figure 6.4 shows a frequency chart for

	Task Name	Low Duration	Base Duration	High Duration	Gantt Chart November 22, 1964
1	Set up on 6th floor	18 min	20 min	24 min	
2	Shooting	0.9 min	1 min	1.2 min	
3	Go downstairs and wait for the bus	8.1 min	9 min	10.8 min	
4	Ride a bus	4.5 min	5 min	6 min	
5	Take a taxi	13.5 min	15 min	18 min	
6	Go home	1.8 min	2 min	2.4 min	
7	Walk from the home	10.8 min	12 min	14.4 min	
8	Shooting police officer	0.9 min	1 min	1.2 min	
9	Walk towards the theatre	22.5 min	25 min	30 min	
10	Arrest	0 min	0 min	0 min	

Figure 6.2. Schedule of Oswald's project.

	Risk Name	Assigned to task	Probability	Impact	Score	
1	Oswald discovered during escape	Assigned to 7 tasks	41.0%	38.8%	15.9%	▭
2	Oswald discovered on 6ᵗʰ floor	Assigned to 2 tasks	34.6%	15.5%	5.4%	▭
3	Walk takes longer	Assigned to 2 tasks	21.7%	8.8%	1.9%	▯
4	Bus does not come on time	Task 4: Go downstairs and wait ...	60.0%	0.0%	0.0%	
5	Bus trip takes longer	Task 5: Ride a bus	50.0%	0.0%	0.0%	
6	Waiting for a taxi	Task 6: Take a taxi	30.0%	0.0%	0.0%	

Figure 6.3. Risk register for Oswald's project.

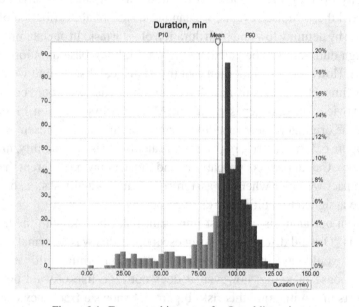

Figure 6.4. Frequency histogram for Oswald's project.

project duration. Because Oswald could be discovered earlier, the "project" can be canceled and duration can be less than 1 h 30 min.

The analysis shows that the chance this project can be completed within 1 h 30 min plus minus 5 min is 33%. The statistical distribution of project duration is quite wide: this indicates that the project was very risky and could mean that either Oswald was either very lucky or had outside help.

Why You Should Use Events as Part of Risk Analysis

In Chapter 5 of this book, we learned about Monte Carlo simulations of project schedules. The input information for Monte Carlo is uncertainties expressed in statistical distributions of project activities' duration and cost. In most cases, these are continuous statistical distributions defined by three point estimates, for example low, base, and high task duration. Applying Monte Carlo to project scheduling was a major step forward in project risk analysis. However, this "traditional risk analysis" has a number of shortcomings.

If you do not have accurate historical data, it is hard to elicit distribution parameters from subject matter experts. Let us assume that we are trying to determine how long it would take a drive to a certain location. If you go to this location regularly, you may already know that it would be say from 30 to 40 min. But, what if you have never travelled there before? To make an accurate estimate you may need to sum up possible delays: it takes longer to leave your neighborhood, there is an accident on the highway, you have trouble locating the correct address at the destination. With this process, you can generate an estimate for your arrival time that takes into account possible delays. In general, defining distributions is not a trivial process. Distributions are a very abstract concept that some project managers find difficult to work with. To define distributions accurately, project managers have to perform a few mental steps that can be easily overlooked, especially with large project schedules. As a result, they assign the same distribution for many tasks at the same time without carefully assessing actual uncertainties.

Statistical distributions can be successfully used if there is a natural randomness in certain activities, repeated many times. For example, your monthly expenditures (groceries, utilities, gas, mortgage, etc.) are always similar from month to month, and unless there a major problem it will be between $1,000 and $2,000. It is easy to manage, because you know what to expect. You would simply leave $2,000 in your bank account to compensate for this randomness. You may not need to do any analysis at all. However, if you have an uncommon event (broken car, broken furnace, etc.), it is harder to manage. Situations can be very uncertain. It may cost $500, but it could be $5,000. You will not know until you see the bill. Should you keep extra money in your account or you just accept this risk? If you need savings, how much is adequate?

In addition, project managers perform certain recovery actions when a project slips. In most cases, these actions are not accounted for by Monte

Carlo if uncertainties are defined by statistical distributions. In this respect, Monte Carlo may generate overly pessimistic results (Williams, 2004).

One of the solutions is to combine risk events with uncertainties defined by statistical distributions, as we did it in Oswald's project example.

Project risk analysis with events has been used (Virine and Trumper, 2007, 2013) since the early 2000s. This approach is sometimes referred to as "Risk Drivers" (Hulett, 2009, 2011). RiskyProject by Intaver Institute was one of the first software applications that performed project risk analysis with events. From the computational perspective, using statistical distributions and risk events are very similar. Risk events can be modeled using discrete or custom statistical distributions as part of "traditional" Monte Carlo process. The trick was how to make risk events a relatively simple process from the user perspective: it had to work in such a way that risks (with probabilities and impacts) from risk registers could be assigned to project activities and resources. Currently, there are a number of software tools which facilitate risk event analysis.

Project Risk Analysis with Events: A Psychological Perspective

One of the main problems with "traditional" Monte Carlo is that uncertainties defined in statistical distribution have one or more root causes; however, the root causes are an implicit rather than explicit property. For example, when we assign a statistical distribution that is between 3 and 5 days, this uncertainty could be because of weather, performance of team members, problem with suppliers, etc. The issue is the probabilities and impacts of each risk event can be different and it is difficult to tell how these risks would contribute to statistical distributions of task duration without quantitative analysis.

Another issue related to 'traditional' Monte Carlo is *confirmation bias*. According to confirmation bias, people actively seek out and assign more weight to evidence that confirms their hypothesis, and to ignore or underweight evidence that could discount their hypothesis (Nickerson, 1998; Darley and Gross, 2000). As a result, people often try to find evidence that supports their hypothesis and ignores evidence that contradicts their hypothesis. Using 'traditional' Monte Carlo with statistical distribution, project estimates (including low and high values) can be intentionally or unintentionally defined to satisfy a preconceived project finish time and cost. But risk events are usually identified separately (separate time, separate meeting, different experts, different planning department) from the schedule model and then are assigned to the schedule. This allows project teams to separate the base project estimates from the impacts of risk. In other words, the task duration, start and finish times, cost, and other project input parameters are influenced by motivational factors to a much greater extent than risk event and this helps to reduce the impact of confirmation bias.

'Traditional' Monte Carlo also suffers from the *anchoring heuristic*. According to anchoring heuristic, people rely on a single piece of information when making decisions (Wilson *et al.*, 1996; Chapman and Johnson, 1999; Quattrone *et al.*, 1984). A more specific case of anchoring is called *insufficient adjustment*: people "anchor" on a current value and make insufficient adjustments for future effects. How does this work out in a project? Imagine at a planning meeting, the project manager asks the team how long it will take to complete a particular task. One of the senior team members quickly offers an estimate. Because it is the first value available all subsequent discussion about the tasks duration becomes anchored around the original estimate, even if it is completely wrong. So if the first estimate is 20 days, one of the other team members who originally was going to provide an estimate of 30 days changes his estimate to 25 days because of the anchoring effect. At which point, further investigation of a more accurate duration is unlikely. Then once the base estimate is set (e.g. 22 days), the team will tend to be anchored close to this value when they estimate low and high durations. They may multiply the duration by 0.9 and 1.1 to come up with low and high estimates. So they end up with an estimate been biased by anchoring and a probability distribution that is too narrow. Because risk events allow people to more accurately estimate what would happen if a risk occurs, analysis using risk events are less affect by anchoring and insufficient adjustment.

The probability of events can be easily calculated based on historical data, which can mitigate the effect of the *availability heuristic* (Tversky and Kahneman, 1973, 1974; Gilovich *et al.*, 2002). According to availability heuristic, people make judgments about the probability of the occurrence of events by how easily these events are brought to mind. Low and base estimates in 'traditional' Monte Carlo suffer from the availability heuristic to a significantly greater extent than risk events. For example, a scheduler may recall primarily instances of the particular task that was completed early. The team may have had a small celebration or his manager came by and congratulated him on a job well done. This will make them more easy to remember and more likely to impact the scheduler's and the estimate will be too optimistic. Compound events can be easily broken into smaller events. The probability of events can be calculated using the relative frequency approach where probability equals the number of times an event occurred during a similar task or project divided by the total number projects in which it was listed. In 'traditional' Monte Carlo simulations, the statistical distribution of input parameters can also be obtained from the historical data; however, the procedure is more complicated and often not practical.

Another psychological effect is called *optimism bias* or *planning fallacy* (Lovallo and Kahneman, 2003; Buehler *et al.*, 2010). It is a cognitive bias that causes a person to believe that they are less likely to experience a negative event than others. Because of this fallacy, project managers tend to create overly optimistic estimates despite their best efforts. Optimism affects our estimates of the probability of risk events occurring and their impacts and the distribution used in 'traditional' Monte Carlo simulations. In the first case, it leads to a reduction in probabilities and impacts of risks. In the second case, it contributes to overly optimistic low and high estimates. However, the problem with overly optimistic low and high estimates may have significantly greater impact on the accuracy of project schedules than overly optimistic probabilities and impacts estimate for individual risk. The reason is that when tasks are affected by multiple events, the cumulative impact of these events tends to provide a more accurate analysis than a standard three point estimate.

There are number of other psychological effects such as overconfidence that affect risk analysis in both 'traditional' and risk-based Monte Carlo. While, using risk events, instead of or in addition to three point estimates, will not completely eliminate the impact of our psychological biases, it will help mitigate their negative impact.

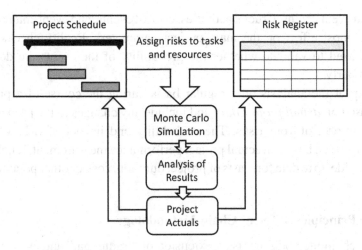

Figure 6.5. Basic steps of project risk analysis with events.

Basic Steps of Project Risk Analysis with Events

Project scheduling and analysis using events the following steps (Figure 6.5):

1. Create a *project schedule* model using best-case scenario estimates of duration, cost, and other parameters. In other words, project managers should use estimates that they are comfortable with, which in many cases will be optimistic.
2. Define a list of events and event chains with their probabilities and impacts on activities, resources, lags, and calendars. This list of events can be represented in the form of a *risk register*. Events from risk register should be assigned to tasks and resources.
3. *Perform Monte Carlo simulations.* The results of Monte Carlo analysis are statistical distributions of the main project parameters (cost, duration, and finish time), as well as similar parameters associated with particular activities. Based on these results, you can determine the chance the project or activity will be completed on a certain date and cost.
4. *Analyze of results.* The results of Monte Carlo analysis can be expressed as a risk adjusted project schedule. You can also use specific percentiles to set "risk adjusted" schedule margin and management reserves sensitivity analysis helps identify the crucial activities and critical events

and event chains. Crucial activities, critical events, and event chains have the most effect on the main project parameters. Reality checks may be used to validate whether the probability of the events are defined properly.

5. Repeat the analysis on a regular basis during the course of a project based on *actual project data* and include any changes to the probability or impact of your risks. The probability and impact of risks can be reassessed based on actual project performance measurement. It helps to provide up to date forecasts of project duration, cost, or other parameters.

Basic Principles of Event Chain Methodology

Event chain methodology is an extension of "traditional" and event-based quantitative risk analysis. It is a logical formula to model and analyze a wide variety of different problems related to managing uncertainties in project schedule.

> Event chain methodology is an uncertainty modeling and schedule network analysis technique that is focused on identifying and managing events and event chains that affect project schedules.

Event chain methodology is based on six major principles:

1. *Principle* 1 deals with single events; as we learn above, single events are used to define uncertainties in project schedule; event chain methodology adds notions of moment of risk, probabilistic risk impact, risk alternatives, and states.
2. *Principle* 2 focuses on multiple related events or chains of events; we will learn it in Chapter 7 of this book.
3. *Principle* 3 defines rules for visualization of the events or event chains using Event chain diagrams; we will learn it in Chapter 8 of this book.
4. *Principle* 4 deals with specific aspects of Monte Carlo simulations as part of Event chain methodology; we will learn about this and next two principles in Chapter 8 of this book.
5. *Principle* 5 deals with the analysis of the schedule with event chains; we will learn about this and next two principles in Chapter 9 of this book.

6. *Principle* 6 defines project performance measurement techniques with events or event chains.

Some of the terminologies used in Event chain methodology comes from the field of quantum mechanics. In particular, quantum mechanics introduces the notions of excitation and entanglement, as well as grounded and excited states (Griffiths, 2004; Manoukian, 2006). The notion of event subscription and multicasting is used in object oriented software development as one of the types of interactions between objects (Fowler, 2002; Martin, 2002).

State of Activity, Moment of Event, and Excitation States

An activity in most real life processes is not a continuous and uniform process. Activities are affected by external events that transform them from one state to another. The notion of state means that activity will be performed differently as a response to the event. This process of changing the state of an activity is called excitation. In quantum mechanics, the notion of excitation is used to describe elevation in energy level above an arbitrary baseline energy state. In Event chain methodology, excitation indicates that something has changed the manner in which an activity is performed. For example, an activity may require different resources, take a longer time, or must be performed under different conditions. As a result, this may alter the activity's cost and duration.

The original or planned state of the activity is called a *ground state*. Other states, associated with different events are called *excited states* (Figure 6.6). For example, in the middle of an activity, requirements change. As a result, a planned activity must be restarted. Similar to quantum mechanics, if a significant event affects the activities, it will dramatically affect the property of the activity, for example, cancel the activity.

Event effect can be *assigned* to:

- one or many activities,
- material or work resources,
- lags,
- calendars.

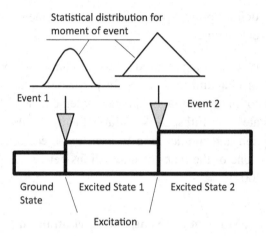

Figure 6.6. Events cause activity to transform from ground states to excited states.

Event assignment is an important property of the event. It is part of the risk properties that we discussed in Chapter 1 of this book.

An illness of a project team member is a good example of an event that can be assigned to a project resource. This event may delay all activities to which this resource is assigned. If an event is assigned to resources, the impact of event will be reduced based on amount of units this resource is allocated to the activity. For example, if a project team member is working on the activity only 50% of time, impact of event "illness" will be reduced by 50%.

Similarly, resources, lags, and calendars may have different grounded and excited states. For example, the event "Bad weather condition" can transform a calendar from a ground state (five working days per weeks) to an excited state: non-working days for the next 10 days.

Each state of activity, in particular, may *subscribe* to certain events. It means that an event can affect the activity only if the activity is subscribed to this event. For example, an assembly activity has started outdoors. In the ground state, the activity is subscribed to the external event "Bad weather". If "Bad weather" actually occurs, the assembly should move indoors. This constitutes an excited state of the activity. This new excited state (indoor assembling) will not be subscribed to the "Bad weather": if this event occurs, it will not affect the activity.

Event subscription has a number of properties. Among them are:

- In general, the impact of an event is the property of the state rather than the event itself. It means that the impact can be different if an activity is in a different state. For example, an activity is subscribed to the external event "change of requirements". In its ground state of the activity, this event can cause a 50% delay of the activity. However, if the event has occurred, the activity is transformed to an excited state. If in an excited state "change of requirement" occurs again, it will cause only a 25% delay of the activity because management has performed certain actions when the event first occurred.
- Probability of occurrence is also a property of subscription. For example, there is a 50% chance that the event will occur. Similar to impact, the probability can be different for different states. Probability can be applied to the duration of task or state, or to the unit of time. For example, there is a 30% probability that this event will occur within 2 days.
- Excited state: the state the activities are transformed to after an event occurs.
- Moment of event: the actual moment when the event occurs during the course of an activity. The moment of event can be absolute (certain date and time) or relative to an activity's start and finish times. In most cases, the moment when the event occurs is probabilistic and can be defined using a statistical distribution (Figure 6.6). Very often, the overall impact of the event depends on when an event occurs. For example, the moment of the event can affect the total duration of the activity if it is restarted or cancelled. Below is an example how one event which causes restart activity with a probability of 50% can affect one activity (Table 6.1). Monte Carlo simulation was used to perform the analysis. Original activity duration is 5 days:

Events can have negative (risks) and positive (opportunities) impacts on projects. For example, one event can cause a delay of activity. Another event can cause acceleration of activity.

Risk impact types related to duration and cost of activities can be:

- Delay activity, split activity, or start activity later; delays can be defined as fixed (fixed period of time) and relative (in percent of activity duration); delay also can be negative.

Table 6.1. Moment of risk significantly affects the activity duration.

Risk description	Risk most likely occurs at the end of the activity (triangular distribution for moment of risk)	Equal probability of the risk occurrence during the course of activity	Risk occurs only at the end of activity
Moment of time chart	Event 1	Event 1	Event 1
Mean activity duration with the event occurs	5.9 days	6.3 days	7.5 days
90th percentile	7.9 days	9.14 days	10 days

- Restart activity; total duration of activity depends on moment of risk.
- Stop activity and restart it later if required.
- End activity.
- Cancel activity or cancel activity with all successors, which is similar to End activity except the activity will be marked as canceled and impact the calculation of the activity's success rate.
- Fixed or relative increase or reduction of cost.
- Redeploy resources associated with activity; for example, a resource can be moved to another activity.
- Execute events affecting another activity, group of activities, change resource, or update a calendar. For example, this event can start another activity such as risk response plan, change the excited state of another activity, or update event subscriptions for the excited state of another activity.

The impacts of events are characterized by some additional parameters. For example, a parameter associated with the risk impact type "fixed delay of activity" is the actual duration of the delay.

Local and Global Risks

Events can be *local*, affecting a particular activity, group of activities, lags, resources, and calendars, or *global* affecting all activities in the project or all activities which are subscribed to this risk. Global events may affect activities regardless of their state. Global risks can simplify assignment of events as they do not require you to assign risks to each activity separately.

In the 1968 movie and play "Producers" directed by Mel Brooks, producer Max Bialystock (Zero Mostel) and accountant Leo Bloom (Gene Wilder) try to produce a show that would purposely flop, so they could legally keep all of the extra money. Their main risk is "Success of the play." It is a global risk. However, the risk "Failure to procure the play Springtime for Hitler: A Gay Romp with Adolf and Eva at Berchtesgaden from Franz Liebkind" is a local one: it only affects one task: "Procurement of the play."

The risk "success of the play" can affect all activities regardless of time if it occurs. But here is another situation. Do you remember the potential computer problem which could have occurred on January 1, 2000, the Y2K bug? Some computer software used only two digits to store calendar years. When the clock struck midnight on December 31, 1999 and the computer clock switched from 1999 to 2000, there was a risk that some software would stop working. For many projects it was a global risk, but it could affect only activities running during this time. The Y2K risk is a *time-dependent global risk*. The moment when this type of risk would occur may be defined by a statistical distribution. For example, a risk "Failure of construction crane" can affect all activities related to construction of a building, but most likely it would occur shortly after the installation of the crane.

Risk Alternatives

Max and Leo persuade playwright Franz Liebkind to sign over the stage rights to the play by convincing him that they want to show the world "the Hitler you loved, the Hitler you knew, the Hitler with a song in his heart." But would happen if Franz Liebkind does not sell the rights to his play? In other words, what if the risk "Failure to procure play Springtime for Hitler" occurs? First of all, Max Bialystock's and Leo Bloom's project would be delayed, because they would need to source out and procure another equally bad play. How long would this take? Most likely it would require a few attempts, which needs to be reflected in estimate of the risk's impact. This would lead to the set of multiple mutually exclusive *risk alternatives*.

In addition, one event can have multiple impacts. For example, Max and Leo may incur additional costs, which also depend on the number of attempts they need to do to purchase the stage rights for other plays. It is important to remember that mutually exclusive risk alternatives can belong to the same category. Different mutually exclusive risk alternatives may have different moments of risk. Risk impacts can be defined using a statistical distribution (probabilistic risk impact) or a single value. Table 6.2 shows a risk assignment table:

Risk: Failure to procure play. Ground State

This would mean that there is:

- a 20% chance that duration will increase by 3 days, or,
- a 10% chance that duration will increase by 6 days, or,
- a 5% chance that duration will increase by 9 days, or,
- a 1% chance that the task will be canceled.

Cost related risk impact types belong to a different category "cost and income." There is a 5% chance that cost would increase by $200 and 1% chance that cost would increase by 5%.

Risk probability within a category equals the sum of all mutually exclusive risk alternatives. In our case, it equals 36% of the duration and scope category and 6% for cost and income category. Total probability of the risk equals the maximum probability between two categories and equals 36%.

Table 6.2. Risk alternatives for risk "failure to procure play."

Alternative	Probability	Category	Impact type	Impact
1	20%	Duration and scope	Fixed delay	3 days
2	10%	Duration and scope	Fixed delay	6 days
3	5%	Duration and scope	Fixed delay	9 days
4	1%	Duration and scope	Cancel task	N/A
Total	36%			
1	5%	Cost and income	Fixed cost increase	$200
2	1%	Cost and income	Relative cost increase	5%
Total	6%			

Table 6.3. Sampling for the risk with multiple alternatives.

Iteration	1	2	3	4	5	6	7	8	9	10
Random number	0.31	0.73	0.93	0.56	0.17	0.44	0.23	0.66	0.82	0.05
Delay (days)	2	0	0	1	3	2	2	0	0	3

Sometimes one risk alternative may have a positive impact or be an opportunity, but another alternative have a negative impact or be a threat. In this case, the risk will be both a threat and an opportunity. In fact, most risks belong to this category, however, either the probability of the opportunity is small or we simply dismiss it. In the book "Robinson Crusoe" by Daniel Defoe the risk "Arrival of native cannibals to the island" was a threat. But they brought with them the prisoner Friday, which was an opportunity for Robinson Crusoe.

How are Risk Chains Calculated?

Risk chains are used in Monte Carlo simulations. Internally, in any project risk analysis software, risk assignments have statistical distributions. Let us assume that we have a risk impact type "Fixed delay" with three alternatives:

1. 20% probability: delay 3 days.
2. 30% probability: delay 2 days.
3. 10% probability: delay 1 day.

We can show this distribution in Figure 6.7. Now let us roll a dice, or in other words get a random number for each Monte Carlo simulation. We can normalize random number from 0 to 1. For each random number, we can get a delay (Table 6.3).

This delay will be used to calculate the duration of the activity which in turn is used to calculate project duration on each iteration of a Monte Carlo simulation.

Probabilistic Risk Impact

Max Bialystock and Leo Bloom had to select an actor to play Hitler. The problem was they need to select an actor so bad that it would guarantee

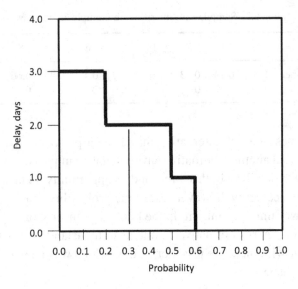

Figure 6.7. Calculation of delay.

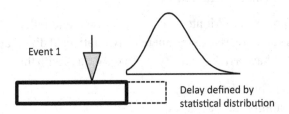

Figure 6.8. Probabilistic risk impact.

that the show would fail. There is a risk that a suitably bad actor might not show up at the first audition and they would have to schedule a second. This second audition would most likely take 1 h, but could last anywhere between 30 min and 3 h. In this case, risk impact type is "delay" and impact value is represented by a statistical distribution (Figure 6.8).

Chapter 7

Event Chain Diagrams

"I think by drawing, so I'll draw or diagram everything from a piece of furniture to a stage gesture. I understand things best when they're in graphics, not words."

Robert Wilson
American experimental theater stage director and playwright

Relationships between project risks can be very complex. Risks can be assigned to different activities and resources, have different probabilities and impacts, and have correlations or act as triggers for each other. Due to this complexity, we recommend visualizing project events and event chains using Event chain diagrams. Event chain diagrams use the familiar structure of a Gantt chart to visualize the relationships between project risks. State tables are also a useful tool and can be used to define the state of an activity. This chapter provides a specification for Event chain diagrams and State Tables along with advice on how to use them effectively.

Why Event Chain Diagrams?

Do you remember the movie "Home Alone"? In this movie, 8-year-old Kevin McCallister, who has been mistakenly left behind when the family goes off on a Christmas vacation, is faced with defending his home against a pair of burglars. We like this example because of how he planned his defense. Like any good project, he needed a plan and in this case, his first step was to create a plan of the house. He used the plan of his house to determine the optimal locations for his booby traps he was going to use to defend his home. Could he have used a written plan instead? Perhaps, but it would be much more difficult as the booby traps had to be installed in

109

a certain order: Kevin assumed that a certain chain of events would occur related to the burglars' invasion of his home. In addition, the house was quite large and it would have been hard to memorize where everything was located. Kevin realized that his traps would be much more efficient if they were set off in a certain order and his drawing helped him to visualize the events of the home invasion before they actually occurred. In fact, Kevin found the diagrams so useful that he used them again in Home Alone 2.

So why do we prefer to use plans, diagrams, and charts as opposed to written descriptions? In business, including project management, we tend to talk about concepts rather than objects and we are much more likely to be remember concepts if they are presented as pictures rather than as words. In psychology this effect is called the *picture superiority effect*. In fact, our brain processes visual and verbal information differently (Paivio, 1971, 1986; Sternberg, 2006). When we store and retrieve information from our memory, we use both words and images. For example, when we hear the words "Project Schedule" we also retrieve an image of the schedule, probably in the familiar form of a Gantt chart. Psychologists also found that images are more distinct from each other than words, which increases the chance that they will be retrieved from memory. The picture superiority effect is used in learning, user interfaces, and advertising. In our book, we also take advantage of this effect by including many pictures so the information will be easier to memorize.

Now that we have convinced you that pictures can be better than words, let's see how it can help you to describe risk events in project management.

Diagrams in Business Processes

Business process diagrams can show three things:

- Actions, such as activities on the Gantt chart.
- Data, such as information in data flow diagrams.
- Combination of actions and data.

Kevin McCallister created the data (plant of the house and locations on booby traps) together with information about actions (how these booby traps were supposed to act).

Traditional visualization techniques include bar charts or Gantt charts and various schedule network diagrams (Project Management Institute, 2013). Although the Gantt chart is named after Henry Laurence Gantt (1861–1919), an American mechanical engineer and management consultant, he was not the first person who invented it (Weaver, 2006). In 1756, 18th-century British polymath Joseph Priestley published the "Chart of Biography," where he plotted 2,000 lifelines as bars on a time scale. He also created "A New of Chart of History" where he presented various historical events on a time scale (Figure 7.1). In 1896, Polish economist and engineer Karol Adamiecki created a method of 'work harmonization' that was based on a chart similar to the modern Gantt Charts. His "Harmonygraph" became a predecessor to modern Gantt charts. At the beginning of the 20th century, charts, very similar to modern Gantt charts, were starting to be used primarily in Germany. Henry Gantt developed his chart around the years 1910–1915. In the beginning, Gantt charts did not include any calculations; planners just estimated start and finish times, and durations of activities, and plotted them on a time scale. After the "critical path method" was developed, Gantt charts were used to present the results of a schedule network

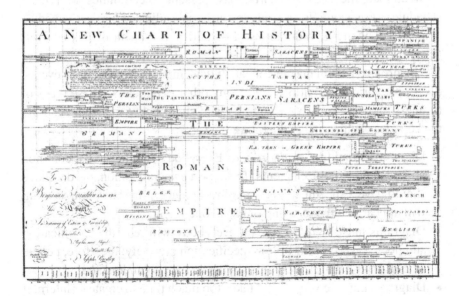

Figure 7.1. A new chart of history by Joseph Priestley.

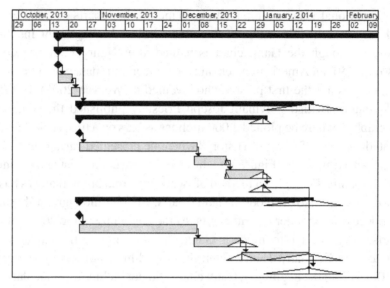

Figure 7.2. Gantt chart with uncertainties in task durations as a result of project risk analysis.

analysis. Other visualization techniques of project schedule include various network diagrams, which are essentially flow charts that show relationships between activities. Gantt charts may present uncertainties in project schedules. For example, a triangle on a risk adjusted project schedule can show low and high durations of activities as a result of risk analysis (Figure 7.2).

In project risk management, analytical models also include events, decisions, various conditions, and many other parameters. These types of business models can be very complex and should be visualized. Here are the key ideas behind many diagramming tools:

- Diagrams should be *standardized*. Everybody should have a common understanding of the elements. To support standardization, the diagrams should have a specification or set of rules that outlines how the diagram will appear and the meaning of each component.
- Diagrams must be *intuitive*. Not everybody will read the specification and not everybody will follow specification precisely: therefore, people who use these diagrams should find them easy to understand.
- Diagrams must be *simple*. If it takes too much time to create or interpret a diagram, the value of the diagram is diminished.

Visual Tools for Probabilistic Business Problems

Visual modeling tools are widely used to describe complex models in many industries. Here are few examples. Unified modeling language (UML) is actively used in the software design (Arlow and Neustadt, 2003; Booch *et al.*, 2005). Visual modeling languages are the next step above simple individual diagrams. They use many diagrams that are related to each other. UML is also used to present sequences of activities, system states, and interactions between different components of a system. Essentially, UML is intended to provide a standard way to visualize the design of a system. In particular, this visual modeling language approach was applied to defining relationships between different events.

Another solution for modeling complex business and technology projects is object-process methodology (OPM) (Yaniv and Dory, 2013; Dori, 2002). It is a bimodal visual and textual conceptual modeling language and an emerging ISO Standard (ISO-19450 "Automation systems and integration — OPM") for system modeling and design. OPM is an easy to use and understand set of standardized diagrams, which help to visualize complex systems in different industries including project management.

A number of diagrams are actively used in the field of decision and risk analysis and risk management. We already discussed some risk management visual tools, such as a risk matrix with different types of information presented on it, frequency histograms and cumulative probability plots which show the results of Monte Carlo simulation, and risk mitigation waterfall charts.

In addition, a number of diagrams are used for project decision analysis. Among them are decision trees, strategy tables, cause-and-effect diagrams, force-field diagrams, mind maps, and various flow charts. Some of them became valuable tools in project management and are included in the Project Management Body on Knowledge (Project Management Institute, 2013). All these diagrams are intended to simplify our understanding of the system, which in our case is projects with uncertainties. Visual modeling languages and diagrams are also applied to probabilistic business problems (Virine and Rapley, 2003; Virine and McVean, 2004). Uncertainties associated with project variables, relationships between uncertain variables and result of analysis, as well as calculation algorithms can be displayed using these diagrams.

Event Chain Diagram Specification

Event chain diagrams are the third principle of event chain methodology. They are intended to show events that affect project schedules. Below is a specification of these diagrams.

1. Single events.
   a. Single events are shown as arrows on the bars on a Gantt chart (Figure 7.3). Arrows pointing down represent *threats*. Arrows pointing up on the Gantt chart represent *opportunities* or an event "Risk Response Plan is executed." Two arrows in one point represent both threats and opportunities for one risk. The particular horizontal position of the arrow on the Gantt bar is not relevant.
   b. Issues are shown as arrows in the circle color of the issue arrow (Figure 7.4).
   c. Closed or transferred risks are shown using dashed lines. Color of the arrow is white. Closed issue is shown in the circle with dashed border line.
   d. Optional. Excited states are represented by elevating the associated section of the bar on the Gantt chart. The height of the state's rectangle represents the relative impact of the event. All excited state of activities should have a textual description. Only states that have different event subscriptions than ground states should be shown.
   e. Optional. Statistical distribution of moment of risk may be shown above activity bar. Is it not recommended not to show uniform distributions for moment of risk as most cases this is the default distribution?

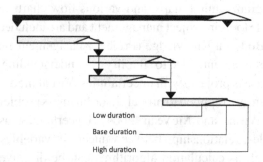

Figure 7.3. Threat and opportunities.

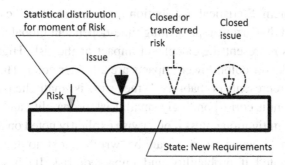

Figure 7.4. Issues, closed risks, state, and moment of risk.

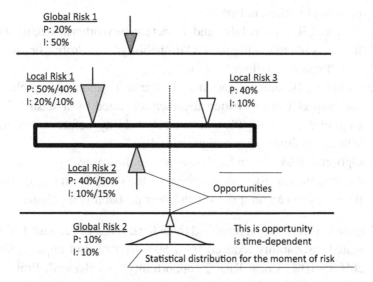

Figure 7.5. Local and global risks with different probabilities and impacts.

f. Global threats are shown at the top of the diagrams pointing down; global opportunities are shown at the bottom of diagrams pointing up. Both threats and opportunities belonging to the same global risk are placed at the top and the bottom of the diagram along the same vertical line (Figure 7.5).

g. Time-dependent global risks, or risks affecting activities running during certain period of time, have a vertical dashed line associated with them. Statistical distribution for moment of risk can be shown around that arrow, representing time-dependent global risk.

h. Colors represent the calculated impact of the risk. Higher impacts are a darker color, lower impacts are a lighter color. The size of the arrow represents probability. If the arrow is small, the probability of the event is correspondingly small. Risk probability and impacts are before mitigation unless it otherwise explicitly noted on the diagram.

i. Optional. Name of risk can be written next to the arrow and highlighted if probability and impact or risk ID is also visible. Sometimes, the same risk will be assigned to different tasks. In this case, the name of the risk will be the same for different arrows pointing to different bars.

j. Optional. Risk probability and impact can be written next to the arrow. It is possible to modify names "Probability:" to "Prob:", or just "P:", and "Impact:" to "Imp:", or just "I:".

k. Optional. Before mitigation and after mitigation, risk probability and impact can be written together separated by a slash "/". For, example: "P: 50%/40%" means "Probability before mitigation is 50%; Probability after mitigation is 40%".

l. Optional. Risk ID can be shown next to the arrow.

m. Many different risks can be shown on the same Gantt bar. If space is limited, you can omit risks with lower probability and impact.

Figure 7.5 shows two global and three local risks. Local Risk 1 (threat) is mitigated: probability reduced from 50% to 40% and impact reduced from 20% to 10%. Local Risk 2 (opportunity) is enhanced. Probability increased from 40% to 50% and impact increased from 10% to 15%.

2. Event Chains

a. Event chains are shown as lines connecting arrows depicting events. Both curved lines or lines containing multiple straight segments are acceptable.

b. Optional. Event chains have a textual description.

c. Optional. Different event chains are presented using different color or line types.

d. If one event triggers another event, event chain lines will have an arrow pointing to the triggered event. If an event chain line does not have any arrows, it means that the chain does not have any triggers; just events that are correlated with each other.

e. Correlation coefficient or probability that one event is triggered by another event is shown on event chain in a rectangular box.

f. Event chains may trigger another activity. In this case, the event chain line will be connected with the beginning of activity with optional arrow.

g. Event chains may trigger a group of activities. In this case, this group of activities will be surrounded by the box or frame and the event chain line will be connected to the corner of the box or first activity within a frame.

Figure 7.6 presents two event chains. "Event chain 1" includes Event 1 that triggers "Event 2" with probability 100%. "Event 2" triggers "Event 4" with probability 50%. "Event chain 2" is shown using different line type. It includes "Event 1" which triggers "Event 3". This is an example of multicasting where one event triggers two events.

Figure 7.7 shows two event chains. "Event 1" and "Event 3" are correlated with each other with correlation coefficient 0.3. Event 2 triggers activity with probability 50%.

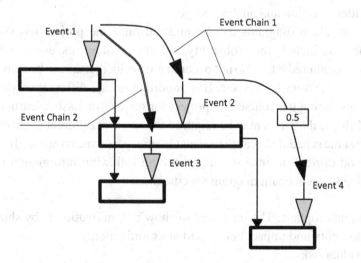

Figure 7.6. Two event chains with multicasting.

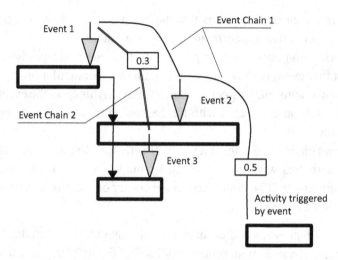

Figure 7.7. Two event chains with correlated events and activity triggered by an event.

How to Use Event Chain Diagrams

The central purpose of event chain diagrams is not to show all possible individual events. Rather, event chain diagrams can be used to understand the relationship between events. Therefore, it is recommended the event chain diagrams be used only for the most significant events during the event identification and analysis stage.

Event chain diagrams can be updated once the project has started. Updates can include the probability and impact of events, events may be removed or altered if they do not occur or are avoided, risks can be converted to issues or lessons learned etc. It is important to save different versions of diagrams during the course of a project for reviews of lessons learned.

Multiple diagrams may be required to represent different event chains for the same schedule because a Gantt chart may become crowded. To avoid busy and difficult to interpret diagrams the following information is not included to event chain diagram specification:

- Mitigation plans. The only way to show risk mitigation is by showing probability and impact before and after mitigation.
- Residual risks.

- Risk cost, risk description, risk categories, impact types, and other risk properties.
- Information about risk alternatives.
- Lessons learned. Analysis of lessons learned could be performed using the original diagrams with updates.
- In case of large schedules, only high level tasks may be included to the Gantt chart for event chain diagram.

All this information in theory could be shown in the diagram, but it would in unintuitive and offer too much information.

Event chain diagrams can be used as part of the risk identification process, particularly during brainstorming meetings. Members of project teams can manually draw arrows between activities linked on the Gantt chart, as well as use any suitable project management or diagramming software. Event chain diagrams can be used together with other diagramming tools.

Table 7.1. Example of state table.

	Event subscription		
	Event 1: Architectural changes	Event 2: Development tools issue	Event 3: Minor requirements change
Ground state	*Probability*: 20% *Moment of event*: any time *Excited state*: refactoring *Impact*: delay 2 weeks	*Probability*: 10% *Moment of event*: any time *Excited state*: refactoring *Impact*: delay 1 week	
Excited state: refactoring			*Probability*: 10% *Moment of event*: beginning of the state *Excited state*: minor code change *Impact*: delay 2 days
Excited state: minor code change			

State Tables

Another tool that can be used to simplify the definition of events is a state table. Columns in the state table represent events; rows represent the states of an activity. Information for each event in each state includes four properties of event subscription: probability, moment of event, excited state, and impact of the event. State tables help to depict an activity's subscription to the events: if a cell is empty the state is not subscribed to the event.

An example of a state table for a software development activity is shown in Table 7.1. The ground state of the activity is subscribed to two events: "architectural changes" and "development tools issue." If either of these events occurs, they transform the activity to a new excited state called "refactoring." "Refactoring" is subscribed to another event: "minor requirement change." Two previous events are not subscribed to the refactoring state and therefore cannot reoccur while the activity is in this state.

Chapter 8

Event Chain Methodology: Managing Event Chains

Failure is not a single, cataclysmic event. You don't fail overnight. Instead, failure is a few errors in judgment, repeated every day.

Jim Rohn
(1930–2009) an American entrepreneur, author and motivational speaker

In this chapter, we will continue to learn about event chain methodology. We will focus on relations between events or event chains. Events may have different types of relationships between them: events can trigger one another or events can be simply correlated with each other. Events can execute activities, which have other events assigned to them. Event chains simply model risk response plans, repeated activities, resource leveling, and other effects in project schedules. We will also learn how to identify and analyze event chains.

Why Event Chains?

Federation Tower is one of largest projects under construction in Moscow, Russia. Originally, it was proposed to include two towers: West (62 stores) and East (93 stories) (Figure 8.1). The two towers would be positioned on one podium with a 506 m spire with elevators and observation desk placed between the towers. East tower is designed to be the tallest building in Europe. The construction of the Federation Tower started in 2003 and West tower was completed in early 2008. However, construction of East tower suffered a number of major setbacks. In late 2007, the construction of the 33–34 levels suffered technical problems, which delayed the project more than five months. In November 2008, the tower construction was

Figure 8.1. Federation Tower construction, April 2014. Partially constructed spire is seen between East and West Towers. Photo by Dinozaurus.

suspended due to lack of funding. In the summer of 2011, work on the tower resumed, but some time was spent on fixing technical problems related to the suspension of the construction. On April 2, 2012 a massive fire on 67th floor of the building caused another delay (Reynolds, 2012). Yet another delay occurred when a main contractor was replaced. In early 2014, a decision was taken to demolish the partially erected spire, which contributed to significant cost increase. In addition, the design was changed and the number of floors increased to 97. Currently, the plan is now to complete the tower in 2016.

We have outlined just a few critical events that have affected the Federation Tower project. Given the unique nature of the tower, there are a large number of technical and organizational problems affecting the project. In fact, it is not only separate events, but a number of chains of events which led to delays and extra costs. For example, the global financial crisis in 2008 led to suspension of construction, which eventually caused design changes and the decision to demolish the spire: a very complex and expensive project by itself. Is it possible to envisage such chains of events? Risks may cause additional mitigation and response activities and even projects, which may have risks by themselves. Such event chains may lead to a dramatic escalation of project costs and major delays.

Event Chain Methodology Principle 2: Event Chain

In Chapter 6, we learned about the first principle of Event chain methodology related to managing single events. Now, we can learn about multiple events related to each other.

Some events can cause other events. These series of events form event chains, which may significantly affect the course of the project by creating a ripple effect through the project (Figure 8.2). Here is an example of an event chain ripple effect:

1. Requirement changes cause a delay of an activity.
2. To accelerate the activity, the project manager diverts resources from another activity.
3. Diversion of resources causes deadlines to be missed on the other activity.
4. Cumulatively, this reaction leads to the failure of the whole project.

Here is how the aforementioned example can be defined using Event chain methodology:

1. The event "Requirement change" will transform the activity to an excited state which is subscribed to the event "Redeploy resources."
2. Execute the event "Redeploy resources" to transfer resources from another activity. Other activities should be in a state subscribed to the "Redeploy resources" event. Otherwise, resources will be not available.
3. As soon as the resources are redeployed, the activity with reduced resources will move to an excited state and the duration of the activity in this state will increase.
4. Successors of the activity with the increased duration will start later, which can cause a missed project deadline.

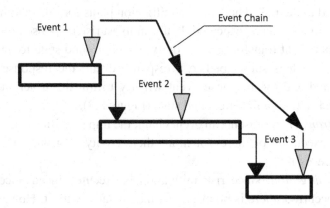

Figure 8.2. Event chain.

Table 8.1. Event chain leads to higher project duration compared to independent events with the same probability.

	Independent events in each activity	Event chain
Mean duration	18.9 days	19.0 days
90th percentile (high estimate of duration)	22.9 days	24.7 days

An event that causes another event is called the *sender*. The sender can cause multiple events in different activities. This effect is called *multicasting*. For example, a broken component may cause multiple events: a delay in assembly, additional repair activity, and some new design activities. Events that are caused by the sender are called *receivers*. Receiver events can also act as a sender for another event.

The actual effect of an event chain on a project schedule can be determined as a result of quantitative analysis. The example below illustrates the difference between event chain and independent events (Figure 8.2 and Table 8.1). Monte Carlo simulations were used to perform the analysis. The project includes three activities of five days each. Each activity is affected by the event "restart activity" with a probability of 50%.

Below, you can find are four different risk management strategies explained using Event chain methodology's event chain principle:

1. *Risk acceptance*: the ground and excited states of activities are subscribed to the risk. There are no mitigation plans for this risk; however, risk response can be executed. In the simplest risk response process, the original event transforms an activity from a ground state to an excited state, which is subscribed to a response event; the response plan is executed and the response event will try to transform activities to a ground state or a lower excited state (Figure 8.3).
2. *Risk transfer*: represents an event chain; the impact of the original event is an execution of the event in another activity or group of activities (Figure 8.4).
3. *Risk mitigation*: since risk mitigation is executed in advance before risk occurred, there is no event chain associated with it. However, risk mitigation will affect event subscription. If risk is fully mitigated (probability would become zero), activities will not be subscribed to this event.

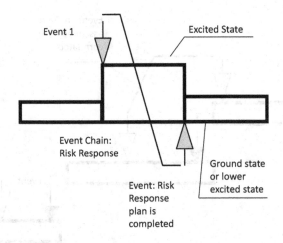

Figure 8.3. Event chain diagram of risk acceptance with risk response.

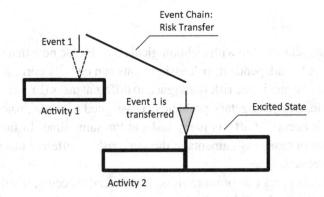

Figure 8.4. Event chain diagram of risk transfer.

4. *Risk avoidance*: original project plan is built in such a way that none of the states of the activities is subscribed to this event.

Types of Event Chains

In the example above, we saw how one event triggered a whole chain of events. It may not be always the case. There are a number of different types of event chains:

1. Risks are independent. If one risk occurs, it would not affect another risk and vice versa. For example, risks related to project financing would not

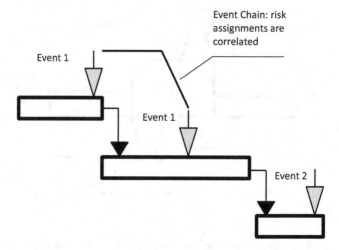

Figure 8.5. Correlation of risk assignment.

have any relationship with technological risks. Please note that although risks can be independent, risk assignments can be fully correlated. This situation occurs if one risk is assigned to different tasks (Figure 8.5). For example, risk "Budgetary problems" is assigned to many project tasks. When it occurs, it affects many tasks at the same time. In fact, in the majority of cases assignments of the same risk to different tasks should be correlated.

2. One risk triggers one or more risks. If risk sender occurs, it will trigger Risk Receiver. But if Risk Receiver occurs without this trigger, it would not affect the Risk Sender. What if one risk is assigned to multiple tasks? Let us assume that all assignments of Risk Receiver are correlated. If Risk Receiver is triggered by Risk Sender, Risk Receiver will occur in all tasks. For example, risk "Budgetary problems" is assigned to many tasks. This risk could be triggered by risk "Change of company's ownership." In this case "Budgetary problems" will occur in all tasks to which it is assigned at the same time. Another situation is where the Risk Sender affects the Risk Receiver less than 100% of the time base on a certain probability. For example, if the risk "Budgetary

problems" occurs, it will trigger the event "Redeploy resources" 50% of the time.

3. Risks are correlated, but do not act as triggers. In this case, if one risk occurs, another one may occur and vice versa. In this relationship, there are no specific sender or receiver risks defined, rather the relationship is defined by a correlation coefficient. For example, a correlation coefficient of 0.5 means that risks would tend to occur together 50% of the time. Correlation coefficients are an additional property of event subscriptions. During Monte Carlo simulation, these correlation coefficients will be used in the sampling process. In reality, correlation coefficients of less than 1 are rarely used.

There are a number of other 'exotic' ways to define risk correlations. Risks may occur only under certain conditions. For example, Risk Receiver will occur only if two or more Risk Senders occur. It is possible to model these types of conditions using ground and excited states of the activities. However, though it is possible to define very complex conditions, these should be used sparingly and only when the expected impact of these chains is very significant.

How are Event Chains Calculated?

The simplest way to define correlation between two risks is seeds. However, this works only when we need to ensure 100% correlation between risks. As we discussed in Chapter 5, each distribution has a seed and each risk has a statistical distribution. If seed is the same for two risks, the risks will correlated. Due to linear congruence, which we discussed in Chapter 5, all sequences of random numbers will be identical if seeds are the same. Figure 8.6 shows a sequence of random values for two risks with a cost impact. The first risk has three alternatives (20% chance of cost increase by $3,000, 30% of cost increase by $2,000, and 10% chance of cost increase by $1,000). The second risk has one alternative: 50% chance of cost increase of $2,000. Both risks are correlated.

Table 8.2 shows a risk correlation calculation of Monte Carlo simulations for the same example. Risk 1 has 60% probability and Risk 2 has 50%

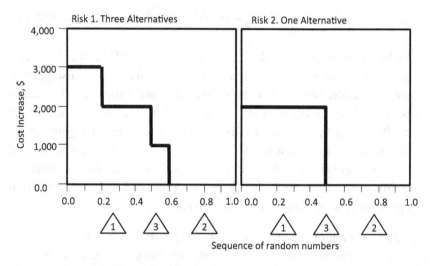

Figure 8.6. Generation of sequence of random number for two risks.

Table 8.2. Example of risk correlation.

Iteration	1	2	3	4	5	6	7	8	9	10
				100% correlation between risks						
Risk 1	*		*	*		*	*	*		
Risk 2	*			*			*	*	*	

probability. Star (*) means any cost increase, and empty space means that cost increase is zero.

In case of 100% correlation, Risk 2 occurs every time Risk 1 occurs, but Risk 1 can occur one more time because the probability of Risk 1 is higher than the probability of Risk 2. When we use correlation coefficients or if there is a Sender/Receiver relationship between risks, Monte Carlo sampling needs to be performed to ensure predefined correlation conditions are accounted for.

Event Executing Other Activities and Event Driven Branching

One of the risk impact types is execution of activity and group of activities. But what if executed activity has risk events assigned to it as well? In this

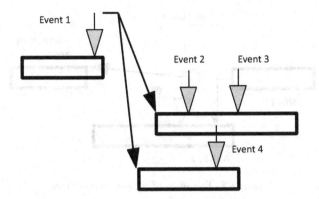

Figure 8.7. Event driven branching.

case, it will be implicit event chain. Moreover, let us assume that sender event has multiple alternatives. For example, event "Fire on the 67th floor during construction" may cause:

1. Delay of 67th floor construction — 0.5% probability.
2. Execute new task: Repair of 67th floor — 0.5% probability.
3. Execute new task: Large Repair from 66th to 68th floor — 0.1% probability.

Total probability of risk will be 2.5%. The effect, when risk alternatives cause execution of different activities or group of activities, is called *event driven branching* (Figure 8.7). It is important to know that tasks "Repair of 67th floor" or "Large Repair from 66th to 68th floor" may also have other risks, for example, "Budgetary Problems." This is what in fact occurred with the Federation Tower.

Repeated Activities

Sometimes, events can cause the start of an activity that has already been completed. This is a very common scenario: sometimes, a previous activity must be repeated based on the results of a succeeding activity (Figure 8.8). Modeling of these scenarios using Event chain methodology is simple. The original project schedule does not need to be updated, as all that is required is to define the event and assign it to an activity that points to the

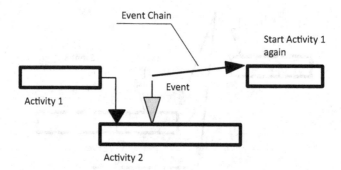

Figure 8.8. Execution of activity second time.

previous activity. In addition, a limit to the number of times an activity can be repeated must be defined.

Execution of Response Plans

Risk response efforts are considered to be events, which are executed if an activity is in an excited state. Risk response events may attempt to transform an activity from the excited state to the ground state.

If an event or event chain occurs during a project, it may require risk response efforts. In some cases, risk response plans can be created. Risk response plans are an activity or group of activities (small schedule) that augment the project schedule if a certain event occurs. Risk response plans can be defined as a part of the original project schedule and only executed under certain conditions. However, in these cases, the project schedule may become very convoluted due to multiple conditional branches, which significantly complicates the analysis. Event chain methodology offers a solution: assign the risk response plan to an event or event chain. These small schedules are executed only when an event or event chain occurs.

The same risk response plan can be used for different events. For example, the events "Change requirements" and "Delay with component delivery" may execute the same risk response plan (group of activities) "Update original design." If both events occur together, this risk response plan will only be executed once.

Each response plan has an entry point and exit point as shown in Figure 8.9. As a result, the original project schedule and the project schedule with simulation results (with risks and uncertainties) are different.

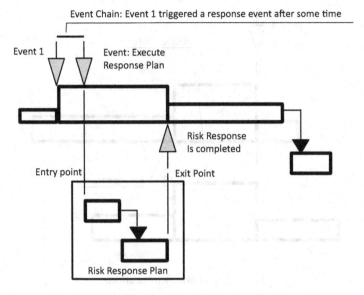

Figure 8.9. Execution of response plan.

With risk response plans, we can have an event chain with three events:

1. Original Event which triggers a response.
2. Event "Execute Response Plan," which executes a group of activities.
3. Event "Risk Response is completed." It is can be depicted as an opportunity because it moves activities to lower excited state.

Delays in Event Chains

Events can cause other events to occur either immediately or with a delay. The delay is a property of the event subscription. The delay can be deterministic, but in most cases, it is probabilistic. If the time of the original event and the delay are known, it is possible to determine when the new event will happen and in some cases, the activity that will be associated with it. For example, original event "Relocation of the business" can cause event "Missing data" sometime after the original event.

Entanglement

In quantum mechanics, entanglement is an effect in which the quantum states of two or more objects have to be described with reference to

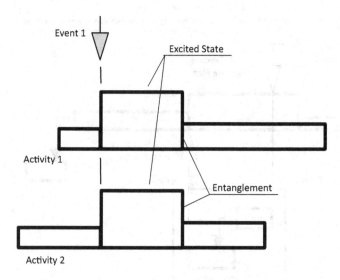

Figure 8.10. Entanglement effect.

each other, even though the individual objects may be spatially separated (Bengtsson and Życzkowski, 2006). In Event chain methodology, entanglement is an effect according to which states of apparently independent activities are changing at about the same time without a common underlying event. We call this effect entanglement for the lack of better term.

For example, after a number of layoffs in the organization, the morale is adversely affected. It affects the performance of all projects and activities including activities, which are not directly related to each other. These apparently independent activities are transferred to an excited state. After a period of time however, performance normalizes and activities tend to return a grounded state (Figure 8.10). This occurs not because of certain events such as management actions, but because of a number of psychological effects. In particular, after a certain period of time, people tend to forget negative events, as long as they do not lead major consequences to the individual.

Resource Leveling Using Event Chains

In standard resource leveling, the algorithm uses a number of criteria to determine how to act on over-allocated activities and which activity

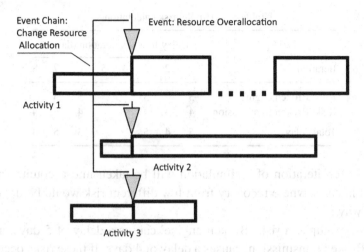

Figure 8.11. Modeling resource leveling using event chains.

should be delayed or split first. In Event chain methodology, this process is simplified through the mechanism of event subscription. Resource leveling is performed on each trial in the Monte Carlo simulation.

Here is an example of a project schedule that includes three overlapping activities with one resource (see Figure 8.11). If overallocation occurs, it triggers an event "Resource overallocation." This event will be multicast to all activities where this resource is present. However, not all activities can be subscribed to this event. For example, Activity 3 may not have a subscription to the event "Resource overallocation." Impact of the event is defined as a property of the event subscription. Excited state of Activity 1 is subscribed to a "split" impact. Excited state of Activity 2 is subscribed to a "Start later" impact. As a result, the choice should be made either to split Activity 1 or start Activity 2 later. The particular choice of the event impact should be made using different criteria: activity priority, predecessor relationship, slack, dates, etc. These criteria are a property of the event "Resource overallocation." In the example, shown in Figure 8.10, the impact of the event is a split of Activity 1.

Parallel Risks

Parallel risks are a way of modeling risk impacts in cases where risks occur simultaneously. If risks are parallel, only the maximum impact of the risk

Table 8.3. Parallel risk calculation.

Iteration	Delay for each iteration (days)							
	1	2	3	4	5	6	7	8
Risk: Broken engine	5		5			5	5	
Risk: Broken transmission	4	4				4		4
Total delay	5	4	5			5	5	4

during each iteration of a simulation will be taken into account. This is useful in cases where recovery from few different risk would be done the same way.

For example, a risk 'Broken engine' causes a delay of 5 days, and a risk 'Broken transmission' causes a delay of 4 days. If these risks occurred together and they were not parallel, the cumulative impact will be 9 days maximum. If they are parallel, cumulative impact will be 5 days. Table 8.3 shows how it works in a Monte Carlo simulation.

How to Define Event Chains

Do you remember the Jurassic Park movies, particularly the first one? We like to use this as an example because of the good risk management examples. What could be more risky than running an amusement park with live dinosaurs? The whole plot of the movie centered on the scientists who were sent to perform a risk assessment of the park before the grand opening. If you remember, paleontologists Dr. Alan Grant and Dr. Ellie Sattler along with mathematician Dr. Ian Malcolm went on a tour which did not end well. Let us take a look how in this particular case, event chains should be identified and managed.

1. Identify risks. There are few potential risks:
   - Bad weather.
   - Safety system, including power at perimeter fence is shut down.
   - Security breach by employee.
   - Dinosaurs are released outside of fence.
   - Dinosaurs' embryos are released.
   - Employee is eaten by dinosaur.

2. Assign these risks to different activities of project schedule.
3. Define event chains. Go through the list of risks and for each risk think about the relationship with other risks. For each risk, try to find a trigger or if there is no trigger try to find how this risk might be correlated with other risks. For example, what can cause a bad weather? The answer is there is no risk in our risk register that can cause bad weather, so we do not have a trigger for it. However, the risk "Safety system, including power at perimeter fence is shut down" can be caused by "Bad weather." Now you can see how we can identify these chains. For example:

- Bad weather + Security breach by employee.
- Safety system, including power at perimeter fence is shut down. Remember corrupted programmer Dennis Nedry who wanted to steal dinosaur's embryos and shit down safety system so he can perpetrate his crime?
- Dinosaurs are released outside the fence.
- Employee is eaten by dinosaur: Donald Gennaro, a business guy, was consumed by Tiranozauras Rex directly from the washroom.

Here is another chain:

- Security breach by employee: employee (Dennis Nedry) stole embryos of dinosaur + Dinosaurs are released outside of fence.
- Dinosaurs are released outside of fence.
- Employee (Dennis Nedry) is eaten by dinosaur + Dinosaurs embryos are released.

4. Create Event chain diagrams.
5. Perform Monte Carlo simulation and determine if project can be completed (project success rate). If risk analysis was really conducted and such event chains identified, the Jurassic Park would never be built. Chance of success of this project would be low, but cost of risk mitigation would be really high.

Here is an interesting observation. Let us assume that there were not any event chains. Each risk by itself will not have a significant probability, but because risks are triggered, this changes the state of other activities and another risk or series of risks are triggered and the result is quite deadly.

In the movie, the mathematician Dr. Ian Malcolm explained it from the perspective of theory of chaos. The theory of chaos involves dynamic systems that are highly sensitive to initial conditions. Perhaps, the theory of chaos is suitable in this case, but we believe that Event chain methodology is much easier way to model Jurassic Park problems.

Chapter 9

Interpreting Results of Quantitative Analysis

Get the habit of analysis — analysis will in time enable synthesis to become your
habit of mind.

Frank Lloyd Wright
American Architect
1867–1959

As we have noted before, the results of project risk analysis need to be
properly interpreted to make meaningful decisions. In this chapter, we will
discuss how to interpret sensitivity charts, frequency histograms, and how
we can use these results to calculate project contingencies. In the end, we
will tie these altogether with Event chain methodology and learn its fifth
principle: how to rank events and event chains based on results of Monte
Carlo simulation.

Interpretation Results of the Analysis

After you have run a Monte Carlo simulation, the unprocessed results are
just a series of statistical distributions. To get any real value, we have to
understand what they mean. One of inherent problems with probabilistic
calculations is that they go against our common sense. In real life, if we
perform a task there is only one result, but Monte Carlo provides us with a
whole range of results (distributions). For example, you are going out for
dinner with your friends and tell your babysitter it will take somewhere
between 2 and 3 h. The babysitter asks if you could be a bit more accurate.
When you think about your answer, you realize that it could be 2 h 15 min,
or it may be 2 h and 45 min even more. If you would like to provide your

babysitter with a more certainty, what should your answer be? Let us see how Monte Carlo simulations help us answer these types of questions.

Many risk analysis software tools offer results in very simple table format (Table 9.1):

Table 9.1. Results of analysis in a simple table format.

Results	Project duration	Project finish time	Project cost
Deterministic	20 days	Feb 20, 2016	$45,000
Low (e.g. P10)	22 days	Feb 22, 2016	$52,000
Base (Mean)	26 days	Feb 26, 2016	$57,500
High (e.g. P90)	31 days	March 3, 2016	$61,400

These results are easy to interpret. This table shows that the mean average duration of the project will increase by six days and $12,500 due to risks and uncertainties.

The results of analysis can be also presented in the form of frequency histograms and cumulative probability plots. In earlier chapters, we examined how to utilize these charts to determine that chance that project or task will be completed before certain dates and below certain costs. These charts can be also useful for quality control of the results of your analysis. Please take a look on Figure 9.1. It represents three very common cases of which you should be aware. In this particular example, we have used a statistical distribution for cost, but similar cases may occur for duration, work, and other parameters.

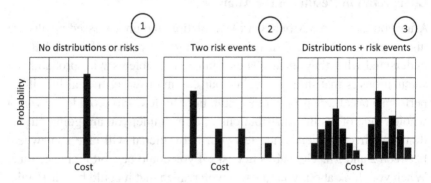

Figure 9.1. Three common cases of statistical distributions.

1. All costs are the same; there are no uncertainties or risk events affecting task or project cost.
2. This task or project has two risk events impacting cost. If there are only two events, why do we have four bars? One of the bars is the original cost (no risks). The second and third bars are costs when the two risks occurred separately. The last bar represents cost when two risks occurred simultaneously.
3. In bimodal distribution, we see the interaction of uncertainty and risk events. In this example, the left group most likely represents cost uncertainty that is defined using a statistical distribution. These distributions model the inherent variability that occurs due to small fluctuations that might occur to cost. The right group most likely represents result of risk events impacting cost. These risk events provide significantly greater impact than "noise", defined by statistical distributions.

Most project risk analysis software applications provide tools for analyzing frequency histograms and cumulative probability plots. We can use sliders or guides to determine the probability that cost or duration will be greater or below certain values. We can also place lines associated with low, base and high estimates of duration and cost which can be expressed as percentiles.

Managing Project Contingencies

Project contingency (also referred to as margin or management reserve) is additional time or budget that can be added to the project plan to account for the possible variance from uncertainty and events and ensure that the project has a high probability of success. Before we discuss how we should set contingency, let us take a look at two common practices that we do not recommend:

1. Project planners are often motivated to create shorter and less costly schedules to win a bid or get a project approved. For example, you are much more likely to have a project approved if you provide an estimate of $700 million as opposed to $1 billion without reducing scope. So how can they reduce estimated costs without reducing scope? It is very

simple actually, just assume that there will be no unexpected problems and reduce contingency accordingly. This approach to project planning is a very common phenomenon for large infrastructure projects (Flyvbjerg, 2005); as the scope is so large, it is easier to hide the true cost of risk. We do not recommend this approach as it tends to lead to large costs and schedule over runs.

2. Project planners in small projects may just choose to add additional contingency to account for all possible issues and therefore they will not be blamed if project is delayed. If you use unrealistically high contingencies, either as schedule margin or management reserve, this requires your organization to hold back resources and results in inefficient use of scarce resources and the inability to take advantage of opportunities.

So if you cannot use these methods, how can we determine a realistic contingency for a specific project? The answer, as you can probably guess, can be determined using the results of the Monte Carlo analysis. Remember, the analysis takes into account risks and uncertainties and provides statistical distributions that tell us what the chance is that we will get a certain result. So, we can extend this to generate risk adjusted contingency. For example, we could determine our contingency based on P80 for cost and schedule. To do this, we would run the Monte Carlo risk analysis and calculate the contingency based on the difference between the original project plan and the P80 results. Once we have calculated this contingency, we would put them into the plan as buffers. During project execution, we would manage the project using the original plan and monitor the buffers. As risk and uncertainties occurs, it will consume the buffer, but as long as the buffer exists, the project would be completed on time and schedule. This approach is part of Critical Chain Method (Project Management Institute, 2013).

Sensitivity Analysis, Tornado, and Scatter Plots

Project managers always want to know which task should they be most worried about, which one could have the most impact on their project? If a task is not on the critical path it may not have any effect on project duration, unless it is impacted by risks. Tasks, which have the most potential to affect the project parameters such as duration or cost, are called *crucial tasks*. This term is used to distinguish it from critical tasks, which are on the critical path of the project schedule.

We can identify crucial tasks using *sensitivity analysis*. In general, sensitivity analysis determines how uncertainties in the output of a mathematical model are impacted by different inputs. In our case, sensitivity analysis determines how uncertainties in project duration, cost, and other parameters are affected by uncertainties in task parameters. Remember the "spring analogy," which we discussed in Chapter 5? Let us assume that each task is a spring and each spring has different stiffness. Tasks with less stiffness will have more uncertainty, that is, they will expand or contract more if impacted by other tasks. We are trying to push or pull on each spring to measure the response on the last task (Figure 9.2). Tasks that have the most effect on the movement of the system of springs (the schedule), are the most crucial tasks. Any risks that are assigned to these tasks need to be given high priority to understand how they can be managed.

We can identify crucial tasks by calculating the correlation between project parameters and task parameters. This is done using correlation coefficients, such as the Spearman or the Pearson correlation coefficient. Spearman is a non-parametric measure of the statistical dependence between two variables. When you perform Monte Carlo simulations, you will get a set of results for duration, cost, and other parameters for each task as well as for the project.

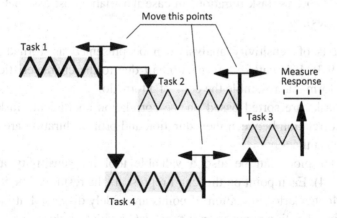

Figure 9.2. Spring analogy for sensitivity analysis.

	Task Name	Correlation Coefficient	Tornado Chart
1	Hiring Key Employees	0.72	
2	Establishing Name and Ownership of Business	0.64	
3	Developing Business Plan	0.50	
4	Renting Facility	0.21	
5	Developing Marketing and Sales Plan	0.18	
6	Analysis of Business Environment	0.10	

Figure 9.3. Example of tornado chart: Project duration vs. task duration.

Let us assume that you want to calculate the correlation coefficient for task duration and project duration. Spearman formula compares the result for each task and the project on each iteration of Monte Carlo simulation. If longer task duration always (100%) corresponds with longer project duration and shorter task duration always corresponds with shorter project duration, correlation coefficient will be 1. If there is no relationship between two variables, the correlation coefficient will be zero. Please note that correlation coefficient does not depend on the nature or units of a variable, so you can calculate correlation coefficient between virtually anything, for example, the lag between tasks and project cost. These are the most common types of sensitivity analysis of a project:

• Project duration vs. task duration.
• Project finish time vs. task finish time.
• Project cost vs. task cost.
• Project success rate vs. task success rate.
• Project cost vs. task duration (in case if variable cost associated with resources).

Results of sensitivity analysis can be presented as Tornado Chart (Figure 9.3). It is called a Tornado chart due to the characteristic shape the bars form that resemble the cone of a tornado.

All tasks are sorted based on the correlation coefficient. Tasks with higher correlation between their duration and project duration are crucial and listed at the top.

Scatter plots can be also a valuable tool for sensitivity analysis (Figure 9.4). Each point on this chart represents the result of one iteration of the Monte Carlo simulation. If points are widely dispersed, it indicates that project duration is not strongly correlated with task duration. If points

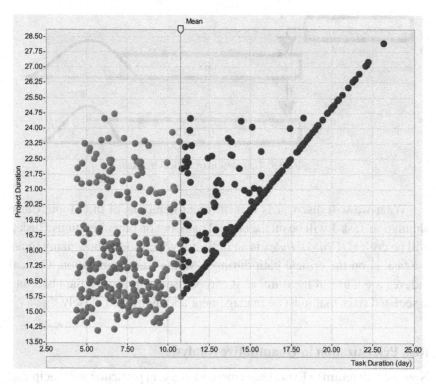

Figure 9.4. Scatter plot: project duration vs. task duration.

appear to be aligned in one direction, it would mean that project and task duration are strongly correlated.

Sometimes different parameters may have "spurious correlation." Spurious comes from the Latin word spurious, which means illegitimate or false. A popular example of this is how people used to think that the stock market was correlated with the length of skirts. As skirts went up, so did stock markets according to this theory. However, most likely this is due to some other confounding factor and therefore, whenever we do see correlations that are unexpected, further investigation is required.

Critical Indexes

Here is an example of project schedule (Figure 9.5). Tasks 1 and 2 have uncertainties defined by a statistical distribution. Let us perform a Monte Carlo simulation of this schedule.

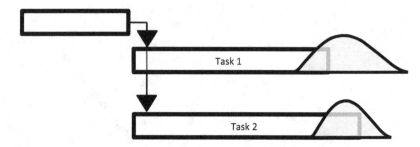

Figure 9.5. Calculation of critical indexes.

What we will discover is that different iterations of the Monte Carlo simulation Task 1 will be on the critical path, but on other iterations, Task 2 will be critical. *Critical Index* is an indicator which shows how many times the task is on the critical path during a Monte Carlo simulation. Critical indexes are a useful measure, as it can be used to prioritize the tasks and associated risks that must be management and monitored closely.

Risk Prioritization in Quantitative Analysis

Now we will return to Event chain methodology, in particular to Principle 5, which deals with the analysis of the schedule with event chains. We can extend this process to use Monte Carlo simulations to prioritize events and event chains. Remember, as part of our explanation of qualitative risk analysis, we learned how to prioritize risks based on the risk score. Now, through the use of Monte Carlo simulations, we can perform a more accurate analysis. Here is an example.

Two pirates, Jonny Death and Orlando Plume found that a treasure chest was buried beneath the parking lot of the Miami Dolphin's Stadium and are planning to dig it out in the morning. However, Captain Barabusa, their arch rival has been keep a close eye on the duo and suspects that they have discovered something and intends to arrive at the parking lot at exactly the same time to steal whatever it is they are digging up. But our two clever pirates have a plan; while Jonny excavates the treasure chest, Orlando will attempt to fool Barabusa by telling him that Jonny has just been hired to repair the sewer and send Barabusa off in the wrong direction. As part of their plan, they created a project schedule (Figure 9.6).

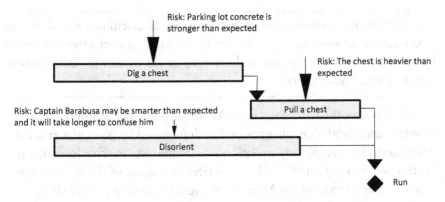

Figure 9.6. Project schedule and risks assigned to tasks.

The final question is how are Jonny and Orlando going to share the treasure? After some discussion, they decide that whoever assumes the most risk should receive the largest share of the treasure. They also agree that the most important risk is that which has the potential to cause the greatest delay in the project. They identified three risks (Table 9.2):

Table 9.2. List of risks.

	Risk	Probability	Delay of the task this risk is assigned to
1	Parking lot concrete is stronger than expected	20%	20%
2	The chest is heavier than expected	20%	20%
3	Captain Barabusa may be smarter than expected and it will take longer to confuse him	90%	80%

Based on this risk breakdown structure, Jonny will have to deal with the first two risks, while Orlando will deal with the last one. Orlando argues that he is assuming the most critical risk (90% chance that this risk will cause 80% delay) and that he deserves greater share of treasure. If we were performing qualitative analysis, where the risks are not assigned to the project schedule, he would be absolutely correct. However, if we use Monte Carlo simulations, the results can be decidedly different.

In quantitative analysis, the impact of risks is calculated based on the correlation between specific changes in duration, cost or other parameter caused by the risk occurring and changes in the overall project duration, cost, or other parameters.

Here is how the risk analysis works in our particular example. In each Monte Carlo simulation, changes in duration caused by particular risk are calculated. For example, in simulation 1 due to the risk "Parking lot concrete is stronger than expected" Task 1 experiences a delay of 0.6 h. The table below shows an example of Monte Carlo results (in hours) (Table 9.3):

Table 9.3. Duration changes on each iteration of Monte Carlo simulation.

Simulation	Task duration increase due to risk 1: Parking lot concrete is stronger than expected	Task duration increase due to risk 2: The chest is heavier than expected	Task duration increase due to risk 3: Captain Barabusa is smarter than expected and it will take longer to disorient him	Project duration
1	0.6 (20% increase of 3 h duration)	0	1.6 (80% increase of 2 h duration)	4.6
2	0	0.2 (20% increase of 1 h duration)	1.6	4.2
3	0	0	1.6	4
4	0.6	0	1.6	4.6
5	0	0	1.6	4
6	0	0	0	4
7	0	0	0	4
8	0	0	1.6	4
9	0	0	1.6	4
10	0	0.2	1.6	4.2
...	...	...	...	...
Correlation coefficient	0.80	0.55	0	

So, the correlation coefficient is calculated between increases in duration caused by specific risks (columns 1–3) and project duration (column 4). Spearman Rank Order correlation coefficient between risk 3 and project duration equals zero. Why? Because the task "Disorient Barabusa" is not on the critical path. Even if the duration of the task increases by 1.6 h

(80%) due to the risk and reaches 3.6 h, it will still be less than the duration of Jonny's tasks: 3 h +1 h = 4 h. It means that risk 3 does not affect project duration at all and the impact of this risk equals 0.

However, the correlation coefficient is not yet the "risk impact." Here is the problem. Let us assume that our project has only one task "dig treasure" and one risk "Parking lot concrete is stronger than expected." What would be the correlation coefficient between changes in duration caused by the risk and project duration? The answer is 100%. It indicates that each time the risk occurs the duration will increase. Now, what happens if this risk increases the duration by 90%, rather than 20%? The correlation coefficient will be the same. Spearman Rank Order correlation coefficient is the same when all values are multiplied by one number.

To avoid this problem, the following calculation algorithm is used:

1. Calculate *correlation coefficient* as a result of Monte Carlo simulation as described above.
2. Calculate the project duration or cost with and without risks. Project duration with risk is the mean project duration. In our case, project duration without risks and mean project duration as a result on Monte Carlo simulations (with risks) equals 4 h.
3. Calculate the *impact coefficient = project duration with risk/(2 × project duration no risks)*. In our case, impact coefficient equals 0.5.
4. Calculated *risk impact* equals *correlation coefficient* multiplied by *impact coefficient*. In our case, impacts will be 40% = 0.8 × 0.5 × 100% and 27.5% = 0.55 × 0.5 × 100% for risks 1 and 2. Impact of risk 3 will be zero.

Project risk register with calculated risk impact and score is shown in Table 9.4.

From this we can calculate that a risk that leads to a doubling of project duration or has an impact 100%. Why two times and not three or five? It is actually an arbitrary value: however; once we adopt this value and use it at an organizational level, it allows us to consistently compare the impact of risks across multiple projects.

Finally, we calculate the risk scores as the risk probability multiplied by the risk impact and rank all risks based on the these scores. So in our story, Jonny should receive the greater share of the treasure because based

Table 9.4. Risk register with calculated risk impact.

	Risk	Probability	Calculated impact	Score
1	Parking lot concrete is stronger than expected	20%	40%	8%
2	The chest is heavier than expected	20%	27.5%	5.5%
3	Captain Barabusa is smarter than expected and it will take longer to confuse him	90%	0%	0%

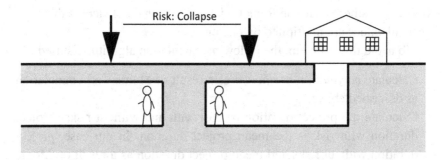

Figure 9.7. Calculating the probability of one risk assigned to multiple tasks.

on the project duration criteria our pirates choose, his risks have the most potential to increase the project duration.

Calculated Risk Probability

In the previous example, we assumed that one risk is assigned one task: a simple 1 to 1 relationship. But what happens if the risk is assigned to multiple tasks? Here is an example. Mexican drug lord El Stuppo wants to escape from jail (Figure 9.7). To do so, he is digging a tunnel from his side, and his associate is digging a tunnel from the opposite side. They are hoping to meet somewhere in the middle. But there is a risk that the tunnel may collapse. So there is a single risk, but we have to assign it to different tasks: "El Stuppo digging" and "Associate digging" with probabilities of 30% and 40% respectively. What would be the total probability of this risk?

Everything depends how these assignments are correlated. Let us assume that the collapse is caused by heavy rain, which can occur at the

Table 9.5. Calculation of probability of risk occurrence for two risk assignments.

Simulation	Assigned to task "El Stuppo digging"	Assigned to task "associate digging"	Total for the risk
1	Occurred		Occurred
2		Occurred	Occurred
3	Occurred	Occurred	Occurred
4			
5			
6		Occurred	Occurred
7			
8			
9		Occurred	Occurred
10	Occurred		Occurred
Probability	30%	40%	60%

same time at both sides of the tunnel. In this case, the risk assignments are correlated and probabilities are equal to maximum probability of both assignments: 40%. If risk assignments are not correlated, then the probability is calculated as is shown in Table 9.5.

Calculated Impact and Probabilities of Event Chain

In additional to calculating probability and impact of individual risk events, we can rank the event chain. To do this, we need to investigate if the event chain is has been fully executed. In some cases one event can occur, but it will not trigger another event. Remember that receiver event may be triggered with certain probability. Then we will calculate the cumulative impact of the event chain, rather than the individual risks.

If an event chain is fully executed, the cumulative impact of this event chain on all tasks to which the events from the chain are assigned is calculated. The next step is to calculate the correlation between event chain impacts and project results. Again, this is a similar process to the analysis we perform on individual risk events and this will allow us to rank event chain based on how they impact specific project parameters.

Chapter 10

Project Performance Measurement with Risks and Uncertainties

Monitoring the progress of activities ensures that updated information is used to perform your risk analysis. While this is true for all types of analysis, it is a critical principle of event chain methodology. In this chapter, we will discuss a simple approach on how to forecast project duration and cost using a partially completed project. We will also briefly review an integrated Earned Value Management (EVM)/Project Risk Analysis approach to managing project performance.

Tracking Project Performance under Uncertainties

The James Webb Space Telescope (JWST) is a new space observatory with a planned launch in 2018 (Figure 10.1). This project is a collaborative effort of 17 countries, including NASA, the European Space Agency and the Canadian Space Agency. The telescope is named after NASA's second administrator James E. Webb (1961–1968), who played a significant role in the Apollo program. The JWST will provide high quality images with a sensitivity range from the long-wave length visible light to the mid-length infrared.

Keeping a complex project such as the JWST on time and budget is a challenge. The original cost estimate for the project was $1.6 billion. As part of this management process, NASA performed an integrated cost and schedule project risk analysis (Druker, 2012). They found that by 2011 about $3 billion had been spent and 75% of its hardware was in production. Due to the cost overruns, the United States House of Representatives voted to terminate funding (Bergin, 2015). Later, funding was restored

Figure 10.1. Full-scale model of JWST in Dublin, Ireland (June 2007).

through compromise legislation signed in the US Senate, but spending on the program was capped at $8 billion. A 2013 estimate put the cost of development and five years of operation at $8.8 billion. Before completion, the project must overcome a number of technological challenges that have and will contribute to the delays and cost overruns (Dance, 2014). One of the challenges is related to the fact that JWST is an infrared observatory that requires all of the optical components to operate at a cryogenic temperature six times colder than your average freezer. Individually, the many risks and technical glitches may be not very significant, but their cumulative impacts contribute to significant delays in the project.

One of the critical problems that most schedulers tackle is forecasting project duration and cost of partially completed projects given that some risks have occurred, some have been mitigated, some still may occur in the future. Information about actual project performance gives additional information that helps to forecast final cost and completion dates more accurately.

Remaining Project Duration and Cost

When we perform project risk analysis, we calculate the project statistical distributions of project duration, finish time, and cost. But let us assume that a project is 60% completed. What would be the statistical distributions for remaining duration and cost of the project? By answering this question, we would be able to forecast project duration and cost at any moment during project execution.

The first step in this process requires us to calculate the remaining duration and cost for individual tasks. Once we have this data, we can then perform Monte Carlo simulations of the complete schedule with the one condition, the simulation starts where the actuals end. There are two ways the analysis can be calculated. Here is an example, you have a task that was originally scheduled to be completed in 10 days, when we receive the actuals, we find that after five days it is only 40% complete.

1. **If we know remaining duration:** Based on our expert experience or historical data, we conclude that the task can be completed in an additional 7–8 days. We define statistical distribution for remaining duration. The task duration on each iteration of Monte Carlo simulation will be the actual duration (5 days) plus duration obtained from statistical distribution, for example, 7.6 days.
2. **We do not have good estimates for the remaining duration and want to calculate it automatically:** In this case, we need to calculate projected duration of the task. In our example, it will be 5 days $\times$ 100%/40% = 12.5 days. For the Monte Carlo simulation, we use the original statistical distribution of the task duration to generate samples e.g. 10.6 days. The base duration will be 10 days. So, the task duration for each iteration for Monte Carlo simulation while taking into account that our task is 40% complete after 5 days is calculated using this formula:

$$\text{Task duration} = \frac{\text{Duration from distribution (10.6 days)} \times \text{Projected duration (12.5 days)}}{\text{Base original duration (10 days)}}.$$

We can calculate task and project costs using the same process using % complete and actual costs.

Here is how a forecast of project or task duration can be presented graphically (Figure 10.2). Low and high estimates of duration can be calculated either by defining remaining duration or by automatically extrapolating using the original duration and statistical distribution.

A probabilistic forecast for duration can be calculated at each phase of the project (Figure 10.3). In reality, the "fork," or the range for statistical distributions of project duration should close over time as there will be less risk and uncertainty as the project progresses until the point where the project is finished and there are no more uncertainties. If the "fork" becomes

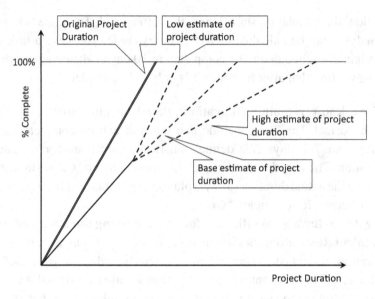

Figure 10.2. Forecast project duration.

wider close to the end of project, it is an ominous signal that a significant risk has been discovered and it does not bode well for your project.

Forecasting Project Duration and Cost with Risk Events

We discussed how the remaining duration can be incorporated into project risk analysis if duration is defined by a statistical distribution. Now, we will examine how it can be done using Event chain methodology.

During the course of a project, we can recalculate the probability of occurrence and moment of the events using actual performance data. The analysis can be repeated to generate a new project schedule with updated costs or duration. But what should be done in cases where an activity is only partially complete and it has certain risk events assigned to it? If the event has already occurred, will it occur again? Or vice versa, if nothing has occurred yet, is there still a chance that it could occur?

There are three distinct approaches to this problem:

1. Probabilities of a random event in partially completed activities stay the same regardless of the outcome of previous events. This is mostly related to external events, which cannot be affected by project stakeholders.

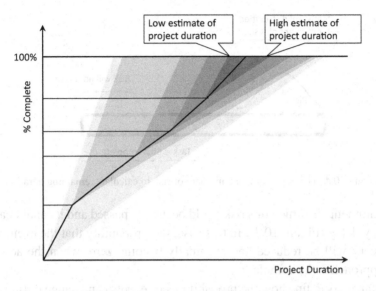

Figure 10.3. Forecast project duration on different phases of the project.

An example might be that a "bad weather" event during a course of one-year construction project can occur 10 times. As it turns out, half year after construction began, bad weather has occurred eight times. Some may hope that because the risk has already occurred more than expected, they can now look forward to relatively benign weather. They would be incorrect. Regardless of the experience of the previous six months, in the remaining half year the event could still occur five times. This approach is related to psychological effect called "gambler's fallacy" or belief that a successful outcome is due after a run of bad luck (Tversky and Kahneman, 1971).

2. Probabilities of events in a partially completed activity depend on the moment of the event. If the moment of risk is earlier than the moment when actual measurement is performed, this event can no longer affect the activity. For example, the activity "software user interface development" takes 10 days. The event "change of requirements" can occur any time during the course of the activity and can cause a delay (a uniform distribution for the moment of the event). Now, if 60% of work is completed within 6 days and the probabilistic moment of the event happens to land in between the start of the activity and 6 days, the

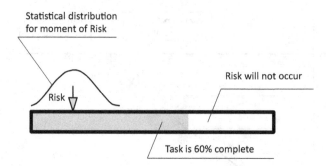

Figure 10.4. Using probabilistic moment of risk to calculate remaining duration.

"moment" in which this risk could occur has passed and it cannot cause any delay (Figure 10.4). In this case, the probability that the event will occur will be reduced and eventually become zero, when the activity approaches the completion.

3. Managers define how the probabilities of events can change during any stage of an activity. For example, the event "change of requirements" occurs, but it could happen again depending on many factors, such as how well the requirements are defined and interpreted and the particular business situation. To use this approach, excited state activities should be explicitly subscribed or not subscribed to certain events. For example, a new excited state after the event "change of requirements" may not be subscribed to this event again, and as a result, this event will not affect the activity a second time.

Monitoring the Chance that a Project Meets a Deadline

We can monitor and show the chance that a project will meet a specific deadline using the chart shown in Figure 10.5. The chance changes constantly as a result of various events and event chains. In most cases, this chance shrinks over time. However, risk response and mitigation plans can increase the chance of successfully meeting a project deadline. The chance of the project meeting the deadline is constantly updated as a result of the quantitative analysis based on the original assessment of the project uncertainties and the actual project performance data.

In the critical chain method, the constant change in the size of the project buffer is monitored to ensure that project is on track. In Event chain

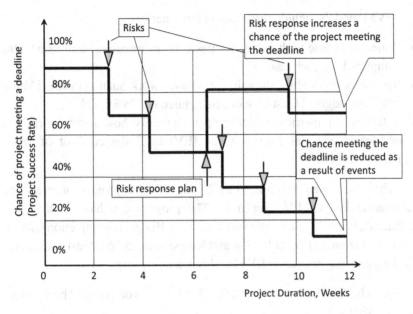

Figure 10.5. Monitoring the chance of project completion on a certain date.

methodology, the chance of the project meeting a certain deadline during different phases of the project serves a similar purpose: it is an important indicator of project health. Monitoring the chance of the project meeting a certain deadline does not require a project buffer. It is always possible to identify particular changes in the chance of meeting a deadline with actual and forecasted events and event chains, and as a result, minimize their negative impact.

Risk Analysis and Earned Value Management

We have shown a very simple way to perform project performance measurement with risk and uncertainties. Many organizations utilize much more advanced framework for measuring project performance called *Earned value management (EVM)*. EVM was first developed in the 1960s, but became a practical methodology late in the last century when it was actively adopted by US government agencies and in particular the US Department of Defense.

EVM models include three main components:

- Project schedule with necessary tracking information, such as percent completed for each task.
- Indicators which show the value of planned work, such as Planned Value (PV) or Budgeted Cost of Work Scheduled (BCWS), and
- Indicators or metrics, which help to quantify how much work was performed, such as Earned Value (EV) or Budgeted Cost of Work Performed (BCWP).

The main idea behind EVM is to measure project progress by calculating EV vs. PV over time. The projects can have many other indicators, including Schedule variance (SV), Budget at completion (BAC), and Cost variance (CV) (Fleming and Koppelman, 2006). Most commonly used metrics for integrated EVM and risk analysis are:

- The Schedule Performance Index (SPI), which is determined by dividing EV by PV.
- The Cost Performance Index (CPI), which is determined by dividing EV by actual cost.

How can we integrate project risk analysis with established EVM processes? Here are the basic steps to integrate EVM/Project Risk Analysis Process (Hillson, 2004):

Step 1. Create the baseline spend plan (BCWS/PV)

1. Create a resource-loaded and cost-loaded project schedule.
2. Identify risks and uncertainties and assign them to the project tasks.
3. Perform Monte Carlo simulation using integrated schedule and cost risk.
4. Risk adjusted project schedule becomes a baseline profile (BCWS/PV); this risk adjusted project schedule can be generated based on certain confidence levels (e.g. 80%).

Step 2. Measure actual project performance and forecast future project outcome (EAC)

1. Record project progress and actual cost spent to date (ACWP), and calculate earned value (BCWP).

2. Review initial time/cost estimates for activities not completed, identify changes, including revised estimating uncertainties expressed as statistical distributions of project duration and costs.
3. Update risk identification, assessment, and quantification: update probabilities and impacts of the risks, review mitigation and response plans.
4. Update project schedule and repeat Monte Carlo simulation; it is done essentially for remaining project work, although the simulations are done using the entire schedule.
5. Select risk-adjusted project schedule defined using certain confidence level as estimate of final project duration and cost (EAC).

Step 3. Evaluate the risk management process effectiveness

1. Select EVM metrics, for example, CPI and SPI to trigger corrective action in risk process and calculate them.
2. Consider modifications to risk processes, for example, perform risk mitigation if CPI and/or SPI cross thresholds.
3. Consider the need to review initial baseline or scope if CPI and/or SPI persistently have unusually high or low values.

In general, we use EVM to manage risk adjusted project schedules. We calculate all necessary metrics at each phase of the project, and then based on these metrics, we perform corrective actions by reducing impact of specific threats or by exploiting opportunities.

Part III

Advanced Quantitative Project Risk Analysis

Chapter 11

More Uncertainties: Calendars, Success Rates, Work and Resources

In this chapter, we will learn about analyzing other uncertainties, related to project schedules. A task or a project can be canceled because of risk events or because they reach a certain deadline. Risk analysis helps to determine a task or a project success rate, which could be an important factor in making project decisions. Probabilistic calendars can be useful in modeling uncertainties in weather or resource availability. Risks and uncertainties can be also be related to work and resource allocation. Resource leveling can be performed as part of project risk analysis.

Deadlines and Success Rate

If you love action movies, you probably have an appreciation of scenes that involve some defusing a bomb. Common to all is that they tend to feature a scene in which for a few very intense minutes, one of the main characters has to defuse a bomb by selecting which wire to cut and avert a catastrophe. Our favorite bomb defusing scene is in Juggernaut (1974), where the British government airlifts a Royal bomb disposal squad to a luxury liner to defuse a number of explosive devices. Other favorites are The Shadow (1994) with Alec Baldwin and Die Hard with a Vengeance (1995) with Bruce Willis.

Success Rate — the chance that a task or project can be completed. A task success rate of 56% means that there is a 56% chance that this task or project will be completed and 44% percent chance that task will be canceled.

What makes these movies so compelling is the deadline: the clock is ticking and if the wires are not cut properly and on time, the hero and any number of innocent victims will perish. For our purposes, we like to describe this bomb defusing as projects. The duration is uncertain as it is unclear how long it will take to defuse the bomb and an early finish may not always be a positive result! However, barring the hero cutting the wrong wire, all activities must be completed before the timer completes the countdown. In other words, there is a chance that the project will not be completed on time. In this case, it is very important to know the success rate that the project will be completed before the deadline and everything ends badly. While in the movies, the heroes rarely think about such things, in our case, if the success rate is low, we need to find another alternative, reduce probability of risks occurring, or avoid it altogether.

First thing we need to do is calculate the success rate, which we can do in the following manner. A simple schedule for the project "Defuse the bomb" has two activities: "Open the device" and "Cut wires", which should take about 1 and 1.5 min respectively (Figure 11.1). The project must be completed in 3 min; otherwise the movie will have an unhappy ending. In

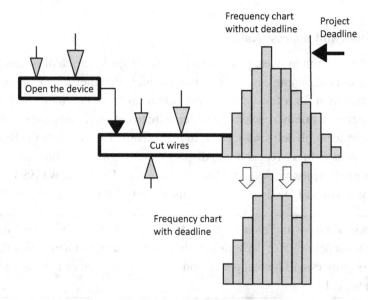

Figure 11.1. Project schedule with deadline.

theory, there is enough time to defuse the bomb, however, both activities have multiple risks that can delay the project.

To calculate probabilistic duration and success rate of the project with risk we need to perform Monte Carlo simulations. We will run the simulation and generate the results on the first frequency histogram. From this, we can see that in 25% of the iterations, the project duration will be greater than 3 min. This converts to a project success rate of 75%. The second (lower) frequency histogram takes into account that the project duration cannot be greater than 3 min regardless of whether the bomb is defused or not. So, in each particular iteration in which duration is greater than 3 min, the iteration is set to 3 min.

More Details about Task and Project Deadlines

Deadlines can affect projects or particular tasks. If a task reaches a project or task deadline it could cause the following outcomes:

1. End task: in this case, duration of task will be reduced, but task success rate will not change.
2. Cancel task: both success rate and duration will be reduced.
3. Reduce success rate: success rate is reduced, but the task duration is not affected.

Project deadlines can be defined by earliest deadline, latest deadline and maximum project duration. Earliest deadlines are rare, but may occur when these are some combinations of finish to finish or start to finish links between tasks in the project schedule or negative lags (Figure 11.2).

Calculation and Presentation of Success Rates

Tasks can be cancelled if:

1. A task reaches a task deadline, as long as deadline leads to cancelation of the task.
2. A task reaches a project deadline, as long as deadline leads to cancelation of the task.
3. A risk with an impact of "Cancel task" or "Cancel task and all successors" occurs and is assigned to the task. For example, if the probability of the

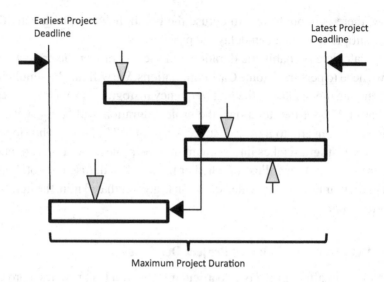

Figure 11.2. Project deadlines.

risk of with these impact is 10%, the success rate of the task will be 90% as long as task cannot be canceled because of other factors.

4. A risk with an impact "Cancel task and all successors" occurs and is assigned to one of the tasks predecessors.

5. Success rates can be reduced due to branching: certain activities may not be executed because a branching condition is met … We will learn about branching in Chapter 11.

Projects can be canceled if the following conditions occur:

1. Any tasks of the project reach a project deadline as long as deadline leads to cancelation of the task.

2. Risks with an impact type "cancel project" occur and are assigned to any task or resources.

In most cases, success rates of projects or tasks are affected by combinations of these factors. When you run a Monte Carlo simulation, any combination of factors can occur during an iteration. On some iterations, a risk impact "Cancel task" can occur, on other iterations a task or project will be reach a deadline. In addition, project or tasks can be canceled due to some "exotic" conditions; for example, cancelations due to resource

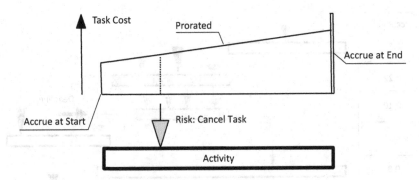

Figure 11.3. Cost of the canceled task.

overallocation or as a result of the execution of a response plan. In most cases, such conditions can be modeled using event chains where the receiver risk of these chains will be an event with impact time "Cancel task" or "Cancel project".

Task cancelation can cause very interesting phenomenon. Sometimes, projects can be affected by many risks, but a project with risks can be shorter than a project without risks. Commonly, risks are threats and increase project duration. However, in the cases of opportunities or risks with an impact that cancels tasks, you can possibly have simulation results where the base duration is less than the original estimate.

If task is cancelled and has a fixed or variable cost, the task cost will depend on the moment of risk (Figure 11.3).

Here is simple example. The task's fixed cost is $5,000 and is accrued at the start. Another fixed cost is $3,000 and accrued at the end. Variable costs are prorated at $100/h. Now, let us assume that the original task duration was 10 h, but a risk occurred and it was canceled after 6 h. The cost after cancelation will be $5,000 + 6 × $100 = $5,600. Fixed costs that accrued at the end are ignored.

Task cancelation may affect summary tasks; however, there could be different rules on how the cancelation of summary task might occur if subtasks are cancelled. The simplest way to deal with it is to have special risk impact types: "Cancel task and all summary tasks" or "Cancel task and immediate summary task." In this case, if a risk occurs it will only impact the task and specified summary tasks.

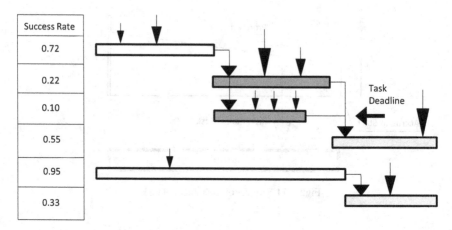

Figure 11.4. Gantt chart shows task success rates.

Success rate can be shown in the Gantt chart, where different Gantt bars will have different colors (Figure 11.4). Green (white color on the Figure 11.4) bars will be associated with higher success rates, yellow (grey color) bar will be associated with medium success rates, and red (dark grey color) bars will be associated with low success rates.

Probabilistic Calendars

Here is a common scheduling issue. Offshore oil drilling in Gulf of Mexico can be affected by bad weather and, in particular, hurricanes. In the case of hurricanes, all drilling is shut down and the crews are evacuated to an onshore location. While the severity of hurricanes can vary, the impact is still largely the same (shutdown, evacuation, startup) so the main issue is what is the probability that a hurricane will occur. In addition, hurricanes can only occur during a specific period: in the Gulf of Mexico, the hurricane season runs from June to November with peak intensity generally in the late summer, early fall. So how do we model this risk?

One of the solutions is to use a time-depended global risk "Hurricane." This risk would only affect activities performed during the hurricane season. It would be possible to assign a statistical distribution for the moment of risk. In this case, we might use a normal distribution as hurricanes are most likely to occur in September/October. However, using a time dependent global risk requires that is has a specific risk impact. For example, a fixed or relative delay, or restart the activity. The problem with this approach is that in reality the impact could vary widely for different activities. Impacts would depend on the actual calendar day when hurricane occurs. For example, if a hurricane occurs during a weekend and holiday, the delay may be shorter.

Another proposed solution to weather modeling is to create a calendar or several calendars that would include non-working days or other restricted schedules that could occur during a hurricane. Once we have developed these "weather" calendars, we then have to assign a probability to how often they will be in effect during a project. For example, we could create a "Hurricane calendar" that has five non-working days in September. Through our research, we know that there is a 10% chance of a hurricane occurring in this area during September. Therefore, during a Monte Carlo simulation, the "Hurricane" calendar would be used as the project calendar in 10% of the iterations and the standard project calendar in the remaining 90%.

In project scheduling, calendars can be assigned to:

- Complete projects (project calendar).
- Individual tasks.
- Resources.

In each case, it is possible to have a probabilistic calendar. Probabilistic project calendars can be used to model other issues in addition to weather. For example, we can create a resource calendar that models the unavailability of a particular resource. If we know that a particular resource will most likely be absent 20% of the time in June, we can create a calendar to model the non-working time and have it run on 20% probability during Monte Carlo simulations.

In project risk analysis software applications, you do not need to define probabilistic calendar explicitly. Instead, you could use a weather modeling tool and define number of non-working days and probability of interruptions because of weather. The tool would then create probabilistic calendars automatically.

Probabilistic Work and Resource Allocation

So far, we have discussed how to define and manage uncertainties in project durations. In many cases, project schedulers use work as input and output parameters. Duration and work are closely related to each other. As a result you may define uncertainties in duration and show the results in the form of statistical distributions of both duration and work. Alternatively, you may define uncertainties in work or units. It is possible to define a distribution for both work and material resources assigned to the particular task. In addition, it is possible to define a statistical distribution for resource allocation units. For example, the bomb defusing expert from the movie "Juggernaut" could be allocated to defuse a particular bomb for 30–70%. However, distribution for units can become very complex and hard to maintain because resource allocations to different tasks should be correlated with each other.

Risk events can also have work or unit related impact type. Here are the examples of risk impact types:

- Fixed or relative work increase.
- Fixed or relative resource allocation unit increase.
- Cancel work of particular resource for particular task.
- Reallocate resource to different task.

Resource peak units, allocation, work, or percent allocation for specific resource can be shown in the chart (Figure 11.5). These charts can show the results of your risk analysis. Each bar of the chart can show low (for

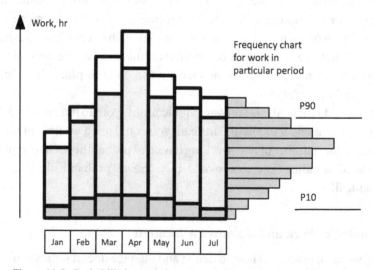

Figure 11.5. Probabilistic work for selected resource or group of resources.

example, P10), base, and high estimates of work or units. Essentially, each bar has a statistical distribution behind this. This statistical distribution does not need to be explicitly shown, but some software will allow you to click on the particular bar and view the distribution. It is also possible to set the chart to show for low, base, and high estimates of work or units separately.

Probabilistic Resource Leveling

In project management, resource leveling is defined in the Project Management Body of Knowledge (PMBOK Guide) (Project Management Institute, 2013) as "A technique in which start and finish dates are adjusted based on resource constraints with the goal of balancing demand for resources with the available supply." In Chapter 8 of the book, we discussed how Event chain methodology can help with resource leveling.

There are two ways to perform a resource leveling as part of quantitative risk analysis:

- During each iteration of a Monte Carlo simulation.
- A deterministic resource leveling generated using the risk analysis.

If we perform resource leveling during each iteration of Monte Carlo simulation, we will generate a statistical distribution for resource allocations during each time interval. This allocation would take into an account all risks and uncertainties in project schedule. Then we would choose a specific percentile of these statistical distributions to use for allocating resources. For example, after the risk analysis we would decide to manage the schedule using P70 value for project finish time. This same P70 percentile would be used for resource allocation.

The drawback to this approach is that resource leveling during each iteration of Monte Carlo simulation may lead to confusing results. For example, sometimes there would be resource over-allocation, even if the resource leveling algorithm was set to ensure no overallocation during each iteration of Monte Carlo simulation. This is because when we show the results for a particular percentile of work or units, it may represent an overallocation. Moreover, resource leveling during each iteration of a Monte Carlo simulation requires a lot of computer memory and computing resources. Because of these issues, we normally recommend performing deterministic resource leveling using the results of a risk analysis. It is just simpler, faster and less confusing. The exception would be in cases where your schedule has many critical risks or significant uncertainties.

Drawbacks of Risk-Based Resource Leveling

The main advantage of resource leveling as part of project risk analysis is that we could ensure that we always have resources to deal with risks and uncertainties in a project schedule. However, this allocation may not be always optimal. The reason for this is that leveling using the results of risk analysis must account for multiple scenarios that traditional leveling algorithms are not designed to deal with. You can imaging in a case where we have a team scheduled to paint a room. In one iteration, the paint does not arrive on time and the activity is delayed, in another the paint arrives on time, but the room is not ready for painting yet, and in another scenario, the paint and room are ready, but the crew is delayed. Resource allocation can handle one scenario, but the risk analysis provides only statistical results of all of these possible scenarios combined and may not provide a particularly good basis for allocating resources.

One of the solutions is to not predefine resource allocations, but to use agile or an incremental approach to resource allocation. With this approach, resource allocation can be adjusted based on actual project performance. Another approach is to periodically run a project risk analysis with resource leveling during project execution and resource allocation can be updated accordingly.

Chapter 12

Scenario Analysis, Branching, and Decision Trees

When we manage projects, we often need to evaluate different scenarios and make decisions based on different objectives. Each scenario may have different risks and uncertainties and scenario analysis may help to analyze the effectiveness of mitigation and response plans as well as calculate the cost of risks. Decision trees and branching are decision analysis processes which can be used as part of scenario analysis.

Multiple Objectives and Multiple Scenarios

On October 1962, the U-2 spy plane overflew Cuba and took photographs that revealed Soviet missile installations that included nuclear missiles, their transports, and tents for fueling and maintenance. This was incontrovertible proof that the Soviet Union had started to deploy ballistic missiles in Cuba in close proximity to the continental US. This event led to the Cuban Missile Crisis (Axelrod, 2009) and provided the backdrop for the movie "Thirteen Days" (2000). The events that unfolded because of these photographs are good case study in how scenario analysis is performed.

The US government was extremely concerned about the imminent installation of hostile ballistic missiles located minutes from major US population centers. Senior government officials headed by President Kennedy are known to have discussed several scenarios on how to respond to the situation including:

- Do nothing: This really did not change the strategic situation that much as American vulnerability to Soviet missiles had existed before the crisis.

Figure 12.1. President Kennedy meets in the Oval Office with General Curtis LeMay.

- Negotiation: Diplomatically pressurize Soviet Union to remove the missiles.
- Secret negotiation: Offer Castro the choice of betraying the Soviet Union or face a full scale invasion.
- Blockade: Use the US Navy to blockade any suspect Soviet supply ships.

- Air strikes: Use the US Air Force to attack all known missile sites.
- Invasion: Full force invasion of Cuba and overthrow of Castro.

The Joint Chiefs of Staff unanimously advised that a full-scale attack and invasion was the only solution. They believed that the Soviet Union would not try to defend Cuba; however (Figure 12.1), Kennedy was not convinced. During these meetings, Kennedy emphasized that the main objective for decision-making was how it would affect the balance of power between the Soviets and the US, specifically they needed a solution that did not shift the balance in favor of the Soviets. While the generals believed that the missiles would shift the balance of power, Secretary of Defense Robert McNamara was of the opinion that the military balance of power would not change. As a result of discussion, they came to a common agreement that the missiles would shift the balance and something would have to be done about them. Based on this scenario analysis, Kennedy eventually chose to set a naval blockade to prevent more missiles from entering Cuba rather than any of the other alternatives that involved overt military action. After some extremely tense days, the blockade strategy worked (helped greatly by secret negotiations between the Kennedy and his Soviet counterpart Khrushchev) and an agreement between the US and Soviet Union was reached. Soviet Union would remove the missiles and dismantle the missile sites, and in exchange the US would publicly declare that they would never invade Cuba without direct provocation. What was not revealed publicly at the time was that the US also agreed to dismantle the nuclear missiles it had recently deployed in Turkey and Italy.

During the Cuban Missile Crisis, the world was teetering on the brink of nuclear war. But with the use of a structured decision analysis process, cooler heads prevailed and a global disaster was averted.

Project Objectives and Indicators

According to the PMBOK® Guide (Project Management Institute, 2013), one of the important steps in project management is "establishing clear and achievable objectives." The Guide defines project objectives as "something towards which work is to be directed, a strategic position to be attained, or purpose to be achieved, a result to be obtained, a product to be produced, or a service to be performed."

When making a decision, a project manager needs to use various indicators to determine which alternatives will best achieve the project's objectives. These indicators are called decision criteria. They may include:

- Economic indicators, such as net present value (NPV), rate of return (ROR), and project cost.
- Project scope indicators, such as number of features implemented.
- Project schedule indicators, such as total project duration, project finish time, duration of particular phase.
- Earn Value Management metrics, such as Schedule Performance Index (SPI), or Cost Performance Index (CPI).
- Resource usage, including material, and work resources.

The indicators that may not be directly related to the project schedule:

- Quality indicators, such as number of defects.
- Safety indicators, such as number of accidents.
- Environmental indicators, such as level of emissions.

Indicators can be used to quantify how different project scenarios are aligned with the project objectives. The idea is to analyze different project scenarios with risks and uncertainties and use these indicators to identify which scenarios are best aligned with the project objectives. Multiple scenarios can be analyzed using a multi-criteria decision-making approach and we will look at a few simple ways we can perform this.

Project Scenario Analysis

Let us assume that we have a residential construction project. The project might be delayed due to permitting process. If the permits are delayed, our project may be delayed and cost more money. We have several options, we could accept the risk and cross our fingers and hope it does not happen. We could choose a mitigation strategy: hire a consultant to assist with the permitting process, but this will cost money. Finally, we could execute a response plan if the risk occurs, which will also have costs associated with it. In any case, this risk can affect a number of tasks and resources and our best course of action before we decide anything is to compare the different scenarios.

Now you have three scenarios:

- Accept.
- Mitigate.
- Response.

We can perform Monte Carlo schedule risk analysis on each scenario. These scenarios must include any other risks and uncertainties that can impact the project as all of them will contribute to the statistical distribution for project cost and duration. The results of the simulations can be presented in different forms, but we prefer using multiple cumulative probability plots (S-curve) (Figure 12.2). Using the results of analysis, you can estimate cost of each scenario based on certain confidence level (80% in our case) and then choose the best course of action. In this case, you use an indicator "project cost" and select risk mitigation scenario. Also, S curves give a very good idea what would be the riskiest scenario: then wider the curve, the more risky the scenario is.

Scenario analysis helps to identify the effectiveness of the different options. Since mitigation and response efforts affect multiple tasks and resources, we need to calculate the entire schedule with and without mitigation and response efforts and compare different indicators including

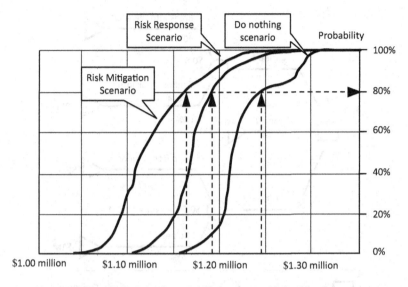

Figure 12.2. Selecting scenarios using multiple S curves.

cost and duration. Project risk analysis software may offer some features that facilitate this comparison. For example, we can save the scenarios as baselines with mitigation plans and without mitigation plans and compare their costs.

We can also rank risks using scenario analysis as each risk in each scenario will have a risk score. It is also possible to isolate the impact of a risk on the project by running two simulations, one with the risk open and the other with the risk closed or disabled. The difference between the two would show the actual cost and delays caused by the risk. Repeat this process with all of the risks and we get a ranking of risks based on the calculated cost or delay caused by each risk. While this method does appear to provide more precision, it also is more time consuming. If you do require a cost of risk, it may be the effort. However, if you are simply looking to rank your risks, the method of risk ranking based on correlation described in Chapter 9 is more than adequate.

Decision Tree Analysis

A group of gangsters are planning to rob a casino in Las Vegas. They have three choices:

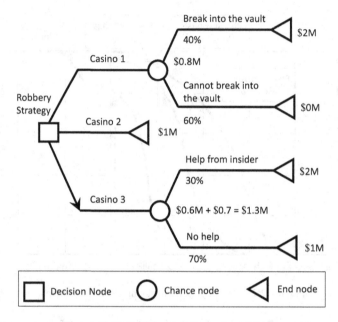

Figure 12.3. Decision tree for casino robbery.

1. August Place casino: will yield $2 million from the vault or but nothing if they cannot crack it. They estimate the probability that they can break into the vault equals 40%.
2. Washington–Washington casino: will yield $1 million.
3. Illusion Casino: will yield $2 million, if they get help from an insider (30% probability) and $1 million without inside help.

We will plot this analysis on a decision tree (Figure 12.3). The decision tree has three different types of nodes:

- Decision node: indicates a juncture where a decision must be made on one branch or another.
- Uncertainty node: indicates that branches have probabilities associated with them.
- End node: indicates an outcome of the decision.

Calculation of decision trees start from left to right. For each chance node, we need to calculate expected value (EV). In our case, an EV is the expected reward from a specific robbery alternative. It is an indicator that we are going to choose the option with the largest EV. EV is calculated as probability multiplied by outcome. For the Casino 1 alternative, the EV is $2 million $\times$ 40% + $0 million $\times$ 60% = $0.8 million. For Casino 2, the EV is $1 million as the probability equals 100%. For Casino 3, the EV is $2 million $\times$ 30% + $1 million $\times$ 70% = $1.3 million.

Using EV as their criteria, the decision for bank robbers is now straightforward. Casino 3 has highest EV even taking into account the uncertainty associated with the possibility that they will not receive any insider help. This is indicated by the arrow pointing from decision node to the Casino 3 branch.

Project schedules can be used to generate decision trees. To do this, we need to create project schedules for each alternative (branch). Alternative scenarios can be represented by different parallel paths through the schedule. Different paths of a project schedule are the result of branching when a predecessor activity has more than one successor activity. The end nodes of the decision tree will represent cost and/or duration of each alternative. We recommend that you simplify the schedule such that any tasks that lie between the chance and decision nodes and are germane to the selection of a particular alternative should be consolidated. It is important to include risks and uncertainties as part of this process as they can obviously have a significant impact on the EVs.

Probabilistic and Conditional Branching

Let us assume that we have a task that has two different scenarios as successors. We will select the scenario to run if the task meets certain conditions. For example, the duration of this task is affected by two events and uncertainty defined by a statistical distribution. These will cause a delay in the task. If the delay is greater than a certain value then Scenario 1 will be selected. If the delay is less than certain value then Scenario 2 will be selected. This process is called *conditional branching* (Figure 12.4) and allows us to set the rules under which certain alternatives or branches will be run. Branching can be also done using cost, work, task finish times, and other parameters. This is useful in cases in which we will have to make a choice based on a condition that can occur. A common example of this occurs in development, when if a component is not available in time, the project will switch to an existing technology that they have available.

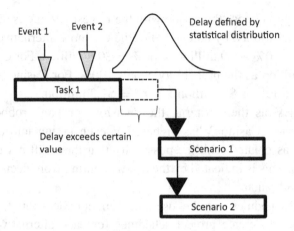

Figure 12.4. Conditional branching.

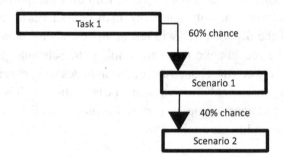

Figure 12.5. Probabilistic branching.

There is also another version of branching (Figure 12.5). In this version, we can select branches based on probability that can be selected randomly based on certain chance, rather than based on predecessor duration, finish time, or cost. In our example, there is 60% chance that Scenario 1 will be executed and 40% chance that Scenario 2 will be executed. This is called *probabilistic branching*. It can be useful when we want to choose different scenarios based on random factors outside of our control. This is often used to model testing activities especially when there is historical data on failure rates. If a scheduled test passes one branch is selected, if it fails another branch is selected. For example in a pipeline, certain sections may fail inspections and need to have connections redone for retesting.

Chapter 13

Probabilistic Cost and Cash Flow Analysis

In projects, cost and schedule are correlated: project activities have resource rates and fixed costs associated with them. When we perform project risk analysis, we can define risks and uncertainties associated with cost at the same time as we define schedule risks and uncertainties. When we perform the risk analysis, we can generate statistical distributions for all project parameters, including cost and schedule, at the same time. With both cost and schedule statistical distributions, we can now plot a joint confidence graph (for cost and schedule) that would provide insight into what the chance is that we can complete the project both on time and within budget.

Integrated Cost and Schedule Risk Analysis

In last few years, the world has experienced a technology revolution that many people are either unaware of or did not appreciate its implications: shale gas production techniques. From 2009 to 2014, oil production in the US has increased by more than 60%. This increase in production placed the US in heady company along with Saudi Arabia and Russia as the leading global producers of oil. This tremendous growth prompted Organization of the Petroleum Exporting Countries (OPEC) to suspend its policy of production quotas, which led to the collapse of oil prices in 2015. How was this enormous growth in US oil production possible?

The world has very significant reserves of oil and gas and our ability to physically extract it has improved immensely; however, this production has to be economical and the main limiting factor is cost. Shale gas and tight oil belong to a category of oil referred to as unconventional oil. To extract them economically, new technologies need to be developed and perfected.

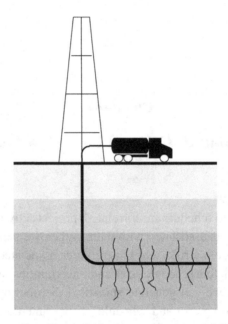

Figure 13.1. Hydraulic fracking and horizontal drilling.

In the case of shale oil, the technological components required to extract it are horizontal drilling and hydraulic fracturing (fracking), or the pumping of a high-pressure water mixture into rock to release oil or gas, were known for many years (Figure 13.1). Over the last 15 years, these and other technologies have dramatically improved, which allowed producers to reduce the cost of oil and gas per unit of production. In 2015, the average full cycle cost of tight oil production was below $50 per barrel. It could be much lower, except for one inescapable issue, oil and gas exploration, and production are fraught with many risks and uncertainties. Geology is one of main uncertainties: there is a built uncertainty in how much oil can be produced from a given play, it may not be able to produce as much oil as planned. But uncertainties related to cost of labor, materials, and services are also very significant. Oil and gas producers work to ensure that they get as much production as possible for the least possible cost. Improved geological characterization and microseismic mitigate geological risks. Reduction of drilling time leads to lower variable costs including labor. For example, only a couple of years ago it could take months to drill a tight oil well: whereas now, it has been reduced to 2–4 weeks. Technological innovations have also helped to reduce the cost per frac, which is now around $100,000 or less, with similar reductions in other completion costs.

Essentially, oil and gas producers' goal is to complete projects on budget to ensure production costs are economical Project risk analysis will help them to determine the chance that project will be completed on budget and indicate the most effective ways to manage project risks and minimize costs. But drilling and completion project costs are directly related to project schedules. If you can drill wells in less time, if you can move equipment more quickly from site to site, and if all materials and services are provided on time, all of this will reduce costs. So we can see that managing project costs and schedules needs to be done at the same time.

Cost Uncertainties

Uncertainties related to cost could be defined different ways (Figure 13.2):

1. We explicitly define a statistical distribution for the fixed cost of each task. For example, fixed cost of a task is between $3,000 and $4,000 and defined by a Beta statistical distribution.
2. As we learned in Chapter 6, risks may have different impact types related to cost: "Fixed and relative cost increase," "Fixed and relative income increase," "Fixed and relative rate increase," and others. These

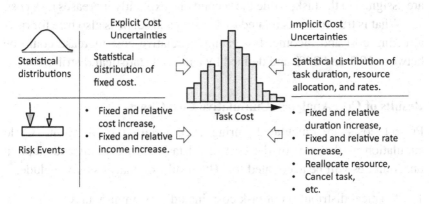

Figure 13.2. Uncertainties in task cost.

risk impact types belonged to the category called "Cost and Income." Risks with these impact types would explicitly define cost uncertainties.

3. If we have uncertainties in task duration, rates and resource allocation expressed as statistical distributions plus we have resources with certain rates assigned to these activities, it would implicitly define input cost uncertainties. For example, if a task duration is between 2 and 7 days and the allocated work resource is $1,000/day, the time dependent cost of the task would be between $2,000 and $7,000.

4. If we have uncertainties in task duration, rates and resource allocation expressed as risk events and resources with certain rates assigned to these activities, it would also implicitly define cost uncertainties. For example, if task cost is $2,000, work resource is $1,000/day, and we have risk "Fixed duration increases by 2 days" with a certain probability, the task's cost be between $2,000 and $4,000.

As we discussed in Chapter 6 of this book, the same risk may have risk impacts related to "Cost and Income" risk category and "Schedule and Scope" risk categories. For example, in oil and gas project risk "Failure to obtain high quality microseismic data" assigned to task "Seismic monitoring" may have two risk impacts:

1. Relative duration increase 20%.
2. Relative fixed cost increase 15%.

The first one implicitly affects cost uncertainties since some resources are assigned to the task, while the second one explicitly increases task cost.

What is true for risks related to duration and scope is also true for risks affecting cost and income. For example, relative cost increase could be between 10% and 20% and defined by a normal statistical distribution.

Results of Cost Analysis: Cumulative Cost Chart

Project costs are calculated during each iteration of a Monte Carlo simulation as the sum of the cost of all tasks. All explicit and implicit uncertainties will be accounted for. The results of analysis may include:

1. Statistical distribution of task cost, including summary tasks.
2. Statistical distribution of project cost.

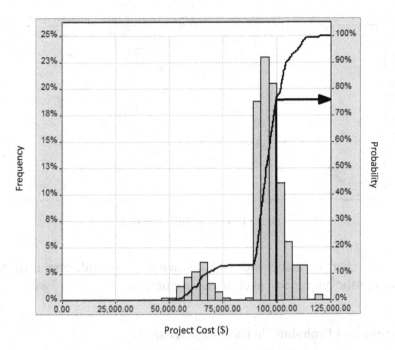

Figure 13.3. Frequency and cumulative probability plot.

3. Ranking of risks based on cost: what risks have the largest potential impact on project cost.

The results of analysis can be presented in the form of frequency or cumulative probability plots, or a combination of the two (Figure 13.3). This chart helps to determine what the chance is that the project can be completed on budget. In this example, there is a 75% chance that project will be cost below $100,000.

Results of cost risk analysis can be also presented on cumulative cost chart (Figure 13.4). Cumulative cost chart shows how project cost increases as project progresses. The chart may show:

1. Cost of projects with risks and uncertainties.
2. Cost of projects without risks and uncertainties (deterministic cost). It is a useful basis for comparison and quality control of the risk analysis.
3. Actual project cost.

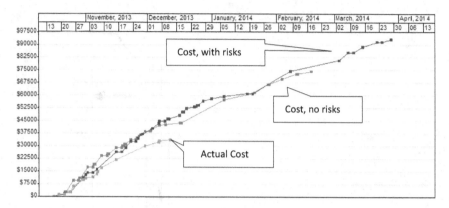

Figure 13.4. Cumulative cost chart.

The chart may also show the difference between deterministic and probabilistic project cost at each moment of time.

Income and Probabilistic Cash Flow Analysis

In project management, we usually complete our project with the final delivery of a product or service. Product marketing and sales is a separate project or operation. But in many cases, as part of risk analysis, it may be useful to analyze all phases of product development. In particular, it is very important for economic evaluation of oil and gas projects. Oil and gas producers must ensure that production is profitable given all uncertainties as we discussed at the beginning of this chapter. Generally, project income is calculated the same way as cost, it just has a different sign: cost will be negative and income is positive. Profit is the difference between income and cost.

In addition to cost uncertainties, the project schedule can include information about income uncertainties. It includes risk "Fixed or relative income increase." It is also possible to assign statistical distributions to income.

As part of risk analysis, we can calculate cost and income for each period of time (weekly, monthly, yearly, etc.). The results of analysis can be presented as a probabilistic cash flow chart (Figure 13.5). Each bar of the chart is associated with statistical distribution. We can calculate low, base,

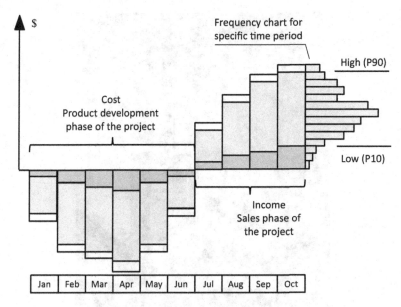

Figure 13.5. Probabilistic cash flow chart.

and high estimate of cost and income. Each estimate can be associated with particular percentile of statistical distribution. For example, low can be P10 and high will be P90.

As part of cash flow analysis, we can calculate a number of key performance indicators that help to determine the economic feasibility of a project. Among them are:

Net present value (NPV): the sum of the present values (PVs) of cash flows over a period of time. Each cash inflow/outflow is discounted back to its PV. According to time value of money theory, time has an impact on the value of cash flows. Particularly, money in hand is worth more than future cash flow. NPV is a measure of value of the project. If the NPV > 0, the project would add no value.

Rate of return: the profit on an investment over a period of time, expressed as a proportion of the original investment. In the case of project management, the return can be calculated as profit of the project divided by incurred cost.

Figure 13.6. Renovation project.

Joint Cost and Schedule Confidence Level (JCL) Analysis

Look at Figure 13.6. What is this? You might think this is a shot of a random manufacturing warehouse under construction. In fact, it is the White House during a comprehensive renovation in 1949–1952 under the Truman administration.

In 1948, architectural and engineering investigations deemed White House unsafe for the President and his family. The scope of the project included the complete removal of the interior, with the exception of the third floor, excavation of a new basement and construction of new foundations, replacing interior walls, refurbishment and replacement windows, and installation of new heating, ventilation, air conditioning, plumbing, electrical, and communications systems. Total budgeted cost was $5.4 million.

Actual construction work started on December 13, 1949. The original schedule called for the work to be finished by late 1951. However, the President was only able to return to the White House on March 27, 1952. Cost escalated due to a number of factors including labor shortages and inflation. Cost overruns amounted to $321,000, but Congress agreed to fund only $261,000 of this, so the total cost of the project was $5.7 million. It addition, they also constructed a secret bomb shelter at a cost of $881,000, but was funded separately.

So the project took approximately 12% longer and cost 6% more than originally planned. President Truman publicly expressed praise for the work, but the night of his return to the White House he wrote in his private diary: "With all the trouble and worry it is worth it — but not 5 1/2 million dollars! If I could have had been in charge of the construction it would have been done for half the money and in half the time!" (Klara, 2013).

We want to ensure projects will be both on budget and on time. This is what President Truman was thinking about. But due to risks and uncertainties, this can be difficult to achieve, as it was the case with the White House renovation. For example, if we try to reduce costs by hiring the lowest bidders, we may end up with less experienced contractors who take longer to complete the work. Or vice versa, when we try to complete projects faster, we hire more people and it costs more.

So, we need to estimate what is the chance that both cost and schedule will end up at certain confidence level. To do this, we perform joint cost and schedule confidence level (JCL) analysis. NASA defines JCL analysis as "a process that combines a project's cost, schedule, and risk into a complete picture" (NASA, 2015). If cost, schedule, or both are above a defined confidence level, it will require management to make some decisions in regards to risk mitigation measures and/or changing the project scope.

JCL analysis is one of results of integrated cost and schedule Monte Carlo project risk analysis. During each iteration of a Monte Carlo simulation, the project cost, duration, and finish times are calculated. This information can be shown on a Joint Confidence chart (Figure 13.7).

Each point of the chart shows cost and finish time or duration of project for each iteration. This chart makes it possible to visualize the chance that both cost and schedule objectives will be met. The crosshair can be moved to a date and cost to obtain their joint confidence.

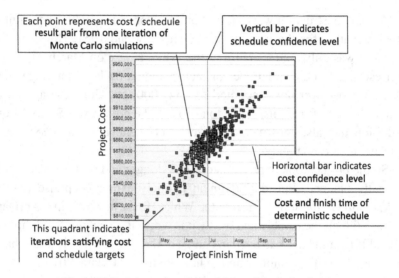

Figure 13.7. Joint cost and schedule confidence level chart.

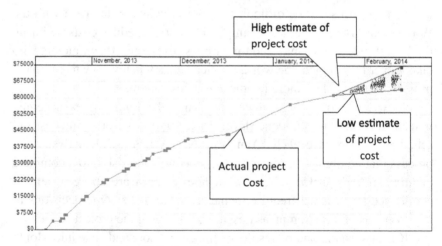

Figure 13.8. Cost of partially completed project.

Cost and Schedule of Partially Completed Project

Cost and finish dates of partially completed projects can also be presented on the scatter plot (Figure 13.8). "The fork" of the right side of the chart represents low and high estimates of cumulative project cost. Each point represents cost/schedule result pair from one iteration of Monte Carlo simulations. This chart helps to visualize total project cost with risks and uncertainties at any moment during project execution. If "the fork" is really wide, the remaining project has too much uncertainty and risks need to be mitigated. In theory, as the project progresses "the fork" should narrow until it becomes a point at the end of the project.

Chapter 14

Non-Schedule Related Risks and Integrated
Risk Analysis

In this chapter, we will learn how to do quantitative analysis of risks that have impacts other than schedule or cost (non-schedule related risks). These risks do not affect cost or schedule directly, but they also can be ranked together with these related risks. In this context, an integrated risk analysis indicates that this is an analysis of risks that impacts several different categories at the same time.

What are Non-Schedule Related Risks?

In the 2011 movie, "We Bought a Zoo," Benjamin Mee (Matt Damon) decides to buy a small zoo together with a new house for his family. He believes that the zoo can be profitable as long as it is ready before the start of the tourist season. However, to prepare the zoo for the opening, Benjamin and his team must overcome a lot of hurdles. The animals must be in good shape and healthy, all enclosures must be constructed to standards, and must be fully certified by extremely strict USDA inspector. These efforts cost a great deal of money and Benjamin had a limited budget. Nevertheless, in spite of these odds, the zoo received the required permit and opened on time.

The zoo business is complex and risky. Critical to understanding this business is that the risks associated with any project in zoo impact not just cost and schedule, but also animal safety, visitor security, public relations, quality of the exhibits, and other potential problem areas. In this case, we

Figure 14.1. Elephant in Denver Zoo. Image by Donlammers.

have the same risks, but with different impact types. In 2015, a devastating flood occurred in Tbilisi, the capital of Georgia. The local zoo was severely impacted by this event and numerous animals escaped during the chaos (North and Grierson, 2015). A hippopotamus was cornered in the main Tbilisi square. Tigers, lions, wolves, and bears prowled the neighborhood of Georgia's capital. In this case, the risk event was a flood, but it had many impact types, including safety, security, and cost.

Look at this enclosure in Denver Zoo (Figure 14.1). The Denver Zoo recently completed a massive project, the Toyota Elephant Passage. The cost was $50 million (Asmar, 2012). How can we ensure that a project such as the Toyota Elephant Passage is completed not only on time and budget, but without sacrificing safety, security, quality, public relations, and meets all regulatory requirements? These non-schedule risk categories must be analyzed together with schedule related categories of cost and duration to improve project decision-making processes. In particular, we need to understand how to quantitatively analyze risks that belong to both schedule and non-schedule risk categories.

Why We Often Ignore Non-Schedule Risk Categories

In almost all cases, project risks affect many different factors: however, during the project risk analysis we often ignore some of these impacts and focus on most obvious and quantifiable duration and cost categories. If we look at a very common risk that many projects face "Budgetary problems" we know that it can affect cash flow, which can cause a delay or cancelation of some project tasks. But this same risk can also contribute to safety or quality if a cash strapped business starts to look for ways to cut corners, but these possible impacts often do not appear on a risk register.

So, why are these impacts often ignored? There are a number of reasons:

1. Risk analysis is compartmentalized across an organization. For example, project schedulers are often tasked to perform schedule risk analysis without analyzing how these same risks could affect other facets of the project or organization. Other factors, such as safety are analyzed by other departments, for example QHSE (Quality, Health, Safety, Environment teams). So, we end up with organizations that are structured in such a way that there is no centralized mechanism to identify, analyze, and manage all impacts of the same risks together.
2. People tend to focus on things that are most tangible to them. Human psychology biases us to make decisions based on information in their working memory that is the most pronounced and distinct. Other information, which could be relevant, are excluded or discounted. As a result, decisions tend to be made based on only a fraction of the total amount of knowledge available (it is just not as easily accessible). Psychologists refer to this as the "focusing effect." Project managers are simply focused on duration and cost of project, even though it is their responsibility to deal with all type of risk impacts.

Non-Schedule Risk Impact Types for Project Task and Resources

If you remember, when a risk is assigned to task and resources we select the type of risk impact. Table 14.1 is an example of how risk assignment that includes non-schedule impacts could appear.

This table is similar to Table 6.1, but includes also non-schedule risk categories. This information is an input for quantitative risk analysis.

Table 14.1. Risk assignment.

Probability	Category	Impact type	Impact
20%	Duration and scope	Fixed delay	3 days
5%	Cost and income	Fixed cost increase	$200
1%	Safety	Safety event	Non-injury accident
10%	Quality	Quality event	One or few minor requirements not met
20%	Technology	Technology event	10%

For each category, there are impact numerical scales (see Chapter 3, "Settings up Risk Matrix"). These scales allow defining numerical values associated with impact of each non-schedule risk category. So, it is possible to quantify the risk impact of non-schedule risks for each risk assignment. Please note that non-schedule risk assignments may have different mutually exclusive alternatives, however, different risk alternatives must belong to the same risk category.

Here is one more thing. In general, total risk probability for all risk categories for one risk should be the same. For example, if we tell that the probability that elephant will break the enclosure equals 1%, it means that it is 1% for cost, safety, legal, etc. In some special cases, for example, if we mitigate risks for specific category, the probability could be different.

Quantitative Risk Analysis with Non-Schedule Risks

Please take a look at this schedule (Figure 14.2).

In this example, we assigned the same risk to two different tasks, and second risk to the third task. We use numerical scales for risk impact; however, it can be assigned using a label which represents an underlying value. Our goal is to rank the risk using quantitative analysis for a single risk category and for all the risk categories. Here is how we proceed:

1. Perform a Monte Carlo simulation. Table 14.2 shows the result of the Monte Carlo simulations for the Safety risk category. Results for Legal category are calculated in similar manner.

   The impact of each risk is a correlation between risk impact and impact for all risks within the same category. In our example, Risk 1 has the

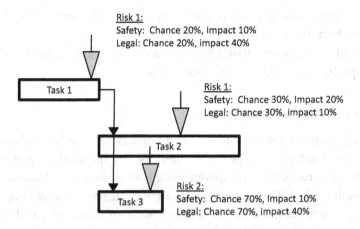

Figure 14.2. Example of a project schedule with non-schedule risk assignments.

Table 14.2. Calculation of risk impact for non-schedule risk.

Iteration	Risk 1, Task 1	Risk 1, Task 2	Risk 2, Task 3	Total impact
1			10%	10%
2	20%	20%	10%	50%
3			10%	10%
4	20%	20%		40%
5			10%	10%
6			10%	10%
7				
8			10%	10%
9				
10		20%	10%	30%
Correlation coefficient	0.87	0.93	0.15	

highest impact and after we multiply this impact by probability, we can calculate the risk score and rank risks within specific risk category.

2. Calculate impact for all categories. Using the same process we outlined for quantitative analysis, we multiply risk impact for each category on the priority assigned to this category, sum the results for all of the categories and repeat for all risks:

$$\text{Total Impact} = \text{Safety Impact} \times \text{Safety Category Priority}$$
$$+ \text{Legal Impact} \times \text{Legal Category Priority}.$$

If the impact for any risk is greater than 100%, the impact for all risks must be normalized.

3. Calculate risk scores: Risk scores equal the calculated impact multiplied by probability. Then we can rank all risks.

Integrated Risk Analysis

It is important to note that if we have impacts for schedule related risk categories (duration or cost), they can also be included as part of the calculation of risk total impact, even though the impacts are calculated using a different method. The total impact for all risk categories is a very important signal for decision-making. The question we sometimes get asked is if we have a risk that has a serious impact, but only on one category should it not have priority. This a common approach, where risks are not prioritized by their overall impact across all categories, but by their single highest impact on any single category. While this may have some merit, we believe that when set up properly, this integrated risk approach provides the best insight on how to manage risks. In many instances, if you have a risk that impacts many risk categories, but only specifically mitigates one impact, it will also act to minimize the impact on other risk categories. Using our zoo example, when they repaired the elephant enclosure, it addressed potential safety, legal, and cost-related problems all at the same time. Therefore, risks with highest overall risk score should have the highest priority.

Part IV

Portfolio Risk Analysis

Chapter 15

Introduction to Portfolio Risk Analysis

In previous chapters, we have covered how to perform risk analysis on individual projects. Projects can be part of a larger portfolio in which projects are strategically selected and managed. Project portfolios can share common risks, mitigation and response plans, and resources. Conversely, these same projects' exposure to these same risks can vary and have different scores for the same risks. One the key goals of project portfolio management is to align and prioritize projects based upon the organization's objectives. Part of this process takes place using an enterprise risk register that contains all the risks the organization faces. Risks from this risk register can be assigned to different projects, and in turn, to each project tasks and resources.

Why Perform Portfolio Risk Analysis?

Climbing Mount Everest, whose peak sits at 8,848 m (29,029 ft.) above sea level, is one of the riskiest projects in the world: by March 2012, Everest had been climbed 5,656 times with 223 deaths. This works out to a fatality rate of 4% (NASA World Observatory, 2016). Outside of conflict zones, it is perhaps one of the most risky activities you could imagine doing during peace time. Add to this, this is for the most part a non-commercial venture (some expeditions do have sponsors), and these climbers are often actually paying tens of thousands of dollars to be part of an expedition that has a 4% of having the worst possible outcome for them.

Let us take a look what each climbing expedition involves. Everest has a number of climbing routes; the two main ones include the southeast ridge from Nepal and the North ridge from Tibet (Everest History, 2016).

Figure 15.1. Everest's North face from the Tibetan plateau. Photo by Joe Hastings.

Expeditions for the southeast ridge ascent usually fly from Kathmandu to the town of Lukla (2,860 m). Before the expedition begins, climbers need to procure all equipment and supplies, hire yaks and human porters, and other logistical preparations. The climbers start the next leg of their journey, the trek up to Base Camp at an altitude of 5,380 m (17,700 ft.). This trek usually takes 6–8 days, which provides a suitable period to begin the adaptation to the extreme altitude. This acclimatization process continues for the next couple of days at base camp as the expedition prepares the upcoming ascent. During this period of time, Sherpas and other experienced climbers set up ropes and ladders in the Khumbu Icefall. The climb now takes place is a series of short ascents from one camp up to another. First, they will climb to Base Camp I at 6,065 m (19,900 ft.). From there, the climbers make their way up to Camp II or Advanced Base Camp at 6,500 m (21,300 ft.). Next is Camp III located on a small ledge at 7,470 m (24,500 ft.). The penultimate step is to climb to Camp IV, where the climbers need to pass the Geneva Spur, an anvil shaped rib of rock, which needs to be ascended using robes. The culmination of the ascent is the push from Camp IV to the summit which usually takes 10–12 h.

This final stage is broken down into several mini climbs. First, the climbers need to reach "The Balcony," which is a small platform at 8,400 m (27,600 ft.). Once they have reached the Balcony, they continue on up to their next goal, the South Summit, a small dome of ice at 8,750 m (28,700 ft.). After this, climbers must perform the "Cornice traverse." Any misstep on this traverse could end up with a fatal plunge of 2,400 m (7,900 ft.). If they complete the traverse successfully, they face one last obstacle. Close to the summit there is a 12 m (39 ft.) rock wall. Once this has been cleared, the climbers have a relatively clear path to reach the summit of Mt. Everest. Unfortunately for our hardy adventurers, they face the same steps with the same challenges on their return route.

Nothing comes easy and we can see that conquering Everest is not just a single long activity, or project, but really encompasses a project portfolio that can last several years if you take into account the projects involved in preparation. Each project within the portfolio involves different objectives and resources and needs to be managed separately: the success of attempt at the summit of Mt. Everest depends on how successfully the leaders manage their project portfolio.

Any project within a portfolio has a number of risks; some of them are shared with other projects, but others are specific to individual projects. In an Everest expedition, a list of critical risks includes:

- Frost bite and cold exposure: Climbers must spend a significant period of time within the "dead zone." The region above 8,000 m where extreme cold means that exposed body parts are at risk of frost bite in a very short period of time.
- Falls: Because of the extreme low temperature, the snow is characteristically extremely hard and difficult to traverse, chance of injury or death is greatly increased.
- Hypoxia or altitude sickness: The atmospheric pressure at the top of Everest is one-third of that found at sea level; as a result, low oxygen levels are required and oxygen tanks and masks are the norm.
- Avalanches: While they can occur at any altitude, in this region they can be especially devastating as the ability of the climbers to react to or recover from avalanche is greatly diminished. Rescue efforts are extremely difficult. In fact, on April 25, 2015 a number of people died at Base camp due to avalanche caused by the Nepal earthquake.

All these risks not only affect safety, but also duration, cost, and success rates of each project and therefore the portfolio. For example, if there is a problem with the transportation of supplies to the base camp, this could delay or potentially cause the cancelation or postponement of the expedition. Because we like movies, we can recall a 1992 movie "K2," about the ascent of K2, the second highest peak in the world. In one scene, the Sherpas (porters) refuse to go forward placing the future of the expedition in doubt. While this makes for good movie drama, it is a scene that has happened many times in Himalayan expeditions.

Let us see how we can manage risks in a project portfolio containing a number of projects that share the same risk register.

Project Portfolio Hierarchy

Project portfolios have the same structure as projects: just like a project can have summary activities and sub activities, a portfolio can have summary projects and sub projects. Below is an example for a project portfolio hierarchy and Gantt chart for the Everest Climbing portfolio (Figure 15.2). In case you are wondering, this is a realistic schedule (Berg International Adventures, 2016), so if you want to try to climb to Everest, you may use it (though we have left out the preparation stages for simplicity). Just perform your risk analysis first.

Each project within a portfolio has tasks, resources, and risks assigned to the tasks and resources. Tasks may have uncertainties expressed as

	Project Name	Dur	Start	Finish	September, 2016					October, 2016				November 2		
					28	04	11	18	25	02	09	16	23	30	06	13
1	⊟ Pre-Climb	18 days	08/30/16	09/22/16												
2	In Kathmandu and Lukla	6 days	08/30/16	09/06/16												
3	Trek to Base Camp	10 days	09/07/16	09/20/16												
4	In Base Camp	2 days	09/21/16	09/22/16												
5	⊟ Actual Climb	18 days	09/23/16	10/18/16												
6	First Rotation Camp I and camp II	4 days	09/23/16	09/28/16												
7	Second Rotation Camp I, Camp II and C8	3 days	09/29/16	10/03/16												
8	Third Rotation Camp I, Camp II, Camp III	3 days	10/04/16	10/06/16												
9	Rest in Base Camp	3 days	10/07/16	10/08/16												
10	Attempt to Reach Summit	5 days	10/12/16	10/08/16												
11	⊟ Departure	15 days	10/19/16	11/08/16												
12	Trip back to kathmandu	12 days	10/19/16	11/03/16												

Figure 15.2. Everest climbing project portfolio.

statistical distribution of duration, cost, and other parameters. We can perform Monte Carlo project risk analysis of each project in the portfolio. The results are shown in Figure 15.2 as triangles: they represent the low, base and high durations of each project. If you are using Portfolio management software usually you can open each project schedule from within the portfolio view. With detailed project views, it is possible to view the statistical distributions of project duration, cost, and other parameters for each project.

Projects within a portfolio can have cross dependencies which can be modeled as predecessor or successor type links. Common resources such as people and materials can also be assigned to different projects within a portfolio.

Prioritization of Projects

People have a tendency to compare and prioritize all sorts of things regardless of how important or difficult it might be. We automatically make judgements: it is an inherent aspect of human psychology. For example, if we listen to a variety of classical musicians, we inevitably make judgments about which musician is superior. Most of us find it quite enjoyable to sit around and discuss and debate these sorts of subjective preferences. However, in many cases such as classical music, it really takes some expertise to distinguish between the qualities of performances of professional musicians. In other cases, we do this intuitively such as the case in a fire; most of us would automatically prioritize invalids and children for evacuation as they are the most vulnerable (Figure 15.3). In project management, we also prioritize different projects and risks, but often do it intuitively without analysis, so while the results are often acceptable, this can lead to inconsistencies. As we have already learned how to prioritize project risks, we will now see how we can extend this process to the actual projects within a portfolio.

Why should we prioritize projects? Here are three important reasons:

1. Projects may require additional resources, which require immediate attention.
2. Project priority can be used to calculate the risk score for the project.

Figure 15.3. Prioritization of saving people during a fire.

3. Risk ranking in an enterprise risk register depends on the priority of project to which this risk is assigned. Projects with higher priority will be given a higher weighting when calculating the risk impact.

There are different approaches on how to prioritize projects. The simplest method is to simply assign different priorities to the project. What are the most important projects for Everest Climbing portfolio? It depends on what do you want to achieve, or your portfolio objective. For example, if your primary goal is to reach the summit, all projects are important with exception of "Descent back to base camp." However, if the primary goal is to ensure you arrive at Base camp, and if conditions allow, you may attempt the summit, all projects before "Actual Climb" have higher priority. If this was the case, you might assign "Pre-Climb" projects a priority of 100% and the "Actual Climb" priorities 80%.

For more complex portfolios, a more sophisticated approach is required. In Chapter 3, we discussed how we can use the *analytic hierarchy process* to prioritize risk categories using pair-wise comparison. We can also use this process to prioritize projects. At its most basic level, you can ask which project is more important: "Descent to Base camp" or "Trek to Base Camp."

You can perform this for each pair of projects in portfolio and calculate the relative priorities as described in Chapter 3.

Another process you can use for complex portfolios is multiple-criteria decision-making (MCDM) or multiple-criteria decision analysis (MCDA) (Ishizaka and Nemery, 2013). For example, if you assemble an airplane or construct a skyscraper, these may require aligning projects with different objectives, and for each objective, a project may have its own priorities. Examples of these objectives might be:

- Complete all projects on time and on budget.
- Retain personnel.
- Improve organizations capabilities.
- Develop new technology that can be applied to future projects.
- Provide high return on investment (ROI).

With these objectives defined, we can then prioritize the objectives. Finally, we can rank projects on how well they satisfy certain objectives. This will allow us to calculate overall ranking of projects within a portfolio.

Project Risk Score

Project risk score is a number or an indicator that helps to rank project risks. Project risk scores can be calculated separately for duration, cost, and other risk categories, such as safety, security, quality, etc. We learned how to calculate cumulative risk impact for non-schedule related risk types in Chapter 14. Calculating risk scores based on the results of qualitative and quantitative analysis is possible, but can be misleading. We recommend using three separate risk scores:

- For project duration.
- For project cost.
- For other non-schedule related risk categories.

There are different ways to calculate project risk score. It is possible to do this based on statistical parameters, such as mean, standard deviation, range, P10 or P90 of a statistical distribution. Here is an example of project duration score calculation formula:

$$\text{Score} = \frac{\text{Duration mean} + \text{Standard deviation of duration}}{\text{Duration original}},$$

where

Duration mean = mean project duration as a result of analysis.

Duration original = original (baseline) project duration with no risks and uncertainties.

   Using the formula above:

- If project does not have duration risks, the Duration score will be equal to 1.
- If the Duration risk score is >1, the project has threats related to duration.
- If the Duration risk score is <1, the project has opportunities related to duration.

   Risk scores for non-schedule or cost risks are calculated in the following manner:

1. For each project and category, there is an array for risk results. For example, if there are two risks "Quality of installation" (probability 50%, impact 30%) and "Quality of manufacturing" (probability 20%, impact 40%), the array for the quality category may appear as shown in Table 15.1:

Table 15.1. Cumulative risk impact using a Monte Carlo simulation.

Monte Carlo iteration	Cumulative risk impact
1	0
2	30% + 40% = 70%
3	30%
4	0
5	40%
6	0
7	0
8	30%
9	30%
10	30%

2. The mean of this array is calculated and multiplied by the weight assigned to each non-schedule risk category.
3. The sum of values from Step 2 is calculated for each project for all risk categories; this number is absolute non-schedule risk score for the particular project.
4. Absolute non-schedule risk scores for all projects are normalized in such a way that:

   • If a project does not have any risks, the score will =1.
   • If a project has opportunities, the score will be <1.
   • If a project has threats, the score will be >1.

In this way, the risk scores for non-schedule risks will be compatible with risk scores for duration and cost.

Enterprise Risk Register

All risks for the portfolio are saved in an *Enterprise risk register*. Risks from an enterprise risks register can be shared across different projects in a portfolio. They can be assigned to projects and to individual tasks or resources. Essentially, each project will have its own "view" or "representation" of an enterprise risk register: some risks from enterprise risk register may not be assigned to a particular project and therefore will not be shown in project's risk register. For example, the risk "Problem with yaks" would not be assigned to the project risk register of "Attempt to Reach Summit," but would be assigned to the project risk register of "Trek to Base Camp." However, regardless of their individual assignments to specific projects, all risks will be saved in the enterprise risk register.

Here is the interesting phenomenon: the ranking of a risk in the enterprise register may be different than for a particular project. "Problem with Yaks" will have a high score for the project "Trek to Base Camp," but at the portfolio level it will be quite low (Figure 15.4). This discrepancy occurs because of two reasons:

1. Cumulative impact of risk "Problem with Yaks" for the portfolio will be low.
2. Project "Trek to Base Camp" to which this risk is assigned will have a lower priority.

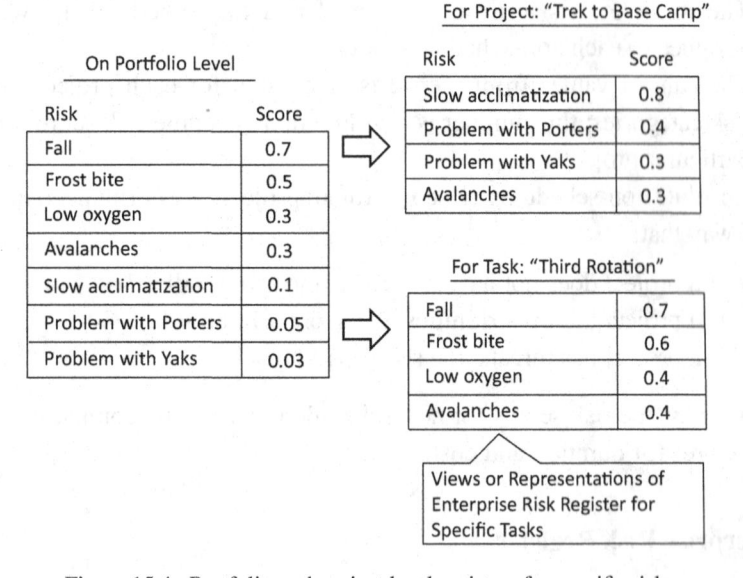

Figure 15.4. Portfolio and project level registers for specific risks.

Therefore, the enterprise risk register at the upper (portfolio) level will look different than a risk register for a particular project. Please note that each summary project within a project hierarchy may also have its own "view" or "representation" of the enterprise risk register, which again may have different risk rankings than the higher level risk register.

Here is how you can use an enterprise risk register:

1. Identify and enter risks in the enterprise risk register. For example, four main risks related to the climbing Everest: fall, frost bites, low oxygen, and avalanches.
2. Open projects and assign risks to appropriate tasks for a particular project. When you assign risks, you enter probability, impact categories (duration, cost, quality, safety, etc.), and impact values (increase duration on 20%). You can do this for each project.
3. Perform Monte Carlo simulations for all updated projects. Risk registers for individual projects are updated and risks are ranked.
4. Save the project. At this point. Project priorities and risk impacts will be used to calculate the risk score of each project. The enterprise risk register for all portfolios is updated including risk rankings.

In addition to risks, enterprise risk register include mitigation and response plans which also can be shared between different projects.

Risk Visibility and Risk Approval Rules

When a new risk is added to a project, it is subject to two properties: approval and visibility. Approval indicates the risk has been approved by management and can be included as part of the portfolio risk register. Visibility indicates where in the portfolio this risk can be assigned: projects, summary projects, or the portfolio. Why is this required? Let us assume that we have a risk "Budgetary Problems" for our Everest expedition. It is not something that we want to share with all of the people in the team; it may cause some team members to leave if they are worried about getting paid or being stranded penniless in Katmandu. Different risks will have different visibility, for example, "Low Quality Carabiners" affect only those projects related to climbing with ropes, so we will manage them at the project or summary project level, rather than the portfolio level.

Each project portfolio usually has *Risk visibility rules* (Figure 15.5). These rules define how risks will be visible when they are first entered in the portfolio. For example, when risk is first added to the register, visibility

Portfolio Level (all projects)		All Summary Projects	
Project	**Visible**	**Project**	**Visible**
📄 Project 1	☒	📄 Project 1	☐
⊟ 🗁 Summary Project 1	☒	⊟ 🗁 Summary Project 1	☒
📄 Project 1	☒	📄 Project 1	☒
⊟ 🗁 Summary Project 2	☒	⊟ 🗁 Summary Project 2	☒
⊟ 🗁 Summary Project 3	☒	⊟ 🗁 Summary Project 3	☒
📄 Project 2	☒	📄 Project 2	☒
Only Immediate Summary Project		**Current Project**	
Project	**Visible**	**Project**	**Visible**
📄 Project 1	☐	📄 Project 1	☐
⊟ 🗁 Summary Project 1	☐	⊟ 🗁 Summary Project 1	☐
📄 Project 1	☐	📄 Project 1	☐
⊟ 🗁 Summary Project 2	☐	⊟ 🗁 Summary Project 2	☐
⊟ 🗁 Summary Project 3	☒	⊟ 🗁 Summary Project 3	☐
📄 Project 2	☒	📄 Project 2	☒

Figure 15.5. Setting up risk visibility and approval rules.

settings are portfolio level, for all summary projects, immediate summary project, or current project.

Enterprise risk management software usually has different roles and permissions for users. Some users will be administrators and have complete access to the system, others will have management roles such as being part of the risk committee, and others will be members of specific projects and will have access only to specific project and/or risks. When a new risk is entered into the system, it may be visible to administrators and some managers, but remain invisible to the majority of users depending on visibility and approval status. Once entered, a risk status can change depending on the review by the risk committee. For example, "Low Quality Climbing Carabiners," was originally identified by a member of a specific project, but after review by the Risk Committee, its visibility has been extended to all climbing projects.

In addition, risk visibility and approval rules can be extended to mitigation and response plans. For example, if the response plan for the risk "fall between Base Camp IV and summit" involves summoning a helicopter, the person who enters this response plan may or may not be an expert in helicopter rescues. If not, the approval process may change the visibility of this response plan to someone with more expertise in this area.

Risk Bubble Chart

One portfolio objective could be related to minimizing risk. In general, we find organizations are very amenable to the idea of maximizing returns with as little risk as possible. Let's say that you have two opportunities: invest in a Zambian based start-up "Eletrocow," which promises to produce artificial milk extremely inexpensively using fusion power artificial cows, or a 300 year old US based company "Shovel and Axe" which as the name suggests produces shovels and axes. The opportunities are on the one hand the Zambian company has a small probability of providing huge return on investment. On the other hand, "Shovel and Axe" has a high probability of providing a small and steady return. If you have a high risk tolerance, you may choose a future as a dairy mogul, if not your future may be less exciting, but in a good way. When managing project portfolios, it is important to

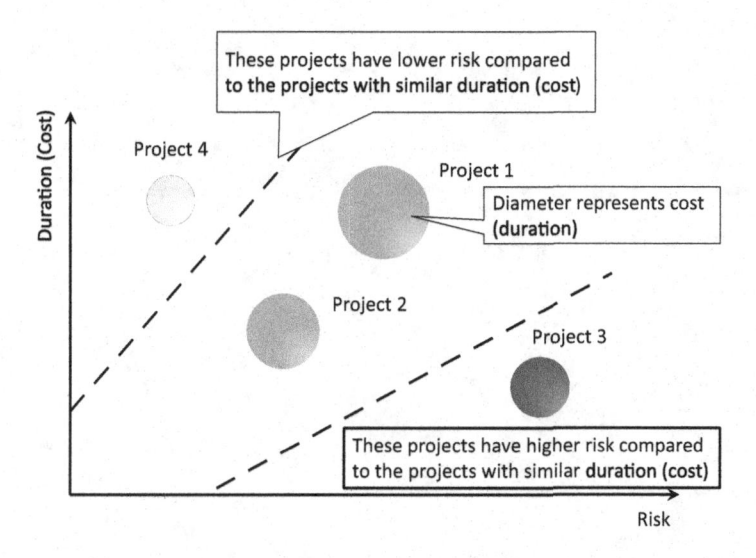

Figure 15.6. Risk vs. duration/cost bubble chart.

ensure that you have your risk balance aligned with your portfolio risk tolerance.

The Risk vs. Duration/Cost chart (Figure 15.6) shows the relative risk associated with project vs. project duration or total project cost. The horizontal axis is a measure of risk, the vertical axis is either duration or cost. Each bubble represents a project and the size of the bubble represents the project cost/duration and risk.

Risk can be expressed as:

- Project standard deviation of task duration or cost.
- Maximum or minimum values.
- Ranges: the difference between maximum and minimum values.
- Certain percentiles.
- Project risk scores.

In a well-balanced portfolio, different projects will have similar levels of relative risk. However, if the relative risk associated with a project is higher than similar projects, the project should be flagged for additional analysis. Alternatively, if project has less relative risk, it may represent an opportunity where additional cost or schedule risk could be transferred to it to mitigate higher risk projects in your portfolio.

Chapter 16

Monte Carlo Simulations of Project Portfolios

Project portfolios tend to be large and complex and any comprehensive analysis of them mirrors this complexity. Because of the unique requirements of portfolio analysis, we have allocated an entire chapter to this topic. Project portfolio Monte Carlo risk analysis requires additional consideration as they can have a large number of projects with interdependencies between projects. This chapter explains a number of modeling methods, which are intended to improve performance of Monte Carlo simulations.

Challenges of Portfolio Risk Analysis

On June 24, 1812, 450,000 men (up to 685,000 according to some estimates) of the Napoleon's Grande Armée, the largest army assembled up to that point in European history, crossed the river Neman and headed towards Moscow (Austin, 2000). Under the guidance of Napoleon, this huge army moved rapidly towards the heart of Russia, Moscow. In September 1812, Napoleon forces entered Moscow, which had been set ablaze by retreating Muscovites. Napoleon's army had made it to Moscow, but the city was empty and spoils were few. After a month, Napoleon realized that he could not sustain the occupation and decided a retreat was in order.

On the long march back to France, the army faced extremely cold weather, starvation, disease, persistent attacks from the Russian army and local peasants, and inevitable desertions, which led to great losses. By November 1812, of the original half a million or so soldiers, only 27,000 fit remained in the Grand Armée, with 380,000 dead and 100,000 captured.

215

The campaign ended on the December 14, 1812 when the last French soldier left Russia and spelled the beginning of the end for Napoleon.

To get a better understanding or what actually happened, Figure 16.1 provides a good illustration. It shows how the invading Grand Armée gradually shrank as it moved across Russia towards Moscow (grey line, from left to right) and back (black line, from right to left). The size of army is proportional to the width of the line. Temperatures during the retreat are plotted on the lower graph.

Napoleon lost this war without losing a single major battle: he lost because his army was not ready for a prolonged military operation across a vast land and in harsh winter conditions. Any war, especially a war on this scale, is a complex project portfolio and each project has many different activities which can be impacted by many different risks. The war of 1812 was an unbelievably complex portfolio. To put this another way, could you imagine taking the entire population of Memphis, Tennessee and ordering them to go by foot or horseback (if they were so fortunate) to Chicago, Illinois over poorly maintained roads and extreme weather? Add in occasional attacks by the local population and Napoleon was planning to live off the land as he had in Central Europe, you can start to grasp the logistical nightmare Napoleon was undertaking.

In the sparsely populated rural Russia of the early 19th century, supplies, including food and forage for horses were scarce and could not keep up with the marching troops. Each battle, each maneuver, each delivery and a supply convoy was essentially a project or even program and in many cases, some of the activities have predecessors and successors in other projects. For example, before a battle, you must have supplies, but the delivery of supplies depends on the security and dependability of the supply chain. This in turn, depends on the army's ability to control the territory that they have already captured. Looking at it this way, we can start to see event chains emerging, where one risk can trigger risks across the project portfolio. In the 21st century, with all of our technology, with just in time communications etc., it is still extremely challenging to manage these types of portfolio risks; in 1812 it was virtually impossible.

Unfortunately for Napoleon's army, any high level portfolio risk analysis that was performed was done poorly. How do we know? If had done it properly, he surely would not have attempted such an undertaking

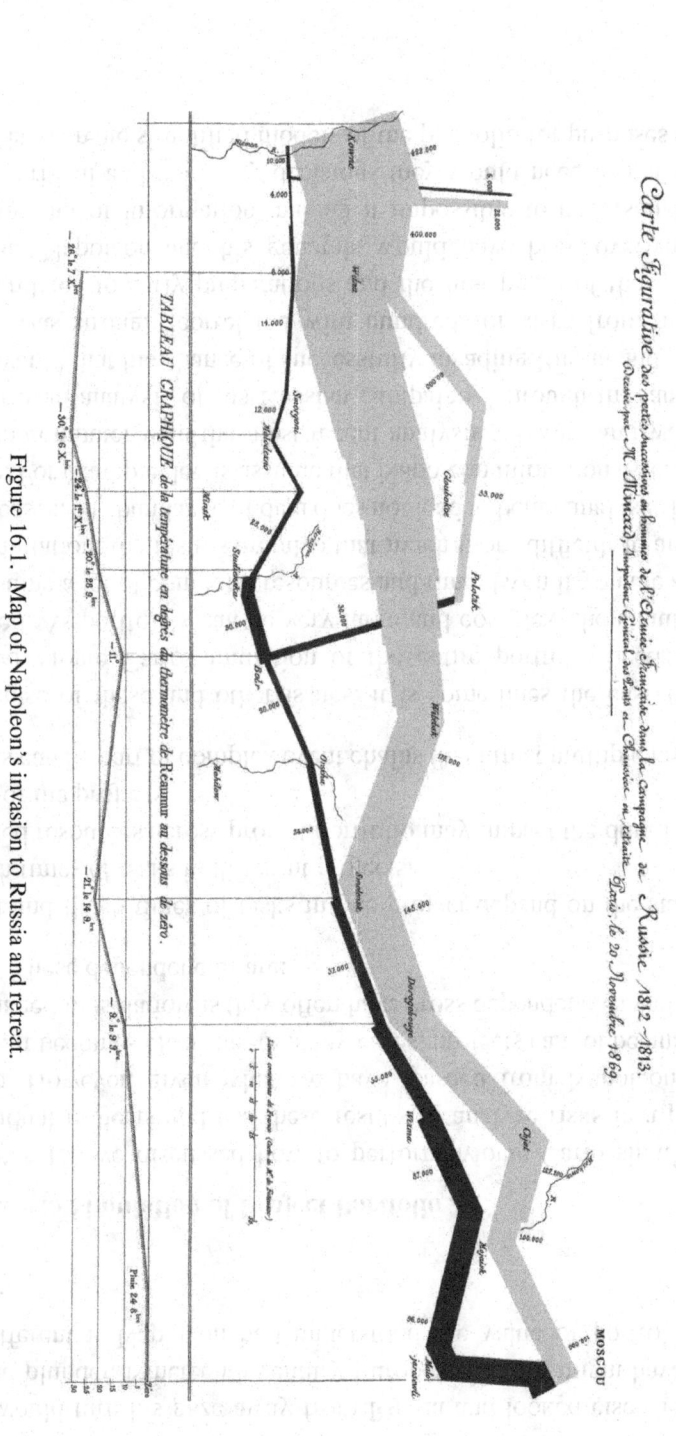

Figure 16.1. Map of Napoleon's invasion to Russia and retreat.

and he would turn his gaze away from Russia and looked elsewhere for glory and plunder. Nineteenth century European history might have been quite different if Napoleon had understood the value of portfolio risk analysis.

Monte Carlo Simulation of Project Portfolio

In Chapter 15, we discussed how to perform Monte Carlo simulations of individual projects and use these results to analyze risks in a project portfolio. However, given what we have learned from Napoleon 1812 invasion, it becomes clear that in many cases, projects cannot be analyzed and managed in isolation as they often have cross dependencies with other projects. These dependencies are:

— Start and finish times of tasks in one project depend on the start and finish times of tasks in different projects.
— Shared resources across project portfolio may impact the duration and cost of the projects.
— Risks can be part of complex event chains that affect multiple projects.

   Because of these and other issues, it is sometimes the case that an integrated Monte Carlo simulation of the entire portfolio needs to be performed. As portfolios can be very large and complex, the simulations can consume a lot of computer resources and time. Even if you are able to run a simulation, the results are also that much more difficult to analyze. In most cases, an abundance of data does not lead to better analysis, but the opposite. For example, let us assume that Napoleon miraculously obtained a modern computer with the most recent analysis software and was able to perform an analysis of his Russian campaign. Through this analysis, he discovered that his chance of successfully invading Russia and seizing Moscow was strongly correlated with hundreds of tasks from multiple projects related to early preparations and the first phase of the invasion of Russia. Napoleon and his generals would have been overwhelmed by the amount of information making it impossible to understand what risks are critical and what key decisions they would need to make. The solution is to create simplified models of the portfolio for purposes of risk analysis.

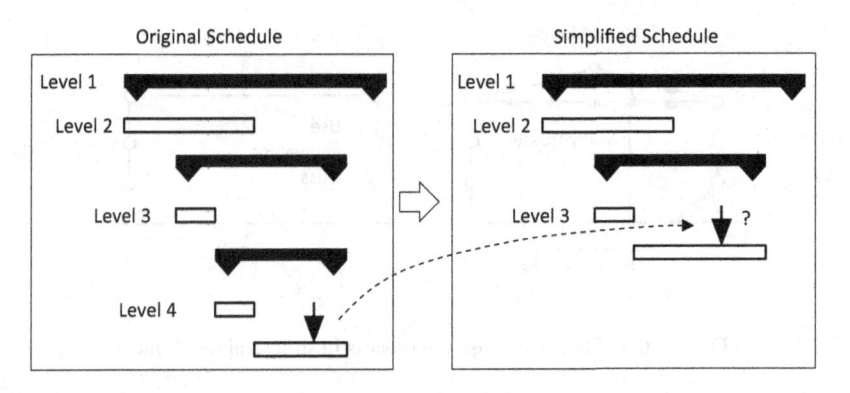

Figure 16.2. Simplifying project schedule base on level.

How to Simplify Project Schedules for Risk Analysis

The idea behind schedule simplification is to create an equivalent schedule that uses a smaller number of tasks, but contains the essential elements (start times, finish times, cost, and precedent network) such that it has enough details to capture the project objectives, without too much detail. This can be a fine balancing act, but there are ways that it can be done, without losing essential data.

The easiest way to simplify a project schedule is to perform a simulation at a specified level of activities and above. The project schedule in Figure 16.2 has four levels (links between tasks are not shown). It is possible to perform risk analysis using only the tasks situated at levels 1–3. Costs, resources, and uncertainties for tasks on level 4 will be allocated to their summary tasks on level 3. There are problems with this approach. It is possible that we could have a risk that is assigned to a single task on level 4. Would it be possible to assign its summary task on level 3? Well, it depends on the risk impact and the task to which it is assigned. The same is true for resources and costs; it may not be possible to create a credible risk model if we roll up the data. So, we can see simplifying the project model may not be equivalent to the original more detailed version.

Another way to simplify project schedules is to use schedule segmentation or "condensation." There is a similar idea in mathematics referred to as *"Model order reduction (MOR)"* (Schilders *et al.*, 2008). It uses a number of techniques to reduce the complexity of mathematical models

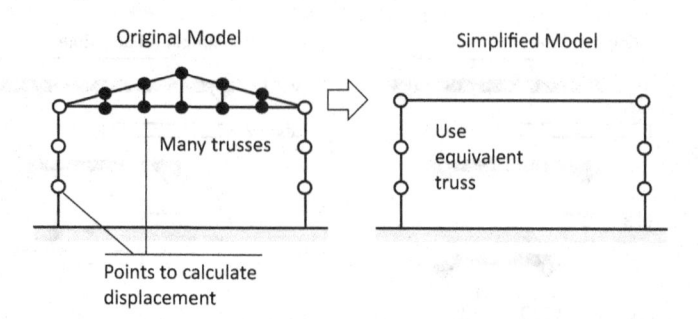

Figure 16.3. Static condensation process in structural mechanics.

in numerical simulations. One such technique is called static condensation (Paz and Leigh, 2001). It is used in structural analysis using the finite element method. Let us assume that you have a structure with many trusses. You need to determine how the structure will react under certain loads. For example, you need to calculate a displacement for different points, including many points within the truss's span (Figure 16.3). These types of structural calculation models can be very large. So to simplify the process, a separate truss is calculated only once. You then create an equivalent model of the truss with only two points, where this truss is connected to the walls. The stiffness of the equivalent truss is equal to the stiffness of the original truss. In this way, the analysis of whole structure is much simpler because all internal points of the trusses are excluded. The calculation model of the structure will be "condensed." After whole analysis is completed it is possible to determine displacements in these internal points.

The idea of condensation can be applied to project scheduling as well. Most schedules contain repeated group of tasks. The whole group may start in different times, but they will have the same risks, costs, and resources. For example, in Napoleon's campaign, they had many groups of tasks related "Battalion marches from point A point B" that can be repeated multiple times for the different battalions. The idea is that these groups of tasks can be "condensed." Here is how we do it (Figure 16.4):

1. Select a group of tasks or projects within a portfolio that has no more than one "entry point" or predecessors and does not have any constraints, such as "Must Start On," or "Start No Later Than."

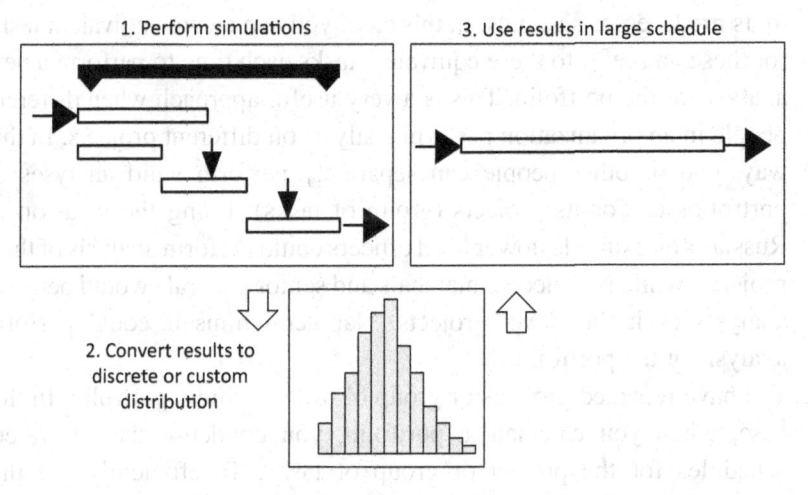

Figure 16.4. "Condensation of the schedule."

2. Run a Monte Carlo simulation of this group and generate a statistical distribution for cost and duration.

3. Convert these statistical distributions into discrete or custom distributions for the whole group. Separate input distributions can be created for cost and duration.

4. Insert this group into the portfolio project schedule as one task with the statistical distributions created in Step 3. The simulation of portfolio will be accelerated because there will be less tasks that will included in the calculation using critical path method. Essentially, this approach "condenses" project schedule.

Another advantage of this is that after the simulation is complete, you can "drill down" to the group of tasks and determine the statistical distributions for cost and duration of individual tasks within the group.

An equivalent schedule for groups of tasks or projects can be used in two ways:

1. You have a project portfolio in which some projects are in execution and others are in the planning stage. Let us assume that you performed an analysis of the same portfolio many times using actual project performance. Certain projects or group of tasks will not change because they have not started yet, however, their start time can be shifted due

to its predecessor's actuals. In this case, you can create equivalent tasks for these and refer to these equivalent tasks each time to perform a new analysis of the portfolio. This is a very useful approach when different people in an organization perform analysis on different projects. In this way, you or other people can separately perform valid analyses of portfolios and/or its projects (group of tasks). Using the invasion of Russia as an example, lower level officers could perform analysis of their projects, while Napoleon's marshals and senior generals would perform analysis of higher level projects. Napoleon himself could perform analysis of the portfolio.

2. You have repeated projects or group of tasks within a portfolio. In this case, when you calculate a portfolio, you condense the equivalent schedules for the project or group of tasks. To efficiently use this approach, you need to find as many repeated group of tasks with the same task duration, cost, risks and uncertainties, and constraints as possible. To ensure that you have these repeated segments you need to minimize number of constraints and link tasks only when it is meaningful. It is especially important to minimize the number of links between projects in your portfolio because it will not only cause problems with segmentation, but also significantly complicate your portfolio schedule.

There is yet another way to accelerate calculations and condense project schedules. Assume that you have a number of sequential tasks. Each of these tasks has a statistical distribution for task duration but does not have any risks or constraints. In some cases, there is an analytical solution for adding statistical distribution together as the statistical distribution for the sum of all tasks is a function of individual statistical distribution.

Why Do We Need to Improve the Performance of Monte Carlo Simulations?

There are a number of reasons why the calculation performance of Monte Carlo simulations can be important:

1. Large integrated project portfolios can consist of tens of thousands of tasks. Sometimes, it is impossible to significantly simplify these portfolios and therefore it would require the ability to perform Monte

Carlo simulation on a large number of tasks. Add resources, cost, and risks and the simulation may take hours.
2. Scenarios are integral to the decision-making framework. In theory, the number of scenarios can be quite significant because it is hard to accommodate all risk responses in one schedule. If a single Monte Carlo simulation can take a long time, running multiple scenarios can add significant time to your analysis.
3. Analysis can be repeated multiple times during project execution based on actual project performance data. This can also be time consuming.

Therefore, vendors of project risk analysis software are in a race to develop more efficient algorithms for Monte Carlo simulations. If you are going to be using Monte Carlo simulation software properly, it is important to be familiar with these algorithms.

Parallel Monte Carlo Iterations

You may wonder, where is the bottleneck that has the most impact on the time required to run Monte Carlo simulations? It is the critical path calculation. While, mathematically it is not a very complex algorithm as it is essentially based on the formula: start time + duration = finish time. The bottleneck is created as it must be run hundreds if not thousands of times. The other calculations related to Monte Carlo simulations, such as the calculation of individual task durations based on risks assigned to this task, or the generation of frequency and cumulative probability plots take much less time. Therefore, software developers of the software are looking to optimize their critical path calculation algorithms. One way to do it is to use multi-processing calculation and graphic processing units (GPUs).

The computer that is sitting on your desk is a marvel of technology and is capable of doing many things at once. One of the reasons for this is multiple processing cores. These cores can perform parallel calculations of each Monte Carlo iteration. All calculations can be done independently and then results merged at the end. As a result, calculation performance can be increased dramatically. Here is how it works:

1. Create a precedence network model with uncertainties and risks and calculate one Monte Carlo iteration. Please note that a precedence

network model for calculation is not the same thing as project schedule. It only includes information necessary to perform calculation using critical path method: start and finish times of tasks, their dependences, information about summary tasks, constraints, and other inputs for calculation. During this step, the task durations and cost are adjusted based on risks. For example, if on this iteration a risk occurs and task duration increases, this new duration will be set in the calculation model.

2. Generate the precedence network model in the computer multiple times and save them to the computer's memory. The number of copies depends on the total available computer memory and number of processing cores. The number of copies of the precedence network should be at least 4 times greater than the number of processing cores because some cores may be unavailable due to unrelated processing tasks such as running the operating system. Send all the models from the memory to the different cores of the computer. Each core will perform critical path calculations.

3. When all calculations are completed, the results are saved back into the memory. Results from each precedence network model are saved in a global data set representing the simulation results of all the tasks and the project.

4. Clean and release memory.

5. Repeat steps from 1 to 5 until desirable number of iterations is achieved or Monte Carlo simulation process converges.

6. Process and generate the results of the simulation from the memory.

Another way to improve performance of Monte Carlo simulation is to use a GPU. The GPU is a specialized computer chip that is used for graphic processing and comes with your computer's graphic card. GPUs are particularly useful for generating 3D graphics as they are extremely fast at performing specific mathematical operations. They can be used to perform Monte Carlo simulations as well as long as the calculation algorithm is programmed certain way. It is even possible to use multiple graphic cards to do parallel computation. This process is called general-purpose computing on graphics processing units (GPGPU). This approach is used widely for different scientific applications (Thompson *et al.*, 2002) and may well be the future of project portfolio simulations.

Conclusions

Imagine your life as an extremely large project portfolio. Everything that you do from the trivial such as preparing breakfasts to the most important such as raising a child represents a project. Each one of your life's projects has risks and if they occur could have a large impact on the course of your life. Risks can be both threats and opportunities, you can take a risk and buy a Powerball lottery ticket, the threat is the loss of a couple of dollars, the opportunity is suddenly being wealthy beyond your imagination and getting to know many of your long lost relatives.

Normally, when it comes to risks in our lives, the impacts can be difficult to either imagine or the effects will not be felt until far in the future and therefore we do not actively manage them and they can cause a lot of hardship. Would not our lives be wonderful if we had a more active role in analyzing and managing risks? We would live healthier lives as we could mitigate lifestyle risks by making healthier choices. We might be more prepared for retirement because we improve the management of our financial portfolio. We could even enjoy more leisure time because we take risks into account when planning trips or other activities and ensure we have risk plans in place (mitigation, responses, contingency, etc.). In reality, though we occasionally perform some mental risk analysis, we tend not to do it often enough because our brains are just not wired that way.

In many cases, what is true in our personal life is also true in business. Very often, we do not perform risk analysis even when there is not any significant barriers keeping you from doing it. In this book, we showed many examples of the disastrous results that can occur when risks are not actively managed. And vice versa, if risk analysis is performed, the results can be quite impressive.

By writing this book, we wanted to reduce one of the barriers in the wider acceptance of risk analysis: knowledge. Part of this is the basic components of the risk analysis and management process:

1. **Qualitative project risk analysis** can start as a very simple mental exercise that will help to answer three basic questions: what can occur, what is a probability and impact of this and what can be done about it.

2. **Qualitative risk analysis can be limited** especially if you are analyzing risks in a project schedule. In this case, quantitative risk analysis can help. The most common method of quantitative risk analysis of project schedules is the Monte Carlo method.

3. **Monte Carlo** helps you to understand how uncertainties can affect your project schedule: what is the chance that a project will be completed on time and on budget, what are the crucial tasks, what level of contingency is appropriate given the uncertainty, and answers to other questions.

4. **Risk events** can be modeled as input uncertainties for Monte Carlo project risk analysis. Risk events from a risk register can be assigned to different tasks or resources in the project schedule. Defining uncertainties using risk events simplifies and improves accuracy of risk analysis. As a result of sensitivity analysis, risks are ranked based their calculated probability, impact, and score. Critical risks can be mitigated or avoided.

5. **Event chain methodology** is an uncertainty modeling and schedule network analysis technique that is focused on identifying and managing events and event chains that affect project schedules. Event chain methodology allows you to account for factors that are not included as part of other schedule network analysis techniques: moment of event, chains of events, execution of response plans under certain conditions, and others.

6. **Event chain diagrams** can be used to visualize complex relationship between different events using Gantt Charts.

7. **Integrated project risk analysis** involves uncertainties in schedule, cost, resources and work, and other parameters. It can be performed as part of Monte Carlo project risk analysis and is particularly valuable when used with event chain methodology. Event chain methodology

integrates analysis of schedule and non-schedule related risks, affecting safety, security, technology, quality, etc.

8. **Probabilistic and conditional branching and decision tree analysis** can be part of quantitative risk analysis and help project managers to make better project choices.

9. **Project risk analysis can be performed on any phases of project** during project planning, project execution, and project close. Risk analysis during project execution integrates information about actual project performance and the actual status of risks including issues. It helps to improve the quality of project analysis.

10. **Risk analysis of project portfolio** helps to manage portfolios. In particular, it is possible to manage risks across an entire, rank projects within a portfolio based on risk exposure, and analyze how uncertainties in relationship between different projects and resources affect the portfolio.

In the end, our advice is to start slowly and add more complexity to your models and techniques as your ability and confidence in the process grows. If you have never performed formal project risk analysis before start with a basic qualitative analysis, ask the questions, what could happen, what would be the impact and what can we do about it. Eventually, you should start to appreciate the value of project risk analysis and apply more advanced methods as described in our book.

Appendixes

Appendix A. Basic Principles of Event Chain Methodology

Principle	Description	
Moment of risk and state of activity (Chapter 6)	Tasks are affected by external events, which transform an activity from one state to another. This moment, when an event occurs, in most cases is probabilistic.	
Event chain diagrams (Chapter 7)	Event chain diagrams are visualizations that show the relationships between events and tasks and how the events affect each other.	
Event chains (Chapter 8)	Events can cause other events, which will create event chains. These event chains can significantly affect the course of the project.	

(Continued)

Appendix A. (*Continued*)

Principle	Description	
Critical events and event chains (Chapter 9)	The single events or the event chains that have the most potential to affect the projects are the "critical events" or "critical chains of events".	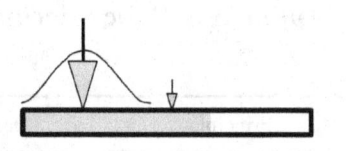
Project performance management with events and event chains (Chapter 10)	Probabilities and impact of events and event chains are changing during the course of a project. It requires new analysis on each project milestone.	

Appendix B. What Can We Get From Monte Carlo Simulation

Once you have completed a Monte Carlo simulation, what questions can we now answer based upon the results? This appendix provides questions we can answer based on the results of Monte Carlo simulations and what presentation tools we can use:

Question	Presentation tool	Comment
What is duration of the mean (low, high) duration of a task or a project with risks and uncertainties?	Project summary or risk adjusted project schedule	The result of a Monte Carlo simulation is statistical distributions of project or task durations. For example, we can tell a low (optimistic) duration that is set at P10.
What level of certainty should I use to ensure that my project will be completed on time with certain probability (e.g. 90%)?	Risk adjust project schedule	Risk adjusted schedule will have all tasks duration, start and finish times calculated based on certain percentile of statistical distributions for these parameters.
What is the probability that a project will be completed on time?	Frequency or/and cumulative probability plots for project duration	Frequency or/and Cumulative Probability plots show the chance that a project will be completed within certain time: e.g. 90% chance that project will be completed within 40 days.
What is my contingency or margin?	Original or/and risk adjusted project schedule	Contingencies or margins are calculated as the difference between the original and the project with risks and uncertainties. It can also be calculated as a difference between results of risk adjusted schedules using different percentiles, such as P70 and P95.

(Continued)

Appendix B. (*Continued*)

Question	Presentation tool	Comment
Does task duration or cost affect the project the most or what are the crucial tasks?	Tornado diagram	Sensitivity analysis is performed using the Monte Carlo simulation. This analysis ranks tasks based on sensitive the project cost or schedule is to the results of the individual task. If a task significantly affects the project, risks associated with this task needs to be given high priority.
What are project or task success rates?	Success rate values or success rate charts	On any iteration of a Monte Carlo simulation, a project or task may be canceled because of risks or deadlines. This will reduce the probabilistic success rate of the project. Success rates are calculated as percentage of Monte Carlo iterations in which project or task is canceled.
What is it the impact of my risk?	Risk register shows the impact of each risk.	The calculated cumulative risk impact can be different than the original impact you entered. The risk can be assigned to multiple tasks or resources, and these tasks may or may not be not on a critical path. Risk impacts are calculated as a result of sensitivity analysis: how project parameters are correlated with the impact of individual risks on individual tasks.
What is the most important risk?	Risk register and risk matrix	Risks are ranked based on risk score, which is calculated as risk probability multiplied by risk impact. Both risk impacts and risk probabilities are calculated as a result of Monte Carlo simulation.

(*Continued*)

What is the chance that project will be on time and on budget at the same time?	Joint confidence level (JCL) chart	Each iteration of Monte Carlo simulations has a certain duration and cost. The JCL chart shows how many times both duration and cost will be less than set percentile.
How often will a task be on the critical path?	Critical indexes shown on the Gantt chart or in a table.	During each iteration of a Monte Carlo simulation, that task may or may not be on the critical path. It is possible to calculate critical indexes which measure how likely the task will be on a critical path.
What is the chance that cash flow during certain period of time will be greater (less) than a certain value?	Probabilistic cash flow chart	Project cost during given time intervals can be different due to risks and uncertainties. Distribution of project cost and income for each time interval can be obtained as a result of Monte Carlo simulation.
What is the chance that resource allocation will be greater or less than a certain value?	Probabilistic resource allocation charts and frequency or/and cumulative probability plots for work.	Resource allocation or how many hours work or material resources will be used during certain time interval is probabilistic. Monte Carlo simulations provide a statistical distribution of work for specific resource for a time internal or particular task. Monte Carlo simulations can also generate a statistical distribution for resource utilization.

(*Continued*)

Appendix B. (*Continued*)

Question	Presentation tool	Comment
What is the forecasted completion date, duration, or cost of a partially completed project?	Project tracking charts or Gantt charts with project tracking information.	Results of actual project measurement help to improve quality of assessment of risks and uncertainties. Particularly, when risks assigned to a task do not occur during certain period of time, the probability of the risk occurring may be reduced. Once a project is in execution, Monte Carlo simulations help to determine project duration, cost, finish time, and other parameters during each phase or milestone of the project.

Appendix C. Project Risk Analysis Software

This table provides an overview of available off-the-shelf project and portfolio risk analysis software presented in alphabetical order.

Software	Vendor	Comment
Project Risk Analysis Software		
@Risk of Project Management	Palisade corporation www.palisade.com	Utilizes Microsoft excel to perform simulations of project schedules, created in Microsoft project. Includes uncertainties in duration and cost defined by statistical distributions.
Acumen Risk	Deltek http://www.deltek.com/	Works as standalone or integrated with other project management software. Includes risk register and uncertainties defined by statistical distributions.
Full Monte	Barbecana http://www.barbecana.com/	Addin for Microsoft project. Integrated with Oracle Primavera. Includes uncertainties in duration and cost defined by statistical distributions.
NetRisk	PMA technologies www.pmatechnologies.com	Supplementary module for PMA Technologies NetPoint. Includes uncertainties in duration and cost defined by statistical distributions.
Safran Risk	Safran software solutions http://www.safran.com/	Works as standalone or integrated with other project management software. Includes risk register and uncertainties defined by statistical distributions.
Polaris	Booz Allen Hamilton www.boozallen.com	Works as standalone and integrated with Microsoft Project. Includes risk register and uncertainties defined by statistical distributions. Performs very fast Monte Carlo simulations.

(Continued)

Appendix C. (*Continued*)

Software	Vendor	Comment
Primavera Risk Analysis	Oracle corporation www.oracle.com	Formerly Pertmaster. Fully integrated with Oracle Primavera. Includes risk register and uncertainties defined by statistical distributions.
RiskyProject Lite and RiskyProject Professional	Intaver institute www.intaver.com	Works as standalone and as an Addin for Microsoft project. Integrated with other project management software, such as Oracle Primavera. Includes full risk register and uncertainties defined by statistical distributions. Includes risk management functionalities for schedule-related and non-schedule risks. Supports event chain methodology.
Portfolio Risk Analysis Software		
RiskyProject Enterprise	Intaver institute www.intaver.com	Enterprise risk register, all project schedules with uncertainties and simulation results are saved in the database. Risks from enterprise risk register can be assigned to multiple projects. RiskyProject Lite and Professional are used as a client interface.

References

AeroWeb 2015. Bell-Boeing V-22 Osprey. Available on: http://www.bga-aeroweb.com/Defense/V-22-Osprey.html. Retrieved September 29, 2015.

Andryushin, I.A., Chernyshev, A.K., Yudin, U.A. 2003. *Pages of History of Nuclear Weapons and Nuclear Infrastructure in USSR*. In Russian. Sarov. Available on: http://window.edu.ru/resource/592/62592/files/ukrosch_ydra.pdf. Retrieved November 20, 2016.

Arlow, J., Neustadt, I. 2003. *Enterprise Patterns and MDA: Building Better Software with Archetype Patterns and UML*. Boston: Addison-Wesley Professional.

Asmar, M. 2012. Denver's Zoo $50M Toyota Elephant Passage opens today. Available on: http://www.westword.com/news/photos-denver-zoos-50m-toyota-elephant-passage-opens-today-5853316. Retrieved January 26, 2016.

Austin, P.B. 2000. *1812: Napoleon's Invasion of Russia*. London: Greenhill Books.

Axelrod, A. 2009. *The Real History of the Cold War: A New Look at the Past*. New York: Sterling Publishing.

BBC News 2014. Yemen raid: US 'unaware' hostage Korkie was with Somers. Available on: http://www.bbc.com/news/world-middle-east-30366455. Retrieved September 28, 2015.

Bengtsson, I., Życzkowski, K. 2006. *Geometry of Quantum States: An Introduction to Quantum Entanglement*. Cambridge: Cambridge University Press.

Berg International Adventures 2016. Climb Mt. Everest with Berg Adventures — Trip Itinerary. Available on: http://www.bergadventures.com/v3_trips/asia/everest-itinerary.php. Retrieved January 22, 2016.

Bergin, C. 2015. James Webb Space Telescope hardware entering key test phase. Available on: http://www.nasaspaceflight.com/2015/01/jwst-hardware-entering-test-phase/. Retrieved January 24, 2016.

Bergen, P., Stermanm, D. 2014. Why hostage rescues fail. CNN. Available on: http://www.cnn.com/2014/12/08/opinion/bergen-sterman-why-hostage-rescues-fail/. Retrieved September 28, 2015.

Booch, G., Rumbaugh, J., Jacobson, I. 2005. *The Unified Modeling Language User Guide*, 2nd edition. Boston: Addison-Wesley Professional.

Bowden, M. 2006. The Desert One Debacle. *The Atlantic*. May 2006. Available at http://www.theatlantic.com/magazine/archive/2006/05/the-desert-one-debacle/304803/. Retrieved September 28, 2015.

Buehler, R., Griffin, D., Peetz, J. 2010. The planning fallacy: Cognitive, motivational, and social origins. *Advances in Experimental Social Psychology*. San Diego: Academic Press, Vol. 43, p. 9.

Chapman, G.B. Johnson, E.J. 1999. Anchoring, Activation, and the Construction of Values. *Organizational Behavior and Human Decision Processes* 79(2): 115–153.

Charleslindbergh.com. 2015. The Flight. Available on: http://www.charleslindbergh.com/history/paris.asp. Retrieved October 31, 2015.

Clemen, R.T. 1997. *Making Hard Decisions: An Introduction to Decision Analysis (Business Statistics)*, 2nd edition. Pacific Grove, CA: Brooks/Cole Publishing Company, Cooke, R.M. 1991. *Experts in Uncertainty: Opinion and Subjective Probability in Science*. Oxford: Oxford University Press.

Dance, S. 2014. Webb telescope at risk of schedule delays, report finds. The Baltimore Sun. Available on: http://www.baltimoresun.com/health/maryland-health/bs-hs-webb-telescope-20141222-story.html. Retrieved January 22, 2016.

Darley, J.M., Gross, P.H. 2000. A Hypothesis-Confirming Bias in Labelling Effects, In *Stangor, Charles, Stereotypes and Prejudice: Essential Readings*. Philadelphia: Psychology Press, p. 212.

David, S. 2015. *Operation Thunderbolt: Flight 139 and the Raid on Entebbe Airport, the Most Audacious Hostage Rescue Mission in History*. London: Hodder & Stoughton Ltd.

Delbecq, A.L., Van de Ven, D., Gustafson, D.H. 1975. *Group Techniques for Program Planning*. Glenview, IL: Scott, Foresman.

Dori, D. 2002. *Object–Process Methodology — A Holistic Systems Paradigm*. New York: Springer.

Druker, E. 2012. Analytical Program Management: An Approach for Integrating Cost, Schedule and Risk. In *Proceeding of the Association of Cost Engineers Conference 2012*.

Dunstan, S. 2012. *Entebbe: The Most Daring Raid of Israel's Special Forces*. The Rosen Publishing Group.

Everest History. 2016. *Ascent Routes on Everest*. Available on: http://www.everesthistory.com/routes.htm. Retrieved January 20, 2016.

Fleming, Q.W., Koppelman, J.M. 2006. *Earned Value Project Management*, 3rd edition. Newtown Square, PA: Project Management Institute.

Flyvbjerg, B. 2005. Design by deception: The politics of megaproject approval. *Harvard Design Magazine*. Spring-Summer: 50–59.

Fowler, M. 2002. *Patterns of Enterprise Application Architecture*. Boston, USA: Addison-Wesley Professional.

Gawande, A. 2011. *The Checklist Manifesto: How to Get Things Right Picador*, Reprint edition. London: UK.

Gentle, J.E. 2004. *Random Number Generation and Monte Carlo Methods*, 2nd edition. New York: Springer.

Gilovich, T. D., Griffin, D., Kahneman, D. 2002. *Heuristics and Biases: The Psychology of Intuitive Judgment*. New York: Cambridge University Press.

Griffiths, D.J. 2004. *Introduction to Quantum Mechanics*, 2nd edition. Addison-Wesley.

Hill, G.W. 1982. Group versus individual performance: Are N + 1 heads better than one? *Psychological Bulletin* 91: 517–539.

Hillson, D. 2004. Earned Value Management and Risk Management: A Practical Synergy. In *Proceeding of PMI 2004 Global Congress Proceedings — Anaheim, California, US*, Available on: http://www.risk-doctor.com/pdf-files/cevb1004.pdf. Retrieved at January 24, 2016.

Hulett, D. 2009. *Practical Schedule Risk Analysis*, New edition. London, UK: Gower Press.

Hulett, D. 2011. *Integrated Cost-Schedule Risk Analysis*, New edition. Surrey, UK: Ashgate Publishing.

Ishizaka, A. Nemery, P. 2013. *Multi-criteria Decision Analysis: Methods and Software*. New Jersey: Wiley.

Klara, R. 2013. *The Hidden White House*. New York: St. Martin's Press.

Lehmann, E.L., D'Abrera, H.J.M. 1998. *Nonparametrics: Statistical Methods Based on Ranks, Revised edition*. Englewood Cliffs, New Jersey: Prentice-Hall.

Lovallo, D., Kahneman, D. 2003. Delusions of success: How optimism undermines executives' decisions. *Harvard Business Review* 81(7): 56–63.

Manoukian, E.B. 2006. *Quantum Theory: A Wide Spectrum*. New York: Springer.

Martin, R.C. 2002. *Agile Software Development, Principles, Patterns, and Practices*. USA: Prentice Hall.

Martinez, L., Raddatz, M., Candea, B. 2014. Navy SEALs Tried Rescuing al Qaeda Hostage Luke Somers. *ABC News*. Available on: http://abcnews.go.com/

International/navy-seals-rescuing-al-qaeda-hostage-luke-somers/story?id=27 413796. Retrieved September 28, 2015.

McNalley, J. 2010. *A Small Book of Random Numbers Paperback*. CreateSpace Independent Publishing Platform.

McRaven, W.H. 1996. *Spec Ops: Case Studies in Special Operations Warfare: Theory and Practice*, New edition. New York: Presidio Press.

Metropolis, N. 1987. The Beginning of the Month Carlo Method. *Los Alamos Science*. Special Issue (15): 125–130.

NASA World Observatory 2016. Mount Everest. Available on: http://earthobservatory.nasa.gov/IOTD/view.php?id=82578. Retrieved January 20, 2016.

NASA 2015. *NASA Cost Estimating Handbook Version 4.0*. Available on: http://www.nasa.gov/sites/default/files/files/CEH_Appj.pdf. Retrieved January 6, 2016.

Nickerson, R.S. 1998. Confirmation Bias: A Ubiquitous Phenomenon in Many Guises. *Review of General Psychology* 2(2): 175–220.

North, A., Grierson, J. 2015. Zoo animals on the loose and deaths feared after Georgia floods. The Guardian. Available on: http://www.theguardian.com/world/2015/jun/14/georgia-floods-deaths-feared-zoo-animals-on-loose. Retrieved January 26, 2016.

O'Hagan, A., Buck, C.E., Daneshkhah, A., Eiser, J.R., Garthwaite, P.H., Jenkinson, D.J., Oakley, J.E., Rakow, T. 2006. *Uncertain Judgements: Eliciting Experts' Probabilities*. Hoboken, New Jersey: Wiley.

Paivio, A. 1971. *Imagery and Verbal Processes*. New York: Holt, Rinehart, and Winston.

Paivio, A. 1986. *Mental Representations: A Dual Coding Approach*. Oxford, England: Oxford University Press.

Project Management Institute 2013. *A Guide to the Project Management Body of Knowledge* (PMBoK Guide), 5th edition. Pa: PMI Newton Square.

Paz, M., Leigh, W. 2001. *Integrated Matrix Analysis of Structures. Theory and Computation*. New York: Springer.

Phillips, L.D. 2006. Decision Conferencing. Working Paper. Operational Research Group, Department of Management. London School of Economics & Political Science. Available on: http://eprints.lse.ac.uk/22712/1/06085.pdf. Retrieved January 16, 2016.

Quattrone, G.A., Lawrence, C.P., Warren, D.L., Souze-Silva, K., Finkel, S.E., Andrus, D.E. 1984. *Explorations in Anchoring: The Effects of Prior Range, Anchor Extremity, and Suggestive Hints*. Unpublished manuscript. Stanford: Stanford University.

Robertson, D., Breen, B. 2013. *Brick by Brick: How LEGO Rewrote the Rules of Innovation and Conquered the Global Toy Industry.* New York: Crown Business.

Reynolds, E. 2012. Huge fire tears through top floors of half-built Moscow skyscraper that is to be tallest in Europe. MailOnline. Available at http://www.dailymail.co.uk/news/article-2124299/Huge-tears-floors-Moscow.skyscraper-tallest-Europe.html. Retrieved November 20, 2016.

Saaty, T.L., Peniwati, K. 2008. *Group Decision Making: Drawing out and Reconciling Differences.* Pittsburgh, Pennsylvania: RWS Publications.

Schilders, W.H., Van der Vorst, H., Rommes, J. 2008. *Model Order Reduction: Theory, Research Aspects and Applications (Mathematics in Industry).* New York: Springer.

Smith, T. 1976. Hostages Freed as Israelis Raid Uganda Airport. New York Times. Available on: http://query.nytimes.com/gst/abstract.html?res=99 02E7DB133DEE32A25757C0A9619C946790D6CF. Retrieved September 28, 2015.

Sniezek, J. A. 1989. An examination of group process in judgment forecasting. *International Journal of Forecasting* 5: 171–178.

Sternberg, R. J. 2006. *Cognitive Psychology,* 4th edition. Belmont: Thomson Wadsworth.

Thompson, C., Hahn S., Oskin M. 2002. Using modern graphics architecture for general-purpose computing: A framework and analysis. In *SIGGRAPH/Internation Symposium on Microarchitecture*, Turkey.

Tversky, A., Kahneman, D. 1971. Belief in the law of small numbers. *Psychological Bulletin* 76: 105–110.

Tversky, A., Kahneman, D. 1973. Availability: A heuristic for judging frequency and probability. *Cognitive Psychology* 5(2): 207–232.

Tversky, A., Kahneman, D. 1974. Judgment under uncertainty: Heuristics and biases. *Science* 185(4157): 1124–1131.

Ulam, S.M. 1983. *Adventures of a Mathematician.* New York: Charles Scribner's Sons, pp. 9–15.

Virine, L., McVean, J. 2004. Visual Modeling of Business Problems: Workflow and Patterns, In *Proceedings of 2004 Winter Simulation Conference*, Washington DC.

Virine, L., Rapley, L. 2003. Visualization of Probabilistic Business Models, In *Proceedings of 2003 Winter Simulation Conference*, New Orleans, LA.

Virine, L., Trumper, M. 2007. *Project Decisions: The Art and Science.* Management Concepts (October 1, 2007) VA: Tyson's Corner.

Virine, L., Trumper, M. 2013. *ProjectThink: Why Good Managers Make Poor Project Choices*, New edition. Surrey, England: Gower Publishing Company.

Weaver, P. 2006. *A Brief History of Scheduling*. Mosaic Project Services Pty Ltd. Available on: http://www.mosaicprojects.com.au/PDF_Papers/P042_History%20of%20Scheduing.pdf. Retrieved November 20, 2016.

Williams, T. 2004. Why Monte Carlo simulations of project networks can mislead. *Project Management Journal* 35(3): 53–61.

Wilson, T.D., Houston, C.E., Etling, K.M., Brekke, N. 1996. A new look at anchoring effects: Basic anchoring and its antecedents. *Journal of Experimental Psychology: General* 125(4): 387–402.

Yaniv, M., Dory, D. 2013. Model-based risk-oriented robust systems design with object-process methodology. *International Journal of Strategic Engineering Asset Management* 1(4): 331–354.

Further Reading

AACE 2011. AACE International Recommended Practice No. 57R-09. Integrated Cost and Schedule Risk Analysis using Monte Carlo Simulation of a CPM Model.

Cretu, O., Stewart, R.B., Berends, T. 2011. *Risk Management for Design and Construction*. RSMeans.

Ghantt, T. 2012. *Project Risk Management: Using Failure Mode Effect Analysis for Project Management*, 1st edition. Plumbline Publishing Group.

Heldman, K. 2005. *Project Manager's Spotlight on Risk Management*. Jossey-Bass.

Hillson, D. 2009. *Managing Risk in Projects (Fundamentals of Project Management)*, New edition (August 11, 2009). Gower Publishing Company.

Hillson, D. 2012. *Practical Risk Management: The ATOM Methodology*, 2nd edition. Management Concepts Press.

Hillson, D., Murray-Webster, R. 2012. *A Short Guide to Risk Appetite (Short Guides to Business Risk)*, New edition. Gower Publishing Company.

Hillson, D. 2014. *The Risk Doctor's Cures for Common Risk Ailments*. Management Concepts Press.

Hulett, D. 2009. *Practical Schedule Risk Analysis*, New edition. Gower Pub Co.

Hulett, D. 2011. *Integrated Cost-Schedule Risk Analysis*. New edition, Ashgate Publishing.

Hulett, D., Nosbisch, M. 2012. *Integrated Cost-Schedule Risk Analysis*. Available on: http://www.projectrisk.com/white_papers/Integrated_Cost-Sch edule_Risk_Analysis.pdf, Retrieved January 14, 2016.

Jordan, A. 2013. *Risk Management for Project Driven Organizations: A Strategic Guide to Portfolio, Program and PMO Success*. J. Ross Publishing (May 16, 2013).

Jutte, B. 2009. *Project Risk Management Handbook: The Invaluable Guide for Managing Project Risks* (May 20, 2009). Mantaba Publishing.

Kendrick, T. 2015. *Identifying and Managing Project Risk: Essential Tools for Failure-Proofing Your Project*, 3rd edition (March 25, 2015). AMACOM.

Mulcahy, R. 2010. *Risk Management Tricks of the Trade for Project Managers + PMI-RMP Exam Prep Guide*, 2nd edition (February 15, 2010). RMC Publications.

Pritchard, C. 2014. *Risk Management: Concepts and Guidance*, 5th edition (December 17, 2014). Auerbach Publications.

Project Management Institute 2013. *A Guide to the Project Management Body of Knowledge*, 5th edition. PMBoK Guide.

Raydugin, Y. 2013. *Project Risk Management: Essential Methods for Project Teams and Decision Makers*, 1st edition (September 10, 2013), Wiley.

Salkeld, D. 2013. *Understanding Risk Analysis: A Guide for Managers*, 1st edition (March 1, 2013). Gower Publishing Company.

Virine, L., Trumper, M. 2007. *Project Decisions: The Art and Science.* Management Concepts.

Virine, L., Trumper, M. 2013. *Projectthink: Why Good Managers Make Poor Project Choices*, New edition. Gower Pub Co.

Walaski, P. 2011. *Risk and Crisis Communications: Methods and Messages*, 1st edition (September 6, 2011). Wiley.

Warren, R. 2013. *Project Risk Management: The Most Important Methods and Tools for Successful Projects*, 1st edition. CreateSpace Independent Publishing Platform.

Glossary

Analytic Hierarchy Process — method of estimation of priorities through pairwise comparisons and relies on the judgments of experts. It can be used in prioritization of project within a portfolio or ranking risk categories.

Global Risk Assignment — see Risk Assignment.

Ground State — in Event chain methodology, an original state of the activity before any events affect it.

Critical Events (Critical Risks) — events that have the most potential to affect the projects. Critical events are determined based of calculation of correlation between cumulative effect of the event on activity cost and duration and total project cost or duration. Critical events can be also determined by sequential disabling selected risk, performing Monte Carlo analysis, and calculating effect of the disabled risk on the project schedule.

Critical Event Chains — in Event chain methodology, event chains that have the most potential to affect the projects.

Critical Index — an indicator which shows how many times the task is on the critical path during a process on Monte Carlo simulation.

Critical Path Method — scheduling algorithms, which calculates start and finish times of each activity, as well as determines critical path, floats, and other schedule parameters. In Monte Carlo simulation calculation, using critical path method is repeated multiple times with different sets of inputs, such as task durations, start, and finish times is they are available, some constraints, etc. These inputs are coming from statistical distributions.

Crucial Task — a task which has the most potential to affect the project parameters such as duration or cost. Crucial tasks are determined as a result of sensitivity analysis: correlation between task parameters such as duration and total project parameters.

Cumulative Probability Plot — a chart which plots cumulative probability vs. value of variable. Cumulative probability chart allows you to analyze the risk associated with variable. Using this plot, you can determine what is the chance that the project will be completed within a given period; or, what is the chance that the cost of the project will be within budget? Cumulative probability charts can be combined with frequency charts using the same variable.

Decision Tree — a tree-shaped diagram used to determine expected value of a project and helps to select a best course.

Earned Value Management (EVM) — is a method of measuring project performance.

Entanglement — in Event chain methodology, an effect according to which states of apparently independent activities are changing at about the same time without a common underlying event.

Enterprise Risk Register — is a risk register which is used for organization or project portfolio. Risks from enterprise risk register can be shared between different projects within a portfolio. They can be assigned to individual project and within projects to individual tasks or resources.

Event Chain Diagram — a visualization of project schedule based on Gantt chart with global and local events, event chains, and optionally with states of activities.

Event Chain — in Event chain methodology, a set of single events linked to each other.

Event Chain Methodology — an uncertainty modeling and schedule network analysis technique that is focused on identifying and managing events and event chains that affect project schedules. Event chain methodology is an extension on quantitative project risk analysis with Monte Carlo simulations.

Event Driven Branching — branching, which occurs when different risk alternatives cause execution of activities of group of activities.

Excitation — process in which activity is transformed from one state to another as a result of event.

Excited State — new state of the activity, which is caused by an event.

Fluctuation (Nose) — uncertainty related to activity's parameters such as duration and cost, which are not caused by the identified event. Fluctuation is expressed as statistical distribution of activity's parameters.

Frequency Histogram or Frequency Plot — a chart which plots the number of samples or probability vs. the value of the variable. Frequency charts allow you to analyze the risk associated with a variable, for example, what is the chance that the cost of the project will be within budget. Frequency charts can be combined with cumulative probability chart for the same variable.

Gantt Chart — a visual representation of a project schedule. Gantt chart shows a bar which represents start and finish times of the different project activities as bar. Gantt chart may show some information, such as links between activities, resources, summary activities vs. subtasks, etc.

Integrated Risk Analysis — is analysis of risks belonging to different schedule-related (duration and cost) and non-schedule (safety, security, quality, technology, environment, legal, and other) risk categories at the same time.

Kurtosis — one of statistical parameters used in Monte Carlo simulations. Kurtosis is a measure of the flatness or peaked nature of a distribution relative to a normal distribution. Kurtosis is a part of results of Monte Carlo simulations for project and for the tasks.

$$\text{Kurt} = \left\{ \frac{1}{n} \sum_{i=1}^{n} \left[\frac{x_i - \mu}{\sigma} \right]^4 \right\}, \tag{1}$$

where μ is mean, σ is standard deviation and n is number of samples (number of Monte Carlo simulations).

Lag — see Probabilistic Lag.

Linear Congruential Generator — an algorithm that generates a sequence of pseudo-randomized numbers using a linear equation. It is used in Monte Carlo simulations.

Local Risk Assignment — see Risk Assignment.

Mitigation Plan — a plan which is designed eliminate to minimize impact of threats and maximize effect of opportunities. Mitigation plan is created during the process of risk identification. Activities associated with mitigation plans are usually part of the schedule and executed together with other activities of the schedule.

Moment of Event (*Moment of risk*) — actual moment when the event occurs during the course of an activity. The moment of event in most cases is probabilistic and defined by statistical distribution.

Monte Carlo Method — the mathematical method used in risk analysis. Monte Carlo simulations are used to approximate the distribution of potential results based on probabilistic inputs. Each simulation is generated by randomly pulling a sample value for each input variable from its defined probability distribution. These input sample values are then used to calculate the results (in schedule risk analysis, they are: project duration, start and finish times, success rate, work, cost, and others). This procedure is then repeated until the probability distributions are sufficiently well represented to achieve the desired level of accuracy. The probability distribution to be used for these inputs is dependent on the types of numbers you want to generate.

Multicasting — In Event chain methodology, a process according to which one sender event (trigger) cause multiple receiver events.

Non-schedule Risk — risk which belongs to non-schedule category, such as safety, technology, public relations, quality, legal, security, and others.

Nose — see Fluctuation.

Opportunity — risk with the positive impact. Threat is opposite of opportunity. Risk can be threat and opportunity at the same.

Percentile — a value on a scale of 0–100 that indicates that percent of a distribution that is equal to or below it. A value in the 95th percentile is a value equal to or better than 95% of other values. In schedule risk analysis, percentiles are results of Monte Carlo simulations for project and for the tasks. Notation P95 indicate 95th percentile.

Potential Loss — see *Risk Cost*.

Precedence Network — a relationship between activities in the project schedule. Activities in project schedules are linked to each other, for example, one activity can start only when the previous one is completed. Precedence network is used in critical path method.

Probability — a chance or likelihood that something will happen. Probability can be expressed in numbers from 0% to 1%, for example, "10% chance of project cancelation." Probability can also be expressed in words such as impossible, unlikely, possible, even chance, likely and certain.

Probability Distribution — a relationship (a table or an equation) between data sample or outcome of a statistical experiment and its probability of occurrence.

Probabilistic Lag — The delay between the finish of the predecessor and the start of the successor task. Probabilistic lags are defined by statistical distribution.

Probabilistic Rate — The rate of pay for the work performed by a resource, defined by statistical distribution. For example, software programmer's rate is between \$50/h and \$60/h. Probabilistic rate is useful for estimation of cost related to work resources, which are not hired yet or material resources, which are not procured.

Probabilistic Resource Allocation — number of units the particular resource assigned to the task defined by statistical distribution. For work resources, it is usually defined as percent. For material resources, it is defined in actual physical units. For example, John can work on the task between 50% and 80% of his time.

Probability/Impact Matrix — see Risk Matrix.

Qualitative Project Risk Analysis — a process of determining project risk probabilities and impacts, risk prioritization, and analysis of mitigation plans without using quantitative methods.

Quantitative Project Risk Analysis — a process of assigning numerical probabilities to the risks and uncertainties and applying quantitative methods to determine impact of those risks on the project schedule.

Receiver Event — in Event chain methodology, it is an event, which is caused by another event (sender or trigger).

Residual Risk — a risk, which remains after original risk occurred and mitigated or transferred. It could be a different risk which arises after mitigation activities.

Response Plan (*Risk Response Plan*) — is an of activity plan which is designed eliminate to minimize impact of threats and maximize effect of opportunities. Response plan is created during the process of project planning, but executed after risk occurred.

Risk — a stochastic event that can be applied to tasks or resources and affects projects. Risks may have different properties. When risks are assigned to task or resources, risk probability and impact should be defined. Risk can belong to different categories. Risk can be threat (risk with positive impact), opportunity (risk with negative impact), or their combination. Risk may have set of mitigation and response plans.

Risk Alternatives (*Event Alternatives*) — in Event chain methodology different mutually exclusive potential impacts of one risk (event).

Risk Adjusted Project Schedule — is a project schedule calculated based on results of schedule risk analysis. Risk adjusted project schedule can be presented based on mean duration, start and finish times, or particular percentile of statistical distribution of start, finish time, and duration.

Risk Assignment — Risk event can be assigned to all tasks or resources (be global) or particular task or resource (be local). The risk should be identified and recorded in Risk Register. When risk is assigned, probability of risk occurrence, risk impact, result, and moment of risk should be defined. If risk event is not assigned to any tasks and resources, it will remain in the Risk Register but will not be used for risk ranking and will not affect project schedule.

Risk Audit — a technique that helps control the efficiency of risk responses as well as the efficiency of the risk-management process.

Risk Breakdown Structure — a hierarchically organized risk register arranged by risk category.

Risk Category — the risk can affect project duration, cost, safety, security, technology, etc., which are called categories. Categories can be schedule-related, such as duration and cost. If risk belongs to schedule related category, the risk impact may change, if schedule changes. Alternatively, non-schedule risk categories are not directly related to project schedule. They include safety, technology, public relations, quality, legal, security, and others. As part of risk analysis, risk impacts and scores can be calculated separately for each category. One risk can belong to different categories. Category is defined when risk is assigned to tasks or resources.

Risk Committee — a group of experts, which ensures that risk identification, analysis and communication is done consistently across organization. For example, risk committee can facilitate risk reviews and approve risks for insertion to the risk register.

Risk Cost — additional cost or loss which is uncured due to the risk. Input data of risk cost is a potential loss: the loss in monetary terms if the risk occurs. It is multiplied on probability of risk to get an *expected loss*. Total risk cost may be calculated by taking into an account cost of risk mitigation, response plans, and residual risk.

Risk Management — a process of identification, analysis, assessment, and control of the risks. Risk management covers the entire risk life cycle: from risks to issues and lessons learned.

Risk Matrix (Probability/Impact Matrix) — The chart presenting risk probability vs. risk impact within matrix. Risk matrix uses different colors (red, green, and yellow) to represent severity of the risk. Risk matrix can be viewed separately for risks and opportunities.

Risk Mitigation Plan — see Mitigation Plan.

Risk Impact — the effect of risk on objectives. Risk impact can be expressed as a label or as a value. Actual value of risk impact depends on what category and what risk impact type it belongs to.

Risk Impact Type — a result if a risk occurs. In quantitative analysis, risk impact types can be schedule-related and non-schedule. Multiple risk impact types can be combined in risk category. In different software, you can customize non-schedule risk impact types, as well enable/disable schedule risk impact types. If a risk is assigned to a task, the impact type can be Increase cost, Delay, Restart, End task, Cancel task, Cancel task + all successors, Cancel Project, and others. If a risk is assigned to a resource, the impact type can be Increase cost, Delay, Restart, End task, and others.

Risk Identification — a process of determining and identifying the properties of potential threats and opportunities.

Risk Monitoring and Control — a process of tracking identified risks, monitoring residual risks, identifying new risks, and executing risk-response plans during the course of a project.

Risk Probability — the chance that event would occur. Risk probability may be different when risk is assigned to different tasks and resources especially if these tasks or resources belong to different projects.

Risk Properties — attributes, associated with the risks. Examples of these risk properties include when risk is created or modified, names of recorded, name of contact, and other information. Organizations usually create a dictionary of risk properties or set of properties which needs to be defined for each risk. Risk Properties can be used for filtering, for example, it is possible to show all risks, which opened after January 1, 2014.

Risk Register — a set of all risks. Includes risk properties, probabilities impact and scores, information about mitigation and response plans, and other information. Risks from Risk Register should be assigned to tasks or resources.

Risk Response Plan — see response plan.

Risk Score or Risk Severity — risk impact multiplied on risk probability. Risk score is usually presented as part of Risk Register. You may sort all risks based on risk score in Risk Register.

Sampling — a procedure that can produce a sequence of values which can be taken from the probability distribution.

Schedule Network Analysis — a technique used to identify start and finish times for the uncompleted activities of a project schedule.

Seed (in Monte Carlo Simulations) — number, which is used as a starting point for Monte Carlo sampling. Seed in most cases is randomly generated.

Semi-standard Deviation — a measure of dispersion for the values falling below the mean or another target value. Semi-standard deviation is calculated the same way as standard deviation, except only samples below mean or target values are used in the calculation. Semi-standard deviation is presented as part of results of Monte Carlo simulations for project and for the tasks.

Sender Event — see Trigger.

Sensitivity Analysis — it is an analysis, which determines how uncertainties in the output of the mathematical model are affected by different inputs.

Skewness — a measure of the degree of asymmetry of a distribution around its mean. If the distribution is skewed to the left, it will have a positive skewness. If it is skewed to the right, it will have a negative skewness. Skewness is presented as part of results of Monte Carlo simulations for project and for the tasks. Skewness is calculated based on formula:

$$\text{Skew} = \frac{1}{n} \sum_{i=1}^{n} \left(\frac{x_i - \mu}{\sigma} \right), \tag{2}$$

where μ is mean, σ is standard deviation and n is number of samples (number of Monte Carlo simulations).

Spearman Rank Order Correlation Coefficient — A non-parametric (distribution-free) rank statistic proposed by Spearman in 1904 as a measure of the strength of the associations between two variables. Particularly, it is used to estimate which task duration, risk, task start date, task cost, risk, etc., affects project duration, finish time, cost success rate the most. Actual formula for Spearman Rank Order correlation includes two sets (arrays) of variables, generated as a result of Monte Carlo simulations (see Lehmann and D'Abrera 1998, pp. 292, 300, and 323).

Standard Deviation — a measure of how widely dispersed the values are in a distribution. It is one of the most important parameters of statistical distribution. Standard deviation equals the square root of the variance. Standard deviation is presented as part of results of Monte Carlo simulations for project and for the tasks. Standard deviation is calculated based on formula:

$$\sigma = \sqrt{\frac{1}{n-1} \sum_{i=1}^{n} (x_i - \mu)^2}, \tag{3}$$

where μ is mean and n is number of samples.

State of Activity — in Event chain methodology, a certain way in which activity is performed. Activities are transferred from one state to another by different events. Original state of activity is called ground state. The state of activities after the event is called excited state. The process of changing states is called excitation.

State Table — in Event chain methodology, a table, which represents activity's states and associated events. State table includes properties of the event subscription.

Statistical Distribution — see Probability Distribution.

Subscription to the Event — in Event chain methodology a set of events, which may affect particular activity in a certain state.

Success Rate — a chance that a task or project will be completed. A task success rate of 56% means that there is a 56% chance that this task will be completed and 44% chance that task will be canceled. Tasks can be canceled when either it reaches a task or project deadline, or if a risk with Cancel task, Cancel task + all successors or Cancel project impact type occurs. Projects can be canceled either when it reaches the project deadline or if a task risk with a Cancel Project outcome occurs.

SWOT Analysis — a technique (strength, weaknesses, opportunities, and threats) used for risk identification and strategic planning.

Threat — risk with the negative impact. Opportunity is the opposite of threat. Risk can be threat and opportunity at the same time.

Time Dependent Global Risk — global risk, which may affect project activities running only during certain period of time.

Trigger (Sender) — is an event which cause a risk. In most cases trigger is a risk itself. In Event chain methodology, trigger is part of event chain.

Variance — a measure of how widely dispersed the values are in a distribution, and thus is an indication of the risk of the distribution. It is calculated as the average of the squared deviations about the mean. The variance gives disproportionate weight to outlying values that are far from the mean. The variance is the square of the standard deviation. Variance is presented as part of results of Monte Carlo simulations for projects and for the tasks. Variance is calculated based on formula:

$$\sigma^2 = \frac{1}{n-1} \sum_{i=1}^{n} (x_i - \mu)^2,\tag{4}$$

where μ is mean, σ is standard deviation, and n is number of samples (number of Monte Carlo simulations).

Index

[Important page numbers are in bold]

Printed in the United States
By Bookmasters